# Storytellers

# Storytellers

*a novel*

BJØRN LARSSEN

josephtailor

ISBN: 978-90-829985-2-8
(paperback edition)

Cover photograph: Hallgrímur P. Helgason
Cover and type design: Ray Grant for josephtailor
Typeset in Baskerville and Born Ready fonts

FIRST EDITION

# Contents

*Those who do not have power over the story that dominates their lives, power to retell it, rethink it, deconstruct it, joke about it, and change it as times change, truly are powerless, because they cannot think new thoughts.*

– Salman Rushdie, "One Thousand Days in a Balloon"

# Monday, March 8, 1920

The thud of the body landing on the good chair sent the dog into hysteria.

Gunnar's gaze moved nervously between the usually calm dog and the unusually silent stranger, who just a few minutes ago had been screaming his lungs out as both men fought the ferociously whipping sleet and wind. The furious barking wasn't helping Gunnar's headache, and the blacksmith squatted with a little groan.

"Come here, Ragnar, good boy. Give me a hug. Now calm down. Sshh..." The dog, unused to visitors of any sort, didn't seem placated. The blacksmith let go of him and stared at the man again. If someone really died here, there would be questions. The authorities might want to inspect the farm, the forge, they might want to look at the shed... Gunnar couldn't think about all those horrible things now, he needed some medication first, to soothe his nerves and allow him to decide what to do next. "Stay alive," he instructed the body. "Watch him for a moment," he instructed Ragnar. The dog continued his furious yapping, paying no attention to the blacksmith slamming the door behind him.

Gunnar returned a minute later with the medication in hand, feeling a bit better already. He shook his head, scattering drops of water, then placed the medication on the kitchen table before entering the room again. Ragnar's cries were hoarse now, but the dog wasn't howling, which seemed to be a good thing. Gunnar carefully lifted one of the man's eyelids with a blackened finger. The stranger's wrinkled face contorted, lips opened in a soundless groan, and Gunnar let out a long breath. Alive. Good. Then he could wait.

The blacksmith knelt next to the dog again, gave him a cold, wet embrace, and stroked the mutt's head. "Ssshhh. It's alright, Ragnar, calm down, boy. We'll get rid of him. Go back to the kitchen." Gunnar lifted the rag dividing the living room – or, more precisely, the only room – from the kitchen, and pushed the dog out with the other hand, firmly, but gently. The muffled barking turned into quiet whimpers. The two men were now alone.

Slush started to melt in Gunnar's bushy hair and beard, and little icy streams ran down his body. They felt like tiny knives, pressing just hard enough to leave marks on the skin, but not hard enough to cut through.

He shivered and looked at the stranger with a mixture of envy and contempt. Even with that pretty woollen coat, thick leather trousers, and the fur-lined boots he still needed someone to save his life, eh? Gunnar was clad in his working pants, shoes that constantly chafed even when they were dry, and two sweaters. No part of him was dry or warm. But he never needed any help.

"H-help," said a weak voice, which Gunnar ignored. It occurred to him now that he had nothing to change into. Had he expected to be out in the storm for half an hour, he would have at least worn his coat. As things were, Gunnar's best option seemed to be keeping his wet clothes on and sitting by the fire until everything was dry. He couldn't afford to soil the nice clothes that he wore only for his weekly visits to Doctor Brynjólf.

"Help...?"

Gunnar ground his chattering teeth. "Do you ever think of other people?" he scolded the man. "I might get pneumonia and die now, and it will be your fault." He demonstratively turned away and knelt by the fire, rubbing his stinging hands, slapping his arms, attempting to force some warmth back into his muscles. Drops of water kept falling from his hair and beard, and Gunnar shivered again. Medication, he remembered, and looked longingly towards the kitchen.

"My ank-kle hurts," whined the man again. Gunnar cast him a disdainful look. The stranger's eyes opened, and his hand wandered up to cover them from the light of a single light bulb dangling from the ceiling. He took in the ursine, dark figure by the fire. "It's the devil," he whispered.

"My name is Gunnar," said the blacksmith, "and I saved your life. The hell are you? You're not Uncle Theodór, are you?"

"I don't know who that is..."

"Nay. You're not fat enough. In any case, keep your hands off my farm." Gunnar dropped to the other chair, which creaked in warning, and started untying his shoes.

"It hurts," wailed the man. He was shivering, his words interrupted by groans. "If you could just p-please help..."

"I've already helped you." Gunnar put the shoes by the fire to dry, then glared at the stranger's boots again. They looked brand new and very comfortable. Gunnar's shoes hadn't been new even when he got them in the first place. "I had the worst day even before all this, let me tell you. What is it with your ankle?"

"I think it's broken."

"So now you want a doctor," grunted the blacksmith, reaching for his shoes again with a groan. This day would never end.

"No, no," said the stranger, attempting to lift himself on his elbow before falling back into the chair with a groan. "No… no doctor. This happened before. It just needs to be… eh…" He muttered something that Gunnar didn't quite catch. "Ah! Stabilised. And iced…" His entire body shivered, and the man cried out in pain again. "Take my left boot off," he whispered. "Cut it off."

"Are you crazy? Those boots must be worth a fortune!"

"I d-don't care about money. For God's sake, I need this boot to come off and you can not tug at it. Please cut it."

"Perfectly good boots," muttered Gunnar through clenched teeth as he stormed towards the forge. "*Certain* people can afford not to care about money," he added, picking an enormous pair of shears. He returned to the room, feeling almost tearful. His own feet were cold and rubbed raw, and those were such beautiful boots, even if they would be too small for Gunnar…

"Please, just do it," said the man. "Yes, I am sure," he added, even though the blacksmith hadn't asked. Gunnar knelt next to him, then started to cut through boot and sock, grimacing in pain himself. A grotesquely swollen, purple foot emerged, with toes sticking out like sickening growths.

"I am not dealing with this," said Gunnar, whose ankle immediately started hurting in sympathy. "I'll go get Doctor Brynjólf. Won't be longer than an hour."

The stranger's sobs stopped as though they had been clipped with the shears as well. "No need for a doctor. It's just pain. It will be alright. I'll tell you… what to do." His breaths were quick and shallow, face a miserable mask. "Just get some pieces of wood… bandage…"

Gunnar shrugged, eager not to have to leave the house again. "Whatever. It's your ankle. You better know what to do though, because I don't. Can you wiggle your toes?"

The old man lifted his head a bit. His pale blue eyes squinted as he tried to focus on Gunnar's hirsute face. "What about my toes?"

"It's important for… feet. If you can't, then Doctor Brynjólf might have to amputate it," the blacksmith pointed out. "But it's your gangrene. You're out of here tomorrow. You can stay in town."

"I don't have gangrene. Can't I stay here until I get better?"

"I'm no innkeeper and this is no inn. It's a forge. I don't like no guests."

Gunnar stopped, as a suspicion formed. "There's nothing for you to find," he added quickly, "nothing at all, *especially* nothing illegal…"

The man's eyes closed again. He didn't seem interested in Gunnar's completely legal possessions, and the blacksmith's shoulders relaxed. "Can you please bandage my ankle now? I will pay."

"Oh? How much? For what?"

"For your discretion, and to stay here until I recover. I gather you have no wife and children?"

"Aye. How do you know that? Discretion? Who *are* you?"

"Good God gracious… Where is my backpack?"

"Under you."

The man scowled. "There's money in it. You can have it."

"How much then?"

"I don't know exactly. About five thousand."

"Did you hit your head out there?" asked Gunnar when his ability to speak returned. "Five thousand kronur?"

"Give or take. I didn't count it." The man didn't seem too fazed by the fortune. Gunnar, on the other hand, couldn't believe what he was hearing. He didn't *count* it? Five thousand would be enough to buy the blacksmith's entire property and possibly some of the surrounding land…

"So, I cut that off too…? The coat, the—"

"Oh no," exclaimed the old man. "Stabilise my ankle, take off my backpack… then my coat… in that order…" He ran out of breath again. "Carefully," he added, his face contorting again.

Gunnar's hands shook as he hurriedly wrapped the swollen ankle, then proceeded to handle the backpack, coat, and their owner in a way he considered incredibly gentle. The stranger in turns cried in pain and berated the blacksmith. When the coat hung from Gunnar's own chair, backpack placed on the seat with great reverence, the blacksmith stood wordlessly next to the chair without touching anything. His wide eyes travelled between the backpack, and the stranger's grey face.

"Just give it to me," sighed the man. His hands moved slowly as he opened the backpack and fished out a black leather satchel. He handed it to Gunnar before closing his eyes again. The satchel was light, but the massive blacksmith slightly faltered. He opened it, looked inside, gasped, then clutched it to his wide chest as if it were an infant. "I don't understand," he whispered. "Why is this happening?"

"Let's discuss things first," said the old man. He tried to straighten himself in the armchair, then winced and returned to his previous position. "I need absolute… secrecy. Nobody can become aware of my…" His lips moved wordlessly again. "…presence here. Not a single person. I had a twisted ankle before–"

"Aye, but could you wiggle your toes…?"

"–And it took a few weeks to recover. It will be perfectly fine. I shall, however, require help, new clothes, food–"

"Nay," interrupted Gunnar again, "not feeding you. I am not a cook. I have a cleaning woman, she cooks too, but she cooks for one."

"Oh? What cleaning woman? What's her name and age?"

"The hell you care? Better tell me what your name is."

"Sigurd," said the man.

"See-ge… wt? That's not an Icelandic name."

"Everybody calls me Sigurd."

"Everybody being?"

"Just everybody." He hesitated briefly. "In America."

Oh, breathed the blacksmith wordlessly. America – the escape for thousands of poor Icelanders, who only started returning when the Great War brought prosperity to their homeland. "Aye. See-gewt," he said, tasting the word – so that was an American name. He wondered what Americans would turn Gunnar Karlsson into. "What are you doing here?" Gunnar's forehead was wet – not from the rain anymore, but from cold sweat. The satchel seemed to be getting heavier. He needed his medication, this was way too much to take in, but maybe the day wasn't so bad after all…

"Travelling," said the old man. He glanced around – hardly anything to see in the undecorated, rock-and-turf room – then had to cover his eyes again. "Can you please switch this light off? It's giving me a headache. Make some coffee, perhaps?"

Gunnar stared at Sigurd for another second or two and then bolted out of the room, nearly hitting his head on the doorframe before hurriedly returning to flip the switch. Once he was in the safety of his kitchen again, his movements slowed down. He cautiously placed the satchel on the table, shook his head in an attempt to clear his mind, and turned towards the stove. Both the kettle and the soup were still warm, they'd be hot in no time. In the meantime, he could finally shake out the contents of the satchel and messily scatter the banknotes all over the table. Colours and numbers danced in front of his eyes as he gently moved the notes around, hardly daring to touch them with his dirty fingers, wondering when he would wake up. A feverish realisation flashed in his head – Sigurd must have robbed a bank…

Gunnar's nose wrinkled. Something was burning… He tore his gaze away from the treasure. It was the soup. It wasn't his fault that he forgot to stir it, anyone would in these circumstances, what a day…

"Here," he said a moment later, handing Sigurd a bowl and a chunk of bread. Gunnar's body might have been in the room again, but in his mind he still couldn't see anything but the money.

"Could you turn that chair? My ankle needs to be elevated." Sigurd paused. "Meaning, it has to be higher than…"

"I know what 'elevated' means," barked Gunnar. "I'll bring you a stool. No wet feet on my chair."

"This soup smells odd…"

"You're welcome. Told you this is no inn. Eat in peace."

As Gunnar uttered those words, he was already on his way to the kitchen, taking Sigurd's coat along, immediately forgetting about the promised stool. He silenced the whistling kettle, burned his fingers as he dropped the pot with the remains of the soup in the sink, then returned to staring at the money, entranced. A single blue 100 kronur note – he had never seen one before – stuck out between other, smaller notes, and the blacksmith had to sit down as his knees felt weak. Suddenly afraid, he jerked his head to look outside, but all he could see was darkness.

The treasure needed to be hidden somewhere safe, and fast. Maybe in the coffee cans…no, that's where thieves would check first. Maybe under the bed upstairs, no – *that* would be the first place… maybe in the chest in the corner, no, too simple, not in the larder, not in the stable… Gunnar's nervous gaze landed on the black door leading to the forge. The heavier of his two anvils stood on a hardwood box, filled with ash and sand for stability. Once you removed the anvil, the lid could be lifted…

*You're rich,* his brain said in disbelief as he put the lid back on, the satchel safely stored underneath. Gunnar stumbled a bit as he walked back into the kitchen. He locked the door, then rested his hot forehead against it, waiting for his rapid heartbeat to slow down. Medication! The situation was so exceptional he almost forgot to take care of his health! Gunnar's hands shook as he made the coffee, adding a generous amount of clear liquid from a bottle to his mug. Some of it spilled as he clumsily re-entered the room.

"What is that smell? That's not coffee."

"None of your business," snapped Gunnar. He held his mug tightly in his hands, both to warm them up more and to protect it from his irritating guest's scrutiny.

"I believe there is prohibition in Iceland," Sigurd said with an unpleasant smirk. "Since 1915, is that correct? Five years and counting. Didn't you notice? Too drunk... perhaps?"

"It's medication. Doctor Brynjólf prescribes it for my nerves and back pain. And lung pain, too."

"You must be very ill. What exactly is it – wait, your doctor prescribes you moonshine?"

The blacksmith's face flushed. "Better tell me who you are. I don't want no bank robber here."

"I paid for your discretion," said Sigurd, "and a lot of money, too..."

"Accidents happen..."

"You would be required to answer a lot of questions..."

"Anybody could fall from such a cliff... how did you even get there...?"

"Stop!" shouted Sigurd. A pounding headache struck, and the tormenting pulse of heat rushed back to his ankle. "One thing at a time," he said, much quieter, closing his eyes again. Everything seemed to be dancing in front of him.

Gunnar took a greedy swig, then tried to scratch his chin with the hand that held the mug. "I, well, uh... What were you doing at that cliff? You can't get there without passing my house first."

"I climbed it."

"You climbed... from the shore to... How?"

"Oh, I'm good at climbing, as well as a few other things."

"Like what?"

"Reading, for instance. Where do you keep your books and newspapers?"

The blacksmith looked around, as if expecting a bookshelf to appear out of thin air. "I don't read no books or newspapers."

In a society of readers, storytellers, and writers, where even the Old Testament was considered entertaining during the winter months – almost as good as The Sagas – this was absolutely unheard of. It had been many years since Sigurd left the country, but he couldn't imagine winters being any different than they had been in his youth, when there was nothing else to do other than keep livestock alive, spin wool, and read or write. But, of course, blacksmiths stood by a fire all day... "What do you do then? You can read, I hope?"

"Aye. I just don't like to. I work, eat, sleep, rest. The usual."

"Yes, yes," said Sigurd. "But what exactly do you *do* when you rest?"

Gunnar held on to his mug with both hands as though his life depended on it. He gently rocked it, admiring the light reflecting off the surface. His hands no longer shook, and he finally started to feel warm. The medication was working. Gunnar's eyes closed, his stiff back relaxed, his nausea disappeared.

"Seriously? You live alone in the middle of nowhere and all you do is work and drink? What sort of godforsaken life is that?"

"Mine. I'm kicking you out tomorrow if you don't tell me what you're up to. Which bank does this money come from?"

"It's not from a bank."

"Where is it from then?"

"It's my inheritance," said Sigurd.

Unnerved, Gunnar drank some more coffee, then wiped his mouth with his nearly dry sleeve. "Okay… then… what are you going to do with it?"

"I just gave it to you."

"Oh," the blacksmith scratched his head, then moved on to his chin. *Lice*, thought Sigurd and shuddered. "So… what were you…?"

"Are you suggesting that you spend every evening drinking by the fire?"

"Aye, it calms me down. I like fire and I like drinking. I don't like strange people who ask me questions when they're supposed to give answers!"

"No need to raise your voice," muttered Sigurd, studying the contents of his own mug.

"I decided. I'm going to take you to town tomorrow. I'll give you back the money…" – Gunnar's voice wavered slightly – "and deliver you to the Sheriff. He'll decide what to do with you. I don't want you here."

"If you do that, the first thing I will tell the Sheriff is that you're making moonshine here. I will also say that I had ten thousand kronur and you kept the rest. They'll rip the place to shreds."

Gunnar gasped. "But I didn't do anything! You stole the money!"

"Inherited," corrected Sigurd with a weak smile. The coffee was surprisingly good and strong. Now that he no longer feared lonely death on the cliff, he was already planning what to do next. Gunnar wouldn't be able to spend too much money before Sigurd was ready to steal it back and depart. The ankle still throbbed with dull pain, but his headache was subsiding.

The blacksmith ground his teeth. "Why does a rich man come to a place like this? To climb my cliff with a backpack full of money just for fun?"

"Stop asking questions," reminded Sigurd.

To his surprise, Gunnar did. Instead, he sat in front of his new lodger, not taking his eyes off Sigurd even for a moment, taking a sip of coffee every now and then. It took maybe two minutes for Sigurd to start feeling uncomfortable under the blacksmith's heavy stare. Every now and then Gunnar's face seemed to double in front of Sigurd's eyes, which made him feel even worse. "Why don't you go and do something?"

"I've got nothing to do today anymore," said Gunnar. "I've had more than enough of today…"

"Yes," said Sigurd, "so I heard." He closed his eyes, but still felt the weight of Gunnar's stare. "Can you stop watching me like that?"

"No. I don't trust you and you don't want to tell me anything. If you don't like me staring, I can put you in the stable. My horse is very discreet."

"I could tell you… something," Sigurd offered, weakly.

"Like what?"

"Some sort of a story. Like in the good old days."

"Your story?"

"Just a story. Let me see… Do you know The Sagas?"

"I know The Sagas back and forth, American. And I know the Holy Bible better than you do. If it got lost, I could write it down again. If you're not going to talk about yourself, you can tell me some other story, but you better make it good."

Sigurd hesitated for a moment. "Alright… There is a story you might enjoy. It's a good one… I think."

"Do people die in it?"

"Yes, they do."

"Fire? Women? Drinking? Fights?"

"Plenty of everything," said Sigurd, exasperated. "What time is it?"

"It's dark outside, that's what the time is. Then it's time to sleep. Then it's time to work. Then it's time to rest."

"So, in other words, is it closer to eight or ten? I lost my watch out there."

"In other words, I don't know nor care."

"Is this some sort of nightmare? You have electricity, but you don't own a single book? You know how to make moonshine, but you don't know what time it is? How can you manage without a clock?" Maybe he *had* actually died on that cliff and this was purgatory, thought Sigurd, worriedly. From what he knew, forges were dark places filled with soot, smoke, and fire. That sounded a lot like hell.

"I don't need no clock. Why would I need a clock? I go to sleep when I'm tired," Gunnar said, then emptied the mug, smacking his lips. "I wake up when I wake up," he continued, his voice a rumble. "I eat, take care of Ragnar – that's my dog – feed Karl – that's my horse – and then I work."

"Surely not on Sundays?"

"Why the hell not? It's a day like any other. I don't let no calendar or clock tell me what to do. I can tell you today is a Monday, because the cleaning woman was here."

"Oh yes, what did you say her name was?"

"I don't know what her name is! The hell you care? She's a mute and an idiot. You just say: woman, do this, do that, and she does. She brings groceries, does the washing, cooks, sweeps the house. Tell me your story, American."

"Bring me a cup of coffee first," sighed Sigurd. "Make it hot. No medicinal additions, *please.*"

Gunnar walked out, muttering to himself. Sigurd's feverish gaze followed. He was now warm, relaxed to the point of nearly falling asleep, his ankle pulsating with heat rather than pain. How traditional, he thought, accepting his coffee. A lot of things have changed in the last thirty years, but stories were still being told by the fire on the cold nights when there was nothing else to do…

He watched the blacksmith make himself comfortable, closed his eyes, and started.

## Then

There was once a young, fearless Icelander named Arnar, who went to seek his luck and fortune in America…

## Now

"Oh, was there," interrupted Gunnar. "But later he returned with a plan, aye?"

Sigurd pursed his lips and stared at the blacksmith until Gunnar muttered an apology and busied himself with his mug.

## Then

There was once a young, fearless Icelander named Arnar, who went to seek his luck and fortune in America. He found the luck almost immediately, when he got hired by a family seeking to move into their new business, dairy production. Arnar found himself with a roof over his head, food on his plate, and just enough money to start building some savings – not quite a fortune, but he was patient. Nevertheless, he felt terribly lonely, having to listen to a language he didn't understand, surrounded by strangers. Fortunately, the family realised that in order for him to work more efficiently it would be good to teach him at least some English, and assigned the task to their youngest daughter, Juana.

The two fell in love the moment their eyes met for the first time. To Arnar, flame-haired Juana looked like summer, radiating warmth and joy. She, on the other hand, couldn't resist the icy blue fire of Arnar's eyes. Bit by bit, as his vocabulary expanded, she began to ask him questions about the mysterious, exotic place he came from, his family, his life. She admired his courage to leave his homeland and come to the New World without a krona…a dollar in his pocket. Arnar admired Juana's otherness and told her so.

Until now, all the ways in which she stood out only caused her to be unhappy. She'd always been made fun of because of her red hair, her unusual name, and the fact that her sisters were already married and had left the house. All Juana had were adventure books, and her future seemed to be limited to making cheese unless she got lucky enough to find a husband of her own. Her father had ideas about who a suitable husband for his youngest daughter would be, but so did she. Their ideas were very different.

"Tell me about your family," said Juana one evening. They were learning words that described family members. "Father, mother, brother, sister…"

"I have two brother."

"Two brothers. Very good! What about your parents?"

"They died," said Arnar, shortly. He'd found out from a letter that arrived many weeks after the funeral. "A long time ago," he added quickly, seeing the smile disappearing from Juana's face. Icelanders approached death sensibly, more focused on life and the work that had to be done. Americans immediately got upset. "It's fine, really…"

"Tell me about your brothers," said Juana. "Are they as good-looking as you?"

Arnar's smile soured slightly. "I've got a twin brother, Ingvar. Definitely not as good-looking as me, though. Sticks his nose in the books all day. He'll be a bishop one day. My other brother, Bjarni, he's a constructor, he builds houses. Nobody's better at it. One day, he'll build wonders no human eye has seen before, but first he'll build my house when I go back one day…"

"Will you go back?" exclaimed Juana, her eyes opening in shock. "Why…?"

"I miss my homeland. I live between the ocean and mountains, volcanoes and glaciers, ice and fire…" Arnar paused. "This here, is work."

"Am I… work as well?"

No, he almost said, watching her slightly trembling lower lip. You are a treasure, a pearl, a diamond… Perhaps it was fortunate that he hadn't learned those words yet. "No. You are my best friend. It would be nice if you could meet my brother."

"Brothers," corrected Juana automatically. "I wish I could go and see that land of ice and fire one day…"

"You could," said Arnar and a silence fell upon them. Juana blushed. So did he.

Finally she spoke again, quieter and slower now. "So, one is the smart one, one is the craftsman… and what about you?"

Arnar's gaze met hers. "I'm the lucky one," he said.

That evening both went back to their bedrooms longing for the other. Arnar found it difficult to fall asleep. When he'd arrived in America, he had believed the fortune he would bring back would be money. Instead, he found a treasure you couldn't put a price on. And Arnar always got what he wanted.

Juana kept thinking about her adventure books, where the heroines discovered new places, new people… sometimes very special men. Could any man really have been more special than the wild and exotic Arnar?

Waterfalls and volcanoes, she thought, amazed by the very idea that those things actually existed outside the books. The ocean and the sky the colour of Arnar's blue eyes. Icelanders called America "the New World". Perhaps it was time for her to discover a new world of her own, one where she would witness wonders she had only read about… and to avoid making cheese all day under her father's supervision.

Unfortunately, her father decided that Juana and the "servant" were spending way too much time together. "He's no company for my daughter," he huffed, as Juana stood in front of him, blushing, her gaze glued to her feet. "Both of you have work to do. He has learned enough. You will never speak to him alone again," he continued. Juana kept staring at her feet, but… her gaze began to turn from ashamed to defiant… forbidden fruit was… much, much sweeter…

### Now

Sigurd's words became slower, then quieter as he found himself slowly drifting into sleep. He awoke with a startle when Gunnar began to snore loudly, slowly sliding off his chair with the mug still in his hands.

"Gunnar," said Sigurd. The only response was another guttural snore. "Gunnar," he repeated louder. "Hey!" he finally shouted, a blunt headache striking again. "Wake up!"

The blacksmith snorted loudly, opened one eye and looked at Sigurd. The fire had almost gone out. "This is not a dream?"

"No," said Sigurd, massaging his temples. "Unfortunately. Where do I sleep?"

"There." Gunnar gestured sideways with his mug, then raised it to his lips, greedily swallowing the last few drops. Sigurd looked where the blacksmith was motioning, but he couldn't see a thing in the dark room. Then he remembered and shuddered.

"On that… pile?"

"My father slept there," slurred the blacksmith. "Twice the man you'll ever be. Or have ever been. You'll be just fine." His eyes started to close again.

"Wake up, you have to move me there!"

Sigurd could have sworn that Gunnar managed to put him on the sheepskins, climb up the ladder, open the trapdoor, then disappear without opening his eyes even for a moment. The ceiling croaked above

Sigurd's head so loudly it sounded as if it were about to break, which probably meant the blacksmith had landed on his own bed upstairs. Sigurd gave the dying fire a longing look. No matter what time of year, the rock-and-turf walls were always damp and cold. A shiver brought a fresh wave of pain. All he could think of was that he had planned to spend this night very differently.

# Tuesday, March 9, 1920

Gunnar threw the sheepskins aside and sat up in bed. The swift movement triggered a headache – something he experienced quite often in the mornings – but staying in the cosy warmth inevitably led to thinking, which led to a visit from the darkness…

Outside, the sun wouldn't come up for another few hours, but Gunnar didn't need light to navigate his house after so many years of practice. He had, however, forgotten about Sigurd and an unexpected, loud snore nearly caused Gunnar to fall off the ladder. Now completely awake, he tiptoed to the kitchen, stroking the rag hanging from the doorframe as he passed. The house was piercingly cold, and the blacksmith shivered despite the fact that he was fully clothed.

Every morning looked the same. He started with lighting the fire in the stove, as it would take a while to get going. In the meantime, he lit the oil lamp – when he had a headache the electric light hurt his eyes. Next, he brushed his teeth. Doctor Brynjólf strongly emphasised the necessity of doing so, and Gunnar followed all the advice he got from the doctor, except for the bits that he didn't. Other than that, the blacksmith didn't concern himself much with personal hygiene. Coal dust had eaten into his hands, arms, face, and had been ground under his fingernails. Perhaps regularly using soap would have helped, but Gunnar believed it to be a waste of money. Every now and then, he took long soaks in a hot spring nearby, but only to ease his back pain. The only other thing that helped, especially in the mornings, was his medication.

As Gunnar waited for the kettle to boil, his fingers danced around the neck of the bottle. His muscles were stiff from the cold, but soon they wouldn't be. His mood would improve, he'd find motivation to work, he'd relax. Gunnar neither understood nor approved of the prohibition. If other people were happy to walk around cold, sore, and stressed out, good for them, he often said to Ragnar. The dog didn't disagree. Once the coffee was ready, the blacksmith added a generous splash from the bottle, took a big gulp, then topped up the mug with some more clear liquid. The taste was awful, but the effects were worth it.

Doctor Brynjólf advised a hefty breakfast, but even the thought of food made Gunnar's innards twist. He blamed it on the smell of the burnt soup from yesterday. In any case, he already felt warmer, his muscles relaxed, his head cleared, his headache was almost gone. Gunnar drank the coffee in big, greedy gulps, refilled Ragnar's bowls, stroked the mutt's head, let him out, then went to take care of Karl. As the blacksmith lovingly combed the mare's mane, he also related yesterday's events. Bored as she looked, Karl was a good listener. Gunnar rewarded her patience with some sugar, then decided he was ready to get on with his day. He'd eat something later.

It was time for Sigurd to wake up. Gunnar picked up a brass pan, nodded to himself approvingly, then struck it with a spoon. If the gong-like noise didn't wake his lodger up, Ragnar's deafening barking must have done it.

"Sorry," said Gunnar to the clearly unimpressed dog, then popped inside the room, remembering to produce a friendly grin. "Morning. Coffee? Breakfast? I can bring it all here."

"Uh," groaned Sigurd, who had forgotten where he was and how he had gotten there. His night had been filled with nightmares. "Gunnar," he said, relieved, recognising the dark, ursine silhouette. His memory began to return bit by bit, starting, for some reason, with Gunnar's uncle Theodór needing to keep his hands off the farm. "Right. Coffee – please – thank you…" He instinctively raised his hand to wind his watch, then the corners of his mouth dropped further. "Do you think you could light a fire and move me to the chair? That would be very much appreciated. I'm really, really cold."

"Fire going all day? Like I can afford… oh. Forgot. Aye, I'll put you in my good chair."

Coffee by the fire was delightful and it put Sigurd in a much better mood despite the dull pain in his tightly bandaged ankle. Probably only God knew how old the "good chair" was. The cracked leather of the heavy armchair somehow felt dry and sticky at the same time. It was, nevertheless, very comfortable. When breakfast arrived, Sigurd was less than delighted to see burnt porridge with a lump of sugar in the middle and a chunk of bread with cod liver oil. The main advantage of the clashing tastes, each of them awful, was that it took Sigurd's mind off the potential lice and the dirt that he could practically feel forming on his skin. The blacksmith straddled his chair, drumming his black fingers on the backrest, impatient. Sigurd was a contrarian and resolved to eat as slowly as possible, but the food tasted so unpleasant he found himself hurrying up just to be done with it.

"Time for work," Gunnar announced the second Sigurd finished. "I can go to town later if you want something. Have a good day."

"Just a moment! Do you have any newspapers around? I need something to do while you're gone."

"I might have some left. Anna gives me old ones to start the fire."

"That's very nice of her. Do you think it would be possible to buy a proper mattress in Klettafjörður? No offence, but this pile, I mean this… bed is absolutely terrible."

"It was good enough for my father…" started Gunnar, but his scowl disappeared almost immediately. "But that was many years ago, aye. I'll see."

"Thank you, I will be much obliged. I would like a pillow, too. And some proper bedding, please. In the meantime, I'll be fine here on your *good* chair. Which I appreciate," Sigurd added quickly, although sarcasm seemed lost on Gunnar, who was now absent-mindedly scratching his head and yawning. "When is your housekeeper coming?"

"On Monday."

"So, in six days," sighed Sigurd. There was no way his ankle would recover in six days. He might have to hide.

"Aye," said Gunnar, his tone strangely grumpy. "Looking forward to the story tonight," he added, then left the room.

The story, thought Sigurd, blood departing from his face. *The* story. He had forgotten that he started telling it. How… why… what was he thinking…? Nothing, he realised. He'd been too feverish to understand how big a mistake he was making. He shivered, his skin covered in goosebumps, cold despite the fire. The ankle responded with blunt pain.

Maybe it was time to tell the story. Perhaps it needed to be told just this one time, to someone who wouldn't understand most of it, who wouldn't know… Not all was lost, Sigurd told himself, relaxing slightly. He just had to add an extra chapter, one in which Gunnar would die.

Gunnar, unaware of his impending doom, entered the forge, saw the anvil and immediately forgot what he had planned to do today.

*You're rich.*

The anvil disappeared along with everything else, replaced by a vision of colourful banknotes.

Ragnar, who kept Gunnar company, curled up into a ball. The cold was piercing. Most people imagined that forges were very hot places and occasionally, in the middle of the summer, they were. But in order to avoid suffocation or heavy metal poisoning windows had to remain open no matter the weather. At least right now it was neither raining nor snowing outside, which Gunnar could tell by the fact that it wasn't raining or snowing inside either. In a moment, he would light the fire and he would heat and hammer the iron. Sweat would drip from his forehead, nose, and stream into his beard and stay there. But he would constantly need to move his feet to relieve the cold, despite two pairs of socks inside his ancient shoes…

*Boots*, he thought, suddenly cheerful. Fur-lined boots with reinforced steel toes. Polished leather. Thick soles. Boots that would last for years. Hell, two pairs, one for work, one to wear outside. In different colours! And sweaters without holes. He immediately forgot his work, instead reaching for his coffee mug. The drink was cold, like everything else, but the added medication would warm him up in no time. So would a fire, but Gunnar needed to see the money again first. Maybe he'd imagined it. Maybe it had turned into straw. His teeth chattering, Gunnar lifted the anvil, opened the satchel and stared at his newfound wealth. You're rich. Without taking his eyes off the 100 kronur note he reached for his mug and chugged its contents. His hands trembled slightly, not only from the cold.

It had been so long since the blacksmith had bought new clothes that he couldn't remember how much they cost, and he couldn't recall ever having owned boots as beautiful as Sigurd's. By Gunnar's standards, 1919 was very profitable, and he had managed to save some money. But he always expected to be punished for any scrap of luck that fate threw his way. He wasn't surprised when almost overnight the economy, no longer aided by the Great War, nosedived. His meagre savings would barely have kept him afloat for another few months, but no longer than that. Now he was lucky, very, very lucky. How painful would the punishment be this time, a voice in his head wondered. "It couldn't be worse than hunger," he muttered under his breath. Just yesterday Gunnar had worried about whether he would be able to keep paying the cleaning woman much longer. Now his focus was redirected towards warm undergarments, multiple pairs of socks without holes in them, leather trousers, fur-lined boots. He would be able to eat meat or fish every day again…!

When he shivered so violently he could no longer ignore the cold, Gunnar folded the 100 kronur note with reverence and carefully placed it in the back pocket of his trousers. Then he lifted the anvil with a groan. Doctor

Brynjólf's voice, reminding him to keep his back straight, sounded in his head. Loud, clear, and too late. But the dull pain and deceptive warmth in his lower back would go away, just like always. Once the anvil was back in place, Gunnar started the electric blower, then absent-mindedly lit the fire with the crumpled old newspapers that Sigurd wanted so badly. He picked up pieces of blackened cotton and pushed them deep into his ears – Doctor Brynjólf's advice. There were many stories written about the romantic ring of the anvil, the sound that ruined the hearing of many blacksmiths. Gunnar stood by the fire, warming up his hands, staring at it, wondering what else he could use the money for…

*Whisky*, he thought, and his mouth began to salivate. Gunnar could almost taste the sweet burn, so much more pleasant than his own produce. Now that he could afford it, he just had to find a way to convince Doctor Brynjólf to double his prescriptions. The blacksmith drained his mug, spat in the fire, and inhaled the sour smell of coal smoke. Gunnar's eyes were open, but the sight of fire was replaced by images of various things he could buy. No matter how good his muscle memory was, there was no way he would be able to work now.

*You're rich.*

A trip to town was in order. Anna, the shop owner, would be pleased to see him, or rather his money. Gunnar had no delusions. But he didn't need her affection. He needed new boots.

Anna and her daughter Brynhildur were busy having a fight.

"What you are wearing is not only inappropriate, but will also give you pneumonia," huffed Anna. "You've got goosebumps all over your forearms. Put on a sweater." Brynhildur, who made her dresses and blouses herself, seemed to enjoy exposing her cleavage to the burning cold. The large cross pendant did nothing to disperse unclean thoughts.

"A sweater over this dress is going to look… inappropriate."

"No, *now* you look inappropriate. Give this to me." Anna twisted a thick knit shawl around Brynhildur's neck and secured it with a heavy green brooch from the "unsold forever" box. "Here."

"You're still treating me like I'm a child," complained her daughter. "I'm a grown up, I can take care of myself." She removed the shapeless brooch and untangled herself from the shawl, trying to look resolute.

"Funny," said Anna. "At your age I was already married for five years. And your sister got married at the age of twenty-seven, same as me.

Happy as a pig in mud. Maybe you take care of yourself too well. Give me that." She started wrapping Brynhildur in the shawl again.

"It's not my fault that Ásta is so egotistic. It was *my* turn. Since when are you pleased about her marrying the merchant's son? She betrayed us!"

"Do not raise your voice at me," huffed Anna, securing the brooch. "Don't you dare take this off. You don't get to marry someone because it's 'your turn'. You need to give them reasons to think you would make a good wife. Put on a nice warm hat." She was rummaging through the "unsold forever" box again.

"I don't want a hat, it will ruin my braids. I don't care what they think, as long as they notice me!"

Anna turned away from the box sharply and hit her daughter with a fierce glare.

"I'm sorry I shouted," said Brynhildur, demonstratively pulling the shawl tighter. "I'm just trying to look warm and welcoming," she continued, then shivered involuntarily. "But it's like they are afraid of me…"

"They're not afraid," huffed her mother. "They think you're a hussy. All these powders, lipstick and whatnot are only going to get everyone to talk about you. And not in a nice way." She pulled a beige woollen hat with pom-poms out of the box. "Here. Wear this."

"That doesn't fit my complexion." Brynhildur pushed away her mother's insistent hands.

"As long as you live in my house, you're going to do what I tell you. Stop moving!"

Brynhildur's lower lip began to tremble slightly just as the doorbell rang. Both women, completely enmeshed in their fight, turned to look at the customer. Their facial expressions were identical: eyes wide open, mouth agape, as if shocked that someone could actually enter the store.

Gunnar, who – as always – tried to open the door so softly the bell wouldn't make a sound, and – as always – failed, froze as well. His heart leapt into his throat, beating faster and harder. Four identical eyes the colour of grass in October stared at him, unblinking. Gunnar's hand convulsively jumped towards the flask in the inside pocket of his coat, he took half a step back and bumped into a shelf. A cookbook fell next to his head and made all three jump. Anna withdrew swiftly towards the back of the store, leaving her daughter to deal with the blacksmith.

He's a bachelor, Brynhildur remembered. An unusually warm smile brightened her face, and her hand absent-mindedly started fiddling with the brooch. As Gunnar squatted clumsily to pick up the book, Brynhildur took in the sight of his wide shoulders. "Gunnar, dear!" When the blacksmith straightened up, she couldn't help but notice his eyes were gentle and displayed vulnerability. "Good news, we sold your roses, so I've got some money for you. Bring us more roses, dear. People come here and ask for them and they get angry when I say we don't have any at the moment. They're very popular decorations for graves." An artist, she thought, creative, perhaps a bit moody, but talented. A drunk, true, but that was fixable...

"Ah," said the blacksmith, whose imagination presented him with the image of a rose-adorned gravestone with his name on it. "I'll, eh, see what I can do. I need some things..." He touched the 100 kronur in his pocket, and blushed. Brynhildur's unblinking stare always made him think about birds of prey. Perhaps he could make do with his old clothes for a bit longer.

"Yes?" she urged him.

"I need, I need... newspapers. And a mattress—"

"Oh my gosh! You're in luck, imagine, Helga just died!" enthused Brynhildur, then quickly cast a look towards her mother. "I mean," she continued in very different tone, "of course, it's very sad and unfortunate... You know Helga? The one with the cats? Used to own the inn? She lives, I mean lived, down the street, on the corner..."

"Aye," said Gunnar. He didn't know Helga. "What about her?"

"Well... she died recently and she lived alone. There's a list of things the family are getting rid of, here, in the window. There should be a mattress, if it's not sold yet. They might still have some chairs too, maybe a sofa..."

Gunnar shuddered at the idea of buying other unnecessary furniture. He was already dealing with more than enough changes in his own homestead. "Just a mattress. And pillows, if they have them. And blankets. Goodbye."

"Just a minute," said Brynhildur quickly, her voice pitched a bit higher than she intended. "You can buy blankets here too, new ones! I just thought I'd mention it for your convenience. And your newspapers! I've got the old ones here for you. Anything else?" The brooch she was fiddling with finally opened, and the shawl fell to the ground. The only person that noticed was Anna, who managed to remain silent by pressing her lips together so firmly that they formed a thin, white line. Gunnar let go of the door handle, then reluctantly turned back towards Brynhildur. A hot ball of dread sat inside his chest and it would remain there until he had a chance to ingest some medication.

"Aye... current newspapers, too."

"Oh? Anything in particular?"

"Just, eh... one of each."

"How nice! Er... why?"

"Interested," he said. "In, um, news. Who knows what could be happening in the world."

Not even Brynhildur's expertise at extricating information from customers was enough to find the reason for Gunnar's newfound interest in the world's welfare. She did, however, manage to liberate him from all the money he had earned through the sale of roses. The moment the door shut, she immediately turned towards Anna. "Imagine!" she gasped. "What do you think this means?"

"What it means," erupted Anna, "is that you are not only a hussy, but also blind and stupid. For Gunnar? He stinks, for God's sake! He's constantly drunk. And look what he's wearing..."

"There is no shame in not being rich..." Brynhildur's voice died out. Anna shook her head, looking at the blush slowly colouring her daughter's face. Brynhildur squatted to pick up the shawl. "I'm cold," she said meekly. "Would you perhaps be able to help me with this brooch, Mother?"

"I'm not as stupid as you think," scoffed Anna, tightening the shawl a bit too much. "If you want to live with a dirty, smelly, *poor* alcoholic, suit yourself..."

"I wonder," Brynhildur said, thoughtfully, "why would the doctor and his wife take so long to conceive? Her being, you know, the doctor's wife and everything? Not that I am suggesting they had any problems, of course."

"Stay away from Gunnar Karlsson is all I am saying..." Her mother's eyes softened. "Of course they didn't have any problems. Although it is very interesting indeed, and perhaps I could visit her mother and ask. But have you seen her? She has such a pretty glow, she must be so happy! And it will be such a lucky child, having Brynjólf as a father..."

It was very kind of Helga to die at such a convenient moment. One of her sons helped load the mattress onto the cart, throwing the pillows in for free. He seemed as uninterested in his mother's final days as Gunnar was himself. The blacksmith overheard a bit of conversation between her sons, concerning the "bloody cats". None of them wanted to take care of the damn pests, and Gunnar departed quickly to avoid being offered one.

Sigurd and Ragnar silently watched Gunnar huff, puff, and curse as he wrestled with the mattress. In the end the blacksmith won. The pile of turf that had previously served as a mattress was ready to be burnt in the fireplace and the blacksmith could finally sit by the fire. He straddled his chair and rested his hands on the backrest, his chin on his hands. "What a day," he remarked, watching Sigurd browsing the newspapers.

Sigurd snorted with laughter, and Gunnar cast him a wounded look. "That's not funny."

"You brought me *The Women's Paper.* That actually is quite funny."

"Go to town yourself next time."

"Oh no, I'm sure it's very interesting. Thank you for the mattress, too. Did you get some bedding as well?"

"Hmm," said Gunnar, scratching his chin with his thumb, looking thoughtfully somewhere above Sigurd's head.

"One step at a time," muttered Sigurd. "So... your father used to sleep here? Do you want to tell me anything about him?"

Gunnar grimaced and turned his face towards the fire. "He knew everything," he said. "He was the best. Smartest, strongest. Taught me all I know and all I forgot."

"Was he a blacksmith too?"

"Aye. Best blacksmith in the country. We built most of this place. Well, he did, but I helped and learned."

Sigurd waited a moment, but Gunnar's speech seemed to be over. "And what about your mother?"

"My mother died." The blacksmith paused. "When I was little." Another pause. "Tell me about your family."

"I'd rather not," said Sigurd.

"Then tell me your story. It's getting dark."

"Those are clouds. It's only afternoon."

"So what? We're not here to argue with Mother Nature. If she decides that it's going to be dark, it's going to be dark."

"Out of sheer curiosity, how much do you work?"

"I work when I feel like it and I feel like it every day. Don't you worry about my work. I've had enough of today as it is."

"Very well. So what time is it?"

"I don't *do* time."

"What does that even mean?"

Gunnar looked at him disdainfully. "Winters, springs, summers.

Day, then night. It's always the same. Go on with your story, now."

Sigurd made a face. "First I would like to know what time it is."

The blacksmith's chair fell on the floor with a loud thump, barely missing Sigurd's bandaged foot. Gunnar towered over the old man, who squealed in surprise. "I. Don't. Know," snapped the blacksmith, their faces nearly touching as he punctuated every word by jabbing his finger in Sigurd's bony chest. He stormed out and, a moment later, the door slammed loud enough to wake Ragnar, who jumped up and started barking. Sigurd's hair stood on end as adrenaline hit him. He realised he'd clearly pushed Gunnar's buttons, but had no idea how or why.

Gunnar didn't go far. He sat on the stairs, drank straight from the bottle, and stared at the mountain tops cut short by heavy clouds the colour of a healing bruise. It looked as though a storm was about to begin, but he could tell from the smell of the air that it wouldn't happen. The clouds hung there for no reason other than to make the world a darker place.

He was too upset not to drink now. The old man made him – it was his fault. All he wanted was to be left alone... yet at the same time there was nothing worse than having to spend time with his own thoughts. Often his mind seemed to be a sophisticated torture device that never stopped until he drank too much to think about anything at all. The story helped, the drinking helped, but nothing could ever really keep the darkness away for long.

Gunnar took another swig, staring forward with unseeing eyes. He would head inside soon. As soon as he stopped feeling the urge to put Sigurd in the stable with Karl and leave him there. As soon as he consumed enough medication to stop his mind from repeating the numbers over and over.

### Then

Arnar didn't have to push Juana towards making a decision. The day that her father sternly forbade her from spending time with the "servant", Juana realised, shocked, that he wasn't the loving and doting parent she believed him to be. He was a tyrant, whose goal was to keep her bound to the mundane and pointless life she led on the farm. Arnar, on the other hand, could offer her passion, freedom, adventures... but would he want to?

The same night, once Arnar let himself in through a window that Juana "forgot" to close in the evening, she could barely wait to ask the question.

"Would you take me to Iceland... one day?"

"Would you like to go…?"

Their gazes met and suddenly there were no doubts or questions left.

"*Já,*" she said, clapping her hands, in her mind already halfway there, "*já,* even tonight if we could, yes!" Impulsively, she kissed him and Arnar realised he made it: he was the luckiest man on Earth. Ingvar could keep his nose buried in his books. Bjarni would effectively be an employee, tasked with building a house for the couple. Paying him wouldn't be a problem, since Arnar knew the family had money and Juana knew where to find it. As he thought about the practicalities, she envisioned the two of them, wrapped in a black cloak, galloping on a black stallion through a thunderstorm. Never mind that her family didn't own a horse like that. She knew from her romance novels that this was what proper elopement looked like.

When Arnar gently touched upon the topic of money, Juana already had a plan of her own, straight from another book she had read. They were not stealing, it was simply a dowry that belonged to her by law once they got married in front of God. Arnar began to explain what else they had to do, but Juana wasn't listening – her imagination suddenly presented her with a group of black-clad men chasing them through the thunderstorm. "Oh no! What if my father finds us?"

"He will never find us. Iceland is big, but few people live there. Nobody will know who you are, where you came from, who your parents are, or where to find them. As long as you don't try to contact your family, we'll be completely safe. Your father is not going to come to Iceland, learn the language, and travel the country to find us. Nobody speaks English there."

Thus reassured, she was ready to depart immediately. Juana knew they would live in a big house surrounded by flowers, which she would tend dressed in beautiful, flowing garments and wide-brimmed hats. Gorgeous, happy children would be running around, laughing as Arnar picked them up in his strong arms to give them a playful tickle. She would have a magic touch, and her garden would be a diamond among others' emeralds. Just like in the books.

"Dear brother," Arnar wrote to Bjarni, "I can't wait to leave this godawful place. If you think you've ever worked hard back home, think again. The weather is horrid, as are the people, and don't get me started on the language – but I'm bringing back a treasure, and I'm not just talking about money. I won't be working for farmers. We'll be independent from day one, thanks to all the money I saved. Think of the most incredible house you can imagine, and we will build it together, no expenses spared. My wife, Juana, is a jewel among women." He hesitated for a moment, counting on his fingers. "Expect us at the end of June."

But a complication soon arose. Juana was unable to hide her excitement and her contempt for the boring life she'd been forced to lead for so long. Her mother promptly noticed the change in her daughter's behaviour and grew concerned. Something was going on, and she had to get to the bottom of things. However, trying to extract information from Juana proved to be impossible. It was nothing, insisted her daughter, it was just spring, the beautiful sunshine, the anticipation of an exciting summer... But the blush on her cheeks, her shining eyes, the tone of her voice made it clear she was lying through her teeth.

"I bet this has to do with that servant," muttered her father when his wife finished her report on the conversation. "This... infatuation has to end, and the sooner the better. Send her away for a few days, there's no need for drama. When she comes back, he'll be gone."

"We never send her away though," answered his wife. "She'll suspect something."

"Who cares? She'll cry a bit when she's back, then she'll come to her senses."

It was he who would be in for a surprise, though, when he discovered that his daughter, the servant, the money in his safe, and two horses had disappeared overnight.

# Wednesday, March 10, 1920

"You healed yet?" Gunnar set a plate on Sigurd's lap and placed the coffee on a stool he had put next to the bed.

Sigurd frowned. "You must be kidding. This is going to go on for a few weeks."

"You look better to me."

"It doesn't hurt as much as it did before. I don't really want to be here either, you know." He bit into the stale bread with cod liver oil – a taste he had forgotten over the years and had hoped never to experience again. Judging by the smell of Gunnar's moonshine, the blacksmith's taste buds had died a long time ago, but Sigurd did not fancy eating greasy mould through the rest of the week.

"Good, because I can't wait for you to leave." The blacksmith looked at the ceiling, scratching his chin thoughtfully. "Once your story is over," he added. Ragnar prodded Gunnar's leg with his muzzle. Gunnar absent-mindedly bent to scratch the dog between the ears, and Ragnar's eyes closed in pleasure. "Is America really that horrible?"

Sigurd looked at the fire. "It depends," he said, reluctantly. "It's a very big place. Think… fifty times bigger than Iceland. Some people are rude, some are nice. Sometimes the weather is great, sometimes it isn't. Like everywhere else. Just different."

"And the language?"

"I speak it," said Sigurd, his facial expression suggesting he had just eaten a lemon. "If I can learn, anybody can. It's hardly a country anyway. It's maybe a hundred years old. They have no history, no ancestors, no Sagas. All they have is money."

"Aaah… I'd like some money."

"You're rich now," Sigurd pointed out. "And I brought the money from America. You've got the best of both worlds. Anyway, don't forget it's just a story." He wished again he'd never started telling it. It had seemed so simple yesterday – he'd just get rid of the blacksmith once his ankle recovered. Now he was realising it wouldn't be that easy. Gunnar was at least twice his size, his shoulders so wide they barely fit through the entrance. But Sigurd's plan needed reworking anyway now that he was stuck here for God knew how long…

"Aye, aye. Just a story. But you need to kill some people next. Not get them married."

"If I start killing people now, everyone will be dead within three days. Also," pointed out Sigurd, "nobody got married."

Gunnar scratched his chin, thinking. "I thought you said 'wife' yesterday," he murmured. "Never mind. I forget things… Anyway. Going to work now." He lifted himself up with a slight groan. Sigurd managed to haggle for a thermos of coffee before the forge door closed, and then he was alone.

Sigurd did not have a plan B. Why would he? Every piece of the puzzle had been in place. He knew who to talk to in order to locate the only speakeasy in Reykjavík. He was happy to buy the pricey drinks, and the men – only God knew what they told their wives – were happy to share everything they knew about Klettafjörður in return. The queer blacksmith's fame had reached even Reykjavík. Sigurd knew he didn't need to worry about getting spotted by guests or family. He had decided to steal a boat, find a good spot to land, scale the cliff, steal Gunnar's horse, and do what needed to be done. Chuckling to himself, he decided to *return* the blacksmith's horse once he was done, leaving absolutely no trace of his presence, except for the corpses he'd leave behind. He'd get back on the boat, return to Reykjavík and leave again, unnoticed, unremembered, victorious.

The plan had seemed perfect, as long as nothing went wrong – and then it had. Sigurd used to take his body for granted. Now that age was slowly creeping on him, his eyesight was no longer perfect. His muscles felt stiff when he woke up. And he had twisted the very same ankle no more than six months ago, walking down a perfectly straight road. No matter what Gunnar's delusions about time were, it waited for no one. Every time he woke up in the morning he was one day closer to death, just like everyone else. And now Sigurd had to waste precious weeks here, hoping that the blacksmith didn't say something stupid to the wrong person. One misplaced word could put an end to everything. He tried to move his ankle, and the flash of pain nearly blinded him.

Sigurd ground his teeth in an attempt to stop the tears of frustration that began to blur his vision. Blinking, he scanned the room again, looking for some distraction. The mismatched chairs angled around the fireplace, a rusty horseshoe hung over the door. A ladder lead upstairs through a trap door. It must have been a typical nineteenth century house at some point, with the kitchen area behind the rag added later. He hadn't gotten a chance to examine the house and figure out whether there was a bathroom of some sort or how many rooms there were in total. It didn't matter much, though. In his current state he couldn't access any of them.

He retrieved The Book from his backpack, recalling Gunnar's words about Sagas and the Bible. Sigurd felt the same way about The Book. There was no sentence he hadn't memorised by now. What made this copy special were the names and addresses written on the last page. He looked, just to make sure – the notes were still there, unaffected by the snow or humidity. Sigurd sighed, closed The Book, and returned it to his almost empty backpack.

He drank some coffee. Flipped through *The Women's Paper* again. Entertained himself by taking the "Which Sort of Dairy Are You" quiz. Short of re-reading the obituaries, he had absolutely nothing else to do. Hours stretched in front of him. Perhaps it was a good thing that he was missing his watch.

### *Then*

"Here we are," Arnar said, proudly. Juana, who had spent most of the trip dozing off in the cart, shook her head, rubbed her eyes and looked around. It didn't seem like they had arrived anywhere in particular. She didn't see any activity or any houses. She shivered in her coat and wished she had believed Arnar when he told her that it was an unusually cold year. The afternoon sunlight was pale and carried no warmth.

"It's late," Arnar said, "but I'm going to find that old bastard Bjarni and wake him up." He clapped his hands in excitement, and Juana couldn't help but smile wearily, even though all she wanted was a warm bed. Bjarni, she remembered, was the builder. She was very curious about his house, knowing it would be impressive, but theirs would be even better. Nothing but the very best for you, Arnar told her every day as the endless trip continued, and she believed him.

"Doesn't he know we're coming?"

"I don't know if he got the letter," said Arnar, slightly sheepish. "I thought we'd have more time. There's a chance the letter was on the same ship as we were."

He dropped to his knees, then knocked on the door of something that resembled a small grassy hill. Juana hadn't even noticed the shack until now.

It had two tiny windows and a door half the size of a grown man. It looked like something to keep dogs or poultry in. She couldn't believe her eyes when the miniature door opened and a man of normal height emerged, crouching through the doorway into the sunlight. He stood up straight and rubbed his eyes, as though Arnar had woken him up. He must have been having an afternoon nap, she thought, envious, then quickly compared the brothers. Arnar was taller, slimmer, definitely stronger. Bjarni, smaller and rounder, wouldn't have talked her into leaving her home.

The men hugged each other and started talking fast and loudly. Arnar had taught her a few basic phrases during the trip, but when he spoke to her, he said them slowly and clearly. Even then she had problems repeating the words, full of sounds she had never heard before. Love made him patient, kind, and happy to repeat everything a hundred times. She repaid him with as much effort as she could muster. But now, at the speed they spoke, she couldn't even make out words. If they used any of the phrases she had learned, she missed them completely. Without warning they stopped and looked at her. Arnar smiled and nodded. This was her cue to say something.

Her lips moved soundlessly as insecurity struck. "*Cy-kl?*" she said. Bjarni chuckled, and Juana immediately became uncomfortable, despite Arnar's encouraging smile and repeated nods. "*Yeah... pantar-risk?*" she said slowly, as if the words were rocks being pulled out of a deep well. She was aware that she'd said, "I American", but she had forgotten how to say "I am". Her lips moved again, but her mind was blank, and Juana stared at her feet. Some random Icelandic phrases came back to her, but she was too tired to remember what they meant.

"*Halló,*" said Bjarni, rescuing her. She rewarded him with a shy half-smile, then brightened further as she watched him struggle with the name "Juana". But she couldn't muster any interest or excitement anymore. "I need sleep," she said to Arnar. "Is there an inn nearby?"

"We're going to stay with him for a while," he answered.

"Oh," she said nervously, "that's nice. Where?"

Arnar looked at her oddly. "Here. That's where he lives."

"Oh... I see..." She swallowed, watching Bjarni crawl back into the "house". "Are we staying here long?" she asked, in an effort to delay the moment they would have to follow Arnar's brother through that door.

"Just until our house is ready. And you know what? If you think his house is big..." He noticed her mouth drop. "...then you're completely wrong – my brother is not a rich man, whether he admits it or not. Ours is going to be much, much bigger!" He spread his arms to indicate how big the house was going to be. "*Much* bigger. Enormous, in fact. Let's just get our things in and go to sleep."

Bjarni must have been extremely poor, thought Juana, and she felt sorry for him. No wonder Icelanders ran away to America. Maybe when their house was ready they could make some space for him. But for now she couldn't see how they would even fit inside. "Maybe we don't need a nap," she said, yawning desperately. "Isn't it better to wait for the night?"

"Oh, my love," said Arnar. "It's the middle of the night now. It never gets dark in the summer. It's part of the magic." Juana was too tired to remember if he had mentioned that. Reluctantly, she crawled inside.

The shack was larger than she expected, but not by much. One room housed everything, with a fire pit in the middle. Everything stank of smoke and dampness. There was one bed, which seemed too small even for Bjarni himself; he gave it to them and curled up on the floor, near the dying embers. From what Juana could see by the light streaming through the hole in the roof and through the tiny windows, the floor was made of dirt. It was too dark to see much and too light to fall asleep, as she quickly discovered. And it was *so* cold. In bed, wrapped in her coat under the sheepskins, she still shivered. The little ray of sun that came through the hole in the roof slowly moved. Despite her exhaustion Juana found herself watching it through half-closed eyes until it reached her face and rested there.

The heroines in books she had read were always forced to go through obstacles in order to reach their happy ending. She'd felt in turns sympathetic and thrilled as she read about their misadventures, comfortably tucked in her lovely, large bed… which she'd never see again. She wouldn't be able to contact her family ever again. At that moment the true meaning behind Arnar's words struck her. *Nobody here spoke English. Her father would never find them.* Juana had nothing but the contents of the bags she had hurriedly packed: money, some clothes, her Holy Bible. A sobering realisation cut through the growing, nauseous feeling. Without Arnar she'd be as good as dead, unable to even say "I am American" correctly. But he loved her and she loved him, and nothing else mattered.

"*Go-tha nokt,*" she whispered to herself. The ray of sun now moved to Arnar's face, but he didn't wake up. The stench of smoke was suffocating her. Maybe it would be better in the morning, she thought before falling asleep.

Breakfast was sparse, but there was a lot of coffee and she nearly cried in gratitude – finally something familiar. Arnar beamed, delighted with everything, and she smiled back. His enthusiasm was contagious. "I'll show you around," he said. "We are in a beautiful place. Everything here is beautiful, but this is an *exceptional* spot. Bjarni and I will start working on our house tomorrow. We're going to draw up the plan today, and no expenses will be spared. Just trust me, my love. You will fall in love with Iceland and see things you've never seen before. Put on your coat, let's have a walk."

Any hopes that she'd had of the "day" being warmer than the "night" were quickly squashed. Confusingly, now that the "night" had apparently ended, it grew darker. Heavy clouds covered the sun, threatening rain.

"How do you know whether it's day or night?" she asked.

Arnar didn't seem to hear her. "Look around," he said, beaming, rubbing his hands for warmth. "Look at the sky. Smell the air. Can you see the mountains?"

Juana looked up. They were commanding, imposing and unfriendly, the peaks hidden in the clouds... oh God, was she seeing snow, in June? Everything seemed grey. The hills in front of her were sharp rocks covered in moss. There were some flowers, sickly and clearly near death. She had never seen a desert but imagined this was what it must have looked like. Yet, Arnar was overjoyed, as if he were showing her the best attraction in the world.

"Have you ever seen mountains like those? We have everything. Mountains and the ocean. Lakes. Hot springs and geysers – wait till you see those! Volcanoes and glaciers!"

*We,* thought Juana. She liked the idea of hot springs much better than the glaciers, and said so.

"They are magical, my love. They are hot even in the middle of the winter. You can enjoy a hot bath, while you're surrounded by snow and ice." Just as she began to envision herself in a magical hot bath, Bjarni emerged from the shack wearing only trousers and a thin blue shirt. Juana looked at him and shivered. She inherited her coat from her two sisters, like most of her wardrobe. It was lined with fox fur with sleeves long enough to cover her hands. Back home she rarely needed more than that to get through a snowy winter, save for a hat and scarf. "It's June," she whined. "Why is it so cold? Aren't you cold?"

"Just a bit, I got too used to your climate. But it's really just the wind that makes it seem cold. And when we have our big house, we'll keep it warm."

Arnar was certainly right about the wind, which pushed itself under her coat, slapping her face, searching for her hands. Juana hadn't brought the winter hat and scarf, despite his insistence at packing all her warmest clothes. "Arnar," she started, nervously looking around, but the surroundings stole her attention again. Thick moss, a few miserable bushes, some purple and blue flowers, greying grass. None of those could provide shelter from the wind. "Where are the trees? I don't see any trees."

His grin barely wavered. "Don't look for what you can't see, look at what you can. Taste the air. We can walk to the ocean from here, or up into the hills. Look at all the flowers, aren't you curious what they are?"

"No," mumbled Juana, but still obediently looked around, trying to muster the enthusiasm she felt was required. Her gaze returned to Bjarni's shack, which now felt like the only safe place in the alien landscape. Homesickness pierced through her heart, and she looked at Arnar's face, seeking reassurance. He was staring at her in an intense way that made her feel both happy and uncomfortable. Shyly, she turned her face away, and the curve of her neck emerged from under the collar of her coat. Arnar stopped breathing for a moment, blown away again by the thought that this otherworldly beauty belonged to him. The greyness of the cloudy day was powerless against the flames of hair flowing freely down Juana's back. He stared in disbelief at her half-closed eyes, long eyelashes, slightly pouting lips. Almost afraid to ruin the vision in front of him, Arnar raised his hand to touch her cheek. A hint of blush appeared on her skin, and her gaze met his again. Her eyes were the colour of dew on young grass, he thought. Arnar couldn't help but imagine the entire country gasping in unison upon seeing the treasure he had brought along.

He beamed proudly until he noticed Bjarni standing with his hands in his pockets, chewing on something, staring at Juana. An unexpected feeling stirred in Arnar's heart. It was only natural that Bjarni would admire her, but he should admire her… with more respect. Surprised by his own reaction, Arnar returned his gaze to Juana's face, noticing she was looking in Bjarni's direction, curious, but shy.

"Say: 'good morning'," he advised.

"*Go-than day inn?*" she asked, uncertain. Bjarni beamed and responded in kind. She still didn't dare look him in the eye, but she smiled, and so did Arnar.

"And 'hello'?"

"*Hay!*"

"That was very good! Now say: 'I speak Icelandic'."

"*Yeh... oh... Yeh turnar... tarnar... islenskoor... kow...*" Her lips still moved, but the corners of her mouth dropped, and her voice grew quieter until it died out. "This is so hard," she mumbled, staring at her feet again. "I will never learn."

Arnar put his hands on her shoulders. "My love," he said gently, "I went to America without knowing a single word and I brought back the most beautiful woman in the world. You're an explorer," he continued. "Just like I used to be. Be patient, and one day very soon you will be able to talk to everyone about everything. And you will never see all there is to see, it would take all your life. This, here? That's the boring part of the country." He could see the dimples emerging. "We're free now. Nobody can tell us what to do anymore."

Juana couldn't help but smile at that, and all was right with the world.

In the afternoon, the brothers started drawing up a plan of their house in the dirt floor with a stick. Juana busied herself with her bags and soon discovered that her worries had been founded. There was no hat, scarf or gloves. She had one small, framed family photo, but there was no suitable space for it, so she just held it and stared at the faces of her parents, sisters, and her own. The photograph was taken when she was barely thirteen. They were all nervous under their glued-on smiles, wearing their Sunday best, standing motionlessly, terrified that the expensive photograph would come out wrong. This was how she felt right now. But the photograph had come out beautifully. The knot in her stomach relaxed, and the older, wiser Juana smiled at the girl on the photograph.

The brothers were arguing. Juana listened intently for a minute or so, but they were not saying "hello", "excuse me", "I'd like to eat something" or "I'm American". She was dying of curiosity. How many rooms would their house have? How big would their garden be? Would they have cows, sheep, horses? How many people would they employ? The questions had to wait though. With nothing else for her to do, it was time to explore the outside on her own, cold or not.

Juana saw two thin cows grazing behind the house. She waved at them. The cows did not wave back. Nevertheless, she felt slightly more cheerful, realising some things were the same everywhere. It looked like Bjarni lived on his own, but Arnar said it was a village, so there must be other villagers, reasoned Juana. She would find them, and soon they would be the best of friends… once she learned the language, of course.

The lack of trees was disconcerting. Surely there must be a forest somewhere nearby, she thought, as she climbed to the top of the mossy hill to better see her surroundings. Even the hill itself was strange. The soil was brick-red, then yellow, even pink. The few purple flowers that sprang up between the rocks were new to her. Juana stumbled on the wet moss and had to use her hands to prevent herself from slipping back down. Her dress was already stained, and her shoes were unsuitable for climbing. When another treacherous rock caused her to fall, bruise her knee and rip the dress on a sharp edge, Juana took it as a clear sign she shouldn't climb any further. She carefully turned around and sat on one of the larger rocks, massaging her knee. She'd get a new dress.

Both the ocean and the sky spread endlessly in front of her. To her left, the weather was clearing, and the water reflected the blue sky; to her right, clouds were gathering and the ocean looked cold and unfriendly. Like everything else, she thought before quickly scolding herself – that was not a thought of an adventurer. Bjarni's shack lay to her left. She could now distinguish another one on her right, then a third. But there was no church, no fields, not even fences! This wasn't a village, it was at best a small settlement.

Juana looked at the ocean again, wondering how far away home was. The frosty wind whipped her mercilessly, and she had to hold on to her dress. Was this really it?

# Thursday, March 11, 1920

"Stop telling me what Iceland looks like," complained Gunnar over breakfast. "I know what it looks like. I don't see what Arnar likes about it so much. Juana is right. It's just damn cold all the time. I only live here because I have to."

Sigurd's forehead wrinkled. "No offence, Gunnar, but how much of the world have you seen? In fact, how much of Iceland have you seen?"

"Enough," growled the blacksmith.

"What about waterfalls? Have you sat by a waterfall, just once in your life?"

Gunnar didn't respond. He was looking at the window behind Sigurd, watching a snowstorm raging outside, listening to the roof creak. Gunnar regularly had to fix leaks in the roof and wasn't looking forward to doing it again. *You're rich,* the idiotic thought reminded, as though he could fix the leaks by sticking money in them.

"You're not listening," said Sigurd. "It's a new world for her. Same as America was the New World for us… There is a lot to see outside Klettafjörður. Have you never felt like travelling? Discovering new places and returning home victorious, richer in experience…?"

"Aye, you sure got some experience there at the cliff. I'd go back, if I were her. Does she go back?"

Sigurd sighed. "You'll see. Think about it as a Saga. The final battle comes at the end." His attention was diverted by the sight of Ragnar, who seemed to be gnawing at his own side. Please, God, no lice, prayed Sigurd…

Gunnar continued to scratch his chin. "Does your story have a title?" he asked.

"*Þetta reddast,*" answered Sigurd without thinking, then covered his mouth with his hand a moment too late.

"Oh," said the disappointed blacksmith. "So, it does all work out well in the end."

"I suppose it depends on how you define 'well'," said Sigurd, angry both with himself and Gunnar. "And whose point of view you're looking from. Anyway, '*Þetta reddast*' is just a saying. Don't read too much into it. I promise it doesn't work out so well for many of the people involved." Damn, damn, damn, he thought. Every day brought another proof that he should have never started telling the story.

Gunnar was nodding, but not listening. His attention had already wandered elsewhere. "I'm going to town today," he announced. "After work. Fresh bread and stuff. Newspapers. Anything else?"

"I'd kill for some books... even just one to begin with...?"

"I can get you more, no problem."

"Maybe just one," Sigurd said, begrudgingly. "Ask for whatever foreign book is selling the best right now. No, let me think... Ask for literary classics. Maybe buy two... and maybe you could get some bedding for me... no, I changed my mind, get me one book, a thick one. Or, maybe two..." he trailed off. "No. This is not good. You can't just start buying books and newspapers all of a sudden. Can I send you to Reykjavík?"

"Can't today. I have to see Doctor Brynjólf. He prescribes me better medicine. The cleaning woman comes on Monday. I'll go then."

Monday seemed months away, but now at least Sigurd would have something to do while Gunnar was away – obsess and worry over the identity of the cleaning woman. "Oh, of course, yes, thank you. So, when you see the doctor in Klettafjörður... say, what time will... I mean... when, um..." His voice broke in uncertainty as he remembered Gunnar's outburst. But the blacksmith didn't look angry. He was looking down at his hands, fiddling with his mug.

"Aye... I have to check on Thursdays," he finally mumbled. Sigurd raised his eyebrows and waited. "If I'm not on time people want to talk to me," Gunnar added reluctantly, still avoiding his guest's curious stare.

"But do you think it will still be light before you return...?"

"Nay, not in this weather."

"It's just that I can't read in the dark..." started Sigurd, then sighed. "Remember, literary classics. And get me *Vísir,* please. And... umm... perhaps also *The Women's Paper*...?" He blushed before dismissing the blacksmith with an irritated hand gesture. "Go. Work."

Gunnar locked himself in the forge, lit the fire, put his hands in his pockets and stared at it. After a few minutes he sighed, picked a chunk of iron from his scrap pile, and started working on a rose. He had to kill some time until his client, a somewhat-known artist whose name he forgot, arrived. She wanted to see how much progress he had made on her elaborate bookcase. He hadn't bothered to start on it yet and didn't feel like it now. This was a good time to make roses. Boring, repetitive projects helped his mind calm down. His hands and eyes did the work while his thoughts curled up like a sleepy cat. Minutes and hours passed by, at times interrupted by swearing when some hot oxide added a new scar on top of the old ones.

By the time the artist arrived, sweat was dripping off Gunnar's forehead. He listened to the woman for about a minute, then tuned her out, nodding every now and then. She seemed pleased enough to listen to her own voice. In his mind Gunnar began going through the list of things that needed to be done once the woman stopped bothering him and left. He needed about an hour to wash a bit here and there, change into his "doctor clothes", look and smell a bit more presentable, allow Karl to transport him to town at her usual speed, then wait at a safe distance just so that he could watch the big clock on top of the tower until it was almost four. There was something else… The woman seemed to have finished talking and was now staring at him questioningly. "Aye," he said, nodding vigorously, "it will be ready soon." This seemed to be the correct answer and, once final pleasantries were exchanged, Gunnar could close the door and breathe with relief.

The rose, nearly finished, lay on the anvil. He put his hand above the metal to check if it was still hot, then picked it up and examined it. It was looking good. Some more shaping, cleaning, then a beeswax finish, and it would be ready to go. But his mind was already chaotically shouting at him – the money, the food, books, bedding, Brynhildur's questions, more medication, *one hundred sixty-six, seventy-four, but first ten,* more medication. Gunnar knew what would happen had he tried to continue. He switched off the blower, sent pieces of oxide into the air with one swipe of his hand, then put the rose back on the gleaming surface of the anvil. The dust in the air made the light look like a divine illumination, and Gunnar's mind quietened for a brief moment in admiration of the beauty he was creating. He marvelled over the contrast between the black, rough flower and the shiny surface of the anvil. *You're rich,* an unwanted thought yanked him back into reality, and all of a sudden the rose was just a chunk of dirty metal covered in ugly oxide. The dust in the air was bad for his lungs, and the reflections of light from the anvil unpleasantly blinding. The silver and black turned into shades of grey, worthless when compared to the colourful banknotes.

"I don't have to do this anymore," Gunnar confided to Ragnar, who was asleep at a safe distance. "I can do anything I want. I'm free." He should have been getting ready, but instead he stood by the anvil, absent-mindedly caressing the smooth surface with calloused fingers, waiting to feel happy. He picked up the rose and tried to crush it in his hand, and smiled proudly when the iron, still warm, resisted. He put it back in the recess in the middle of the anvil.

Gunnar loved this anvil, but there was no escaping the fact that it was old. Corners were no longer sharp, the horn chipped, no longer as round as it should be. He could buy a new one now, he mused, but this thought didn't make him happy either. It felt like a betrayal. This anvil had served his father. The faint feeling of guilt was promptly replaced by the knot of anxiety when he remembered he needed to start preparing for the trip. As he walked towards the door, the rose forgotten, he was already looking forward to returning home.

Doctor Brynjólf's wife was as welcoming and pleasant as always. The protruding belly didn't seem to bother her, other than making her seem even more fragile. Everything here seemed fragile, including the chair Gunnar sat on. It had a soft crimson pillow he was afraid to rip, thin wooden legs that threatened to break, a back rest that he'd never dare rest his back on. She handed him a tiny cup of coffee with a matching saucer and a pretty, tiny silver spoon. Gunnar thanked her profusely, then slowly placed the offering on the table, trying not to touch the white cotton. His hands were not just black and dirty now, but also cold and sweaty. The blacksmith knew he didn't fit in here, in this place full of clean, delicate objects. Everything he owned was sturdy. What was wrong with sturdy? Gunnar didn't know why every time he visited the doctor his breath turned shallow, heartbeat accelerated, throat tightened. What he did know was that he couldn't tell Doctor Brynjólf that he was afraid of his coffee cups.

Brynjólf charged well for his services and for medication, whether it came in the form of a large flask, powders, or small pills. Not even the Sheriff, who was Brynjólf's patient as well, could afford to live so lavishly. *I am rich too*, Gunnar thought without conviction. But what did that change? He admired the big windows – this was not a household where heat was a precious commodity. The colour of dark green wallpaper beautifully complimented the crimson curtains, made of the same soft fabric as the pillow Gunnar was sitting on. The doctor's wife ushered the blacksmith inside just as he had finally managed to distract himself, pondering replacing the oil paint in his kitchen with wallpaper, and the practicalities of such a decision. Her porcelain smile made his heart race in a way that was not at all romantic.

"Your face looks grey," said the doctor, instead of a welcome. He leaned forward, his fingers steepled, his smile warm. This made Gunnar slink back in his chair. "Are you okay? Are things going well?"

"Oh," said the blacksmith, "just as always, just as always." He took off his cap and held on to it to stop his hands from shaking.

"Is your back still hurting?"

"A bit."

"Have you been taking care of your posture while working?"

"Aye," said Gunnar, who didn't. He withdrew just a bit more. The room seemed to be overheated.

Brynjólf shook his head, and the smile started to wane, replaced by the usual concerned expression. "You really should keep your back straight. The pain is just going to get worse and then you won't be able to work. Should I show you again?"

"Nay. I remember."

"The usual, then, I guess," sighed the doctor. Gunnar tried to open his mouth, tried to gather courage to ask for a double dose of medication, but paradoxically couldn't – because he hadn't had any yet. No sound came out, as he watched the doctor put a sticker on the bottle. One spoon three times a day with meals, said the sticker.

"You're not very talkative today."

"Aye. Nay."

"Is something going on? Are you doing… well? Any new customers?"

"Uh… just one. But all is well." Gunnar started to wring his flat cap as if squeezing water out, stared down at his hands, stopped, put the cap on his head, looked back up, tried to smile, pulled the cap off again and started fiddling with it. "*Very* well," he added, crushed by the weight of Brynjólf's curious stare. A little drop of sweat slowly trickled down Gunnar's forehead, stopping at his eyebrow.

"That's it then, I suppose," said the doctor, discreetly looking at the clock hanging over the door. "Let me know if there is anything else I can do for you… and I mean anything."

"Aye. Thank you, Doctor Brynjólf."

Gunnar left, protectively clutching his medication to his chest. Brynjólf shook his head at the closed door and sighed. The doctor had a tendency to mix up his patients every now and then, but Gunnar was impossible to confuse with anyone else. He also seemed very determined to slide down the rabbit hole. Maybe the town's community could come up with some sort of plan, before it's too late, thought the doctor guiltily.

Once he made it outside, Gunnar hid behind the nearest corner. He looked around – nobody – took his little flask out and drank half of its contents in one go – it wasn't a large flask, he'd point out, had anybody asked – he closed his eyes, savoured the burning in his throat, and imagined a black cloud lifting. He put the flask back, then rested his back against the wall and waited. It didn't take long for his heartbeat to become more regular again and his stomach to calm down. Gunnar wiped his mouth on his coat sleeve, spat on the ground, and returned to the street, his walk steadier, his back straighter. *Now* he was ready to visit the merchant.


"I've got things for you," Gunnar announced upon his return. "I bought your bedding. And a book. New sweater and trousers for myself. And very good boots, let me tell you. Bread and eggs. Newspapers…"

"Wait, wait," interrupted Sigurd. "I said not to buy too much…"

"I went to the expensive store – I mean the merchant. Anna will not know. Brynhildur is the worst though," continued the blacksmith, for once able to unload his thoughts onto someone who wasn't a dog. "Needs to know everything. Asking about my back and the mattress. Unbelievable. All she ever does is ask questions. Look at my boots! I've never–"

"Wait a moment, so this Brynhildur works for the merchant…?"

"Of course not," huffed Gunnar. "She's Anna's daughter. I just said."

"Do you know," remarked Sigurd, barely stopping himself from saying something else, "I think the best way to make sure she stops asking you all those questions is not to answer. Just ignore her."

"I do," said Gunnar. "It doesn't help. She's very persistent." He wiped his sweaty hands on the trousers. It was fine now that he had a new pair (brown, soft, thick corduroy, he was assured they would survive for years, as long as he didn't burn holes in them), and no matter how much Sigurd frowned, the new trousers pleased him, and so did the boots.

### *Then*

Visions of being a lady of the house, delegating tasks to servants, had to wait. The house would take months to build. But Juana didn't stay idle. A girl called Helga began to teach her Icelandic, help tend to the cows, gut fish, and prepare meals for the men. "*Sail Helka,*" said Juana every day, and the girl responded, cheerfully, with "*Sail Yuana*". The new variations on her name never failed to make Juana smile briefly before they moved on to learning difficult words, and almost all of them seemed difficult. There was the "ooh" letter which sounded like it ended with a "r", but it didn't. The one that sounded like saying "k" and "l" at the same time. *Yuana* was now a *Pantar-risk*, and before she spoke, she always remembered to say *Af-sakeith*, which she felt should end with "d", but didn't. Helga couldn't speak a word of English, which forced them to speak Icelandic all the time. But, just as Arnar said, Juana realised with relief that it was getting easier every day. She no longer stumbled when greeting Bjarni or Helga. Initially her Icelandic was limited to pleasantries and vocabulary related to food, but Helga was curious and asked a lot of questions, which she then helped Juana answer.

Initially Juana didn't even notice when the sun started setting and the days began to grow shorter. By then she was used to sleeping in an uncomfortable position on the tiny bed, no matter whether it was light or dark inside. The ocean and mountains didn't intimidate her anymore. She had even gotten used to the wind, although she still disliked it. But there was one question that remained unanswered. Every time Juana asked how the house was progressing, Arnar answered in the same way. He wanted it to be a surprise. "You will see it when it's ready," he repeated, always ready to disperse her doubts and worries.

Things improved further when Arnar presented Juana with her first book in Icelandic – the Holy Bible. She read it out loud and Helga, infinitely patient, corrected her pronunciation. So empowered, Juana tried to befriend the other women living within walking distance, but they never progressed past exchanging empty pleasantries – not only because of the language barrier. She couldn't help feeling that they were all very plain. Those women's hands were ruined, faces red and raw, hair dirty and hanging in streaks around their faces. Juana dressed better to milk the cows. She silently disapproved of them, and the women returned her dislike in kind. She did nothing, they said to each other, listening to Helga's reports. As though she were some sort of a princess.

"Jealousy," explained Arnar shortly. "They will never be as beautiful as you, nor will they dress so pretty." He looked at her with a mixture of pride and worry. Juana looked every bit the princess that the women accused her of being. Her clothes were lovely, but impractical. She dressed to look pretty, while other women, including Helga, dressed for work and comfort.

Juana's longing for adventure was intensifying. No books ever ended after three chapters with the words "…and then they worked, not particularly happily, ever after". But while Helga was perfectly polite and helpful, she did not seem to have any interest in doing anything spontaneous. She seemed happy to do most of the chores, help Juana with her education, then go home. Helga rarely spoke of anything but work, until one day she unexpectedly touched on a different subject.

"It's so nice for you to be married," Helga said, without raising her eyes from the fish she was gutting.

"Why is it so nice?" Juana asked, once the meaning of the word "married" had been established.

"It's so hard to get married. Of course," said Helga, blushing modestly, "you have to meet someone first. You have to have enough money to buy land, support your family and one sheep…"

"One sheep," repeated Juana in a flat voice, wondering if there was a chance she had misunderstood that.

Helga nodded, giving up on the fish. "And then you get married."

"And… then?"

"And then you're married. That's it."

"Yes, but what do you *do*?" dug Juana.

"You live, Yuana. You have kids, you work, you read and write. Make sure your family stays warm and doesn't die of hunger." Helga shrugged. "Visit people in the winter. What else is there to do?"

Juana opened her mouth to answer, but she didn't know the words to express her longing. Maybe Helga was right about life. Yet, when the girl departed, Juana found herself staring at the family photograph, trying to hush the echo of Helga's voice saying, "it's so nice for you to be married". She imagined how unimpressed her parents would be and hurriedly put the photograph away. Looking at it made her feel ashamed.

"Arnar," she asked that evening, when he had returned from work and begun to wolf down the fish soup that Helga had made. "When are we going to get married?"

"Soon, my love," said Arnar and put down the spoon to kiss Juana. The only moments of intimacy they had were the rare times when Bjarni was away. "When the house is built and we're living together."

"Can't we go to the church, at least? I miss going to the Mass."

"Why don't you pray here, at home, my love? God is everywhere." He kissed her again.

Juana had more doubts and more questions, but decided to push them aside, as she did so often now. Arnar's arms and kisses made her feel warm and gave her the safe feeling she longed for more than anything else. But, unlike ever before, his hand – gentle, warm, determined – touched her in a way that made fire flow through her veins – all the thoughts rapidly sped away, except a tiny voice that told her to wait – but it felt so good, his head – his hands – the warmth… and it was like this that Bjarni found them, bringing them back to reality with a slap of cold wind from the door he opened.

"Oh," he said. "*Afsakið mig!*" He withdrew awkwardly and closed the door. Juana's brief moment of happiness at having understood the words was rapidly replaced by mortification. They had nearly sinned, no, they had sinned already, and they had been seen by God and man. Arnar laughed nervously, and Juana glared at him.

"There's nothing funny about this," she blurted out.

"No," he agreed, the grin immediately replaced by a sad, loving expression. "I am sorry. I couldn't stop myself…"

"You – we can never do this again, not until we are married." Juana's voice sounded strangled, her face nearly white. "Now everyone is going to find out."

"Bjarni is a discreet man," said Arnar. "I will talk to him. I'll ask–"

"God knows," said Juana. "No matter what you say to Bjarni, God saw everything, He saw our sin…"

"I'm sorry," whispered Arnar. He tried to kiss her cheek, but Juana jerked her head away. "I promise," he said. "I will not do anything you don't want."

"And what is it that you want?"

"All I want is for you to be happy."

When Bjarni returned, soaked from waiting outside in the rain, Juana couldn't look him in the eye. Were they laughing at her? Was Arnar's tone boastful or lecherous? The bed was too small to avoid touching Arnar altogether, and she spent a sleepless night praying for forgiveness.

"We're going to town today," Arnar announced in the morning.

"Are we?" Her voice sounded flat and there were bags under her eyes.

"We are. We've been working so much that I haven't had a chance to relax for weeks."

"That's true… and maybe afterwards I could see how our house is progressing?"

Arnar laughed. "It's nowhere near ready yet, but remember this: we will be living there before winter starts."

Juana suddenly had a thought that made her eyes open wide. He was taking her to church. They were going to marry! Suddenly she no longer felt tired.

The trip took over an hour, and the weather alternated between sunshine and sleet, cold water soaking through Juana's new hat, dripping under her coat. She didn't complain once. Chaotic thoughts rumbled in her head. They would have to buy a new dress first, of course. Who would throw the rice? Her excitement only increased when she saw the first building, then another, and then, God gracious, the church! It was a small building made of rocks and turf, nowhere near what she had imagined, but the cross on top was just as it should be.

A huge smile lit Juana's face. "There it is," she exclaimed, "now we can get married!" She jumped off the horse and stood in front of the building, waiting for Arnar to drop to his knee and offer her a ring, or at least say something. But he stayed behind her, quiet. Juana turned back, beaming with joy. "Where are the wit–" she began, then noticed Arnar's grave expression, and her smile began to wane.

"It's too late," he said. "Oh, my love, don't look at me like that. We just took too long. Everyone thinks we are married since Bjarni found us in bed together. I couldn't tell them we were sinning all this time." He paused for a moment, struck by a worrying thought. "Did you tell Helga?"

"Did I tell Helga," Juana repeated, incredulous. She turned away from him, the sight of the church door blurred by the tears in her eyes. Bjarni was supposed to be discreet, she thought, at first angry, then ashamed again.

"My love," started Arnar, his voice shaky, uncertain, and Juana's anger returned. She abruptly turned back, and Arnar winced. He had never seen her like this before.

"You never intended to marry me," accused Juana, her voice rising dangerously. "Why?" He tried to grab her hands, but she pulled hers away as if burned by hot iron. "Tell me!"

"Don't be angry," he pleaded. "We are as good as married in the eyes of God. Nobody cares, anyway."

"I do!"

"My love... do you know how difficult it is to get a permit...?"

"Yes. It takes one sheep. Go get a sheep, then a permit. I don't see what's so hard about it!"

"But think about it," he begged. "What's the point? Your family is not here and neither is mine, except for Bjarni. We spend all our time with him anyway. Why does it matter?"

"It matters to me and it matters to God! I want to have your family name."

"But you wouldn't have my name," he gently explained. "I thought you knew that by now. That's not how it works here. My name literally means Arnar, son of Jón. Helga is called Hannesdóttir, daughter of Hannes. Nothing would change, my love, nothing. God loves us as we are. It's just a piece of paper. Why would God care about a piece of paper...?"

It wasn't the piece of paper that Juana desired. She wanted a white, puffy dress; a triumphant descent from the stairs of the church; rice thrown in the air; a photographer asking them to pose without moving for minutes. A new name and a wedding band on her finger, sealing their union in front of God...

"What about your other promises? You promised me waterfalls, volcanoes, you promised me hot springs! I want to go to a hot spring."

"We will," Arnar quickly promised, "tomorrow." He looked afraid.

"I want a wedding ring," she demanded.

"Of course, you will have the most beautiful of rings! I will have it ordered for you. Diamond? Ruby? Anything for my wife. Or just gold?"

"What's a traditional Icelandic jewel?"

Arnar's brows furrowed in thought. He didn't know. "Anything you want. You can even have a piece of volcanic rock," he joked. But to Juana that sounded wonderful and exotic, and excitement promptly replaced anger. "I'd like to have a piece of volcanic rock!"

"Lava is everywhere," he laughed. "You're walking on it every day. I will make sure it's a ring like no other. I'll have one made especially for you. You have my word."

She didn't really know what else to ask for. "I'm cold. Can we go to the inn?"

"Hmm... I think the owner of the inn is away, working in the country."

"Oh," said Juana, momentarily thrown off. "Then I want to confess." She pushed the door, but it didn't open, and she looked at Arnar questioningly.

"Hmm," he started, averting his gaze with a guilty expression on his face, and Juana angrily interrupted. "Is the pastor away, working in the country?"

"Aye... He probably is, actually. He's hardly ever here. He's overseeing the children's education in all villages nearby, as well as here in town. He also takes care of the funerals, and…" He nearly said "weddings". "He's old, and that's a lot of work for one man. We'd have to come again on Sunday. But we can visit the merchant," he said. "She's bound to be here, and I want to spend money on my wife." Juana winced at the word but said nothing. *Wife. Husband. Piece of paper.* She felt it was all wrong but couldn't explain why anymore.

"When you came to America," she asked her husband on the way back, "how did you feel?"

He thought about it for a while. "Lost," he answered.

"Did it get better?"

Arnar didn't answer for a minute. "It got better," he said, "when I met you."

Juana spent the rest of the trip chiding herself for her own unrealistic expectations. This wasn't home… no, this *was* home, but she didn't know their customs all that well yet. How strange was the idea of a permit requiring ownership of sheep? The vision of a non-existent crowd throwing rice at her disappeared, as she realised she hadn't even seen rice since they arrived. Juana chuckled to herself as she imagined the villagers throwing salted cod at them, and no longer felt upset.

They went to bed early that evening. Juana was on the brink of falling asleep when Arnar got out of bed. The door opened quietly, and he crawled outside. A minute later he returned, lay next to her again, and soon started to snore. There was nothing unusual about a full bladder, she thought, then dozed off. The next night Arnar woke her up by doing the exact same thing. When it happened three nights in a row, she started to wonder. Was it something he ate? But then – every night at the same time? Juana couldn't remember Arnar ever having done this before, and she lay in the darkness, wondering, hoping he wasn't ill.

The next evening Juana couldn't stop herself from casting suspicious looks at Arnar and she resolved to stay awake to see if he did the same thing again. She was so convinced she was still awake that when Arnar gently shook her shoulder, waking her up, she let out a little alarmed cry. Bjarni muttered something in his sleep, then emitted a snore louder than the noise she had made.

"Sshh," Arnar whispered. "Put on your coat and come outside."

Where are we going, Juana wondered, half-asleep as she crawled through the small door. The cold night air roused her within seconds.

It was cool inside the hut, but outside it was freezing, everything covered in a thin layer of ice, lit by moonlight, and, and…

"Look at the sky," he whispered. Juana obediently raised her eyes, and her mind went blank as her mouth opened in shock.

Something that resembled green fire danced in the sky. The colours moved faster, then slower. They disappeared, then reappeared, regrouping stronger, covering the stars. Their shine was so powerful that the frozen grass appeared greener than during the day, a gleaming colour she had never seen before.

"There," Arnar pointed, and Juana's eyes followed. The flames painted the sky, slowing down, stopping as if teasing, then returning to their dance with renewed energy.

"Is this magic?" she whispered. "Is it mountains changing shape? Is the sky burning?"

"When the nights get longer and darker, this is what God sends us to let us know he hasn't forgotten about us," he whispered back. "It seems dark, aye, but there is light and always will be. When you think things are going bad, remember they will always turn out fine. This is what *petta reddast* means. It will always turn out fine."

Juana shivered from the cold, but she didn't care, fascinated by the magical lights. If there was a pattern to their dance, she couldn't understand it. The green colour was now being licked by a hint of purple, as if the flames themselves were set on fire again. But the fire she had known until now never looked or felt like this, it never obscured the stars or cast a greenish glow. "Are you sure this isn't dark magic?" she whispered and made a sign of the cross.

"This is the fire that burned in my heart every day that I spent in America," said Arnar, holding her hands tight and kissing her cheek. Juana didn't pay him much attention, staring, trying to understand the impossible. Only God or Devil could create something like this, and the beauty convinced her it was God himself. He was giving them their blessing. "This is what happiness looks like," whispered Arnar, and she believed him.

It was at that moment that the realisation struck her, raising goosebumps on her skin: she had been living her adventure without even noticing. She was surrounded by magic, a prize more valuable than any jewel, more astounding than any story she had read before.

That night changed Juana forever.

Arnar had many more wonders to show her. They held hands, listening to the roar of a waterfall, admiring the rainbow that formed over it. "God's blessing," explained Arnar. Juana cried out in fear and excitement when the boiling water from a geyser erupted into the sky. "God's power," explained Arnar. They enjoyed baths in a hot pool that stank of sulphur. "Devil?" asked Juana quietly, worried by the heat and the smell. "Not here," said Arnar, "not in Iceland. God has everything under control." Relieved, Juana reached out to pick up some snow from the shore and watched it melt in her warm hand.

"Isn't everything perfect?" whispered Arnar, massaging her shoulders. But instead of relaxing, Juana tensed. "What is it, love?"

"I would like to see the house," she said reluctantly. "I know, I know, it's a surprise and all, but it's snowing already, and…

"So you'd like a surprise… Perhaps we have one for you…"

"Today…?" she whispered.

"If you like."

"Is it big?"

"Much bigger than Bjarni's."

"Will I have a garden?"

"It's up to you…"

Before he finished the sentence, Juana was already out of the water, energetically drying herself, ignoring the cold air, chiding him for not moving fast enough. She didn't notice his facial expression, excited beyond belief to finally leave the confines of Bjarni's smoky hut and tiny bed. As they approached the new dwelling Arnar began to slow down. Juana, impatient, let go of his hand and broke into a run. Arnar followed, dragging his feet, feeling his breath cease, his stomach knot. The closer they got, the slower Juana's footsteps became, and he caught up with her right before she entered the house.

"You have stove," said Bjarni. "Fire is in stove," he continued in English, very pleased with himself. "Good. Hot good. Two room!" He ran out of the words at that point, so he finished in Icelandic: "All for yourselves. No other house around here even compares to this one." Juana shivered. Hot good, indeed. "Look at those windows," continued Bjarni, too excited to remember he needed to speak slowly. "They are so big! We've made you a good roof and when grass grows on the top it will look incredible. There will be no leaks and, if there are, just come to me. And your garden is going to be…" Bjarni stopped when he realised Juana wasn't listening.

She looked shocked, which pleased him. Of course, she hadn't seen a dwelling as luxurious as this one before. Her pupils widened, mouth half open, and she wrapped herself tighter in the coat that she never seemed to take off. Bjarni's chest puffed out with pride. He spent many years feeling like a loser next to his brothers. Today was his turn to shine.

Juana tried to stop comparing it with her parents' house, she really tried, but the nausea hit the moment she had to bend down just a bit while entering their new house. The lamps were lit, and she could see everything – what little there was to see. Juana swallowed, then forced a smile, but her lower lip trembled. Bjarni didn't expect this sort of reaction, but Arnar did. He wrapped his arms around Juana. "Americans," he mouthed over her shoulder and Bjarni's eyebrows rose in an unvoiced question.

"I want to go home," she wailed. Her fingers convulsively grabbed Arnar's sweater, and Bjarni finally understood what was going on. "I'll bring your bags," he mouthed back at Arnar, then quietly let himself out.

Juana didn't register his departure. All the thoughts she had been pushing away spilled out now, and there was no way to stop them. "I miss my home," she wept, "I miss my parents, oh God, I miss the church so much, and the sunshine! We're living in sin, we stole their money, this is not even a house, my mother would never believe it, I can't stay here…" She continued listing her complaints, her words becoming unintelligible, and Arnar just held her in his strong arms. Finally, sobbing turned into sniffles and one firm resolution. "I want to go home. Take me home, Arnar, take me home. I can't live here. Take me back home."

She tried to push him away, but his embrace tightened. "This is home," he said, as gently as he could. Juana's body shook every few seconds, but she was now silent. Just as Arnar thought her hysteria was over, she repeated in a flat, yet decisive voice:

"Then you stay here and send me home alone. I am going back to my family. I am not going to stay here."

Arnar felt a chill of fear. He had never heard her speak like that.

"But… what about the hot springs? What about the lights? You said you loved them so much," he cried. "What about us? We are one, we are destined to be together, how could you forget?"

"No," she said, glaring at him without a hint of warmth. "I am leaving and going back to my parents." She pushed him away again, and this time Arnar let go of her. "You can do whatever you want. I want the money back. It's my final decision."

He felt the cold tentacles of panic and blurted out the first words that popped into his head. "I don't think your parents would take you back."

Juana's body stilled. Her breath now came in tiny, sharp pants.

"You have ruined your family's name. You stole your parents' money. You ran away with a strange man. You never so much as sent them a letter to tell them where you were. And then… you lived with him in sin ever since, unmarried. As you said. What would you say to them?"

The enormity of the words struck them both at the same moment. Juana tumbled over, and Arnar caught her in his arms.

"I am sorry," he whispered. "I am so, so sorry. I can't believe I said that. Please don't leave me. I will do anything you want. Every single thing." Tears rolled down his face now. "My love, I will… I have… I do not know what came over me. I will never forgive myself for this. I will…" he ran out of words. Juana slowly withdrew, and Arnar dropped to his knees. "I beg you," he burst out in despair, "if you must leave me, I will understand, but take this first." He pulled a small pouch out of his pocket and handed it to Juana. Their eyes met. She didn't lower her gaze as her fingers found the silken string, slowly unwrapped the pouch, and fished out a ring. In the lamplight, the stone came alive, flickering red like a bloodied amber or the finest of wines.

"I forgot," she whispered, turning the ring around, hypnotised by the delicate handwork and the light reflecting from its surfaces.

"I didn't," he whispered back. "Wait till you see it in the sun. They say it looks like blood, and it does; the blood that is in our hearts, in the love and passion that connect us. Can you see?" He stood up again and brought her hand closer to the lamp. "This is gold," he pointed out, "this is white gold. Woven together, like you and me. Always together, and the only thing between us is the red jewel of love. Have you ever seen a ring like this?"

"No," she breathed. The ring changed everything. Neither her sisters nor her mother had ever owned anything like this. The rock was huge, the ring heavy on her finger. "*Elska*," remembered Juana. Love. She would never forget the value of love as long as she had this ring. Juana looked up from the red fire of the volcano to the deep blue fire in the eyes of the man she would now think of as her husband. As painful as his words were, all of them were true. The low, slanted roof, the bed, the small windows that Bjarni praised so much didn't matter, nothing but love mattered. Gold and white gold forever connected by the fire. Passion, love, adventure, she remembered. Exactly what she wanted. A conciliatory smile slowly emerged on her face, and Arnar knew he had won her heart. He vowed never to lose it again.

# Friday, March 12, 1920

"I have to go to town," announced Gunnar, grumpily, "but I don't want to."

Sigurd raised his eyebrows politely, but no explanation came, so he returned to squinting at *The Picture of Dorian Gray*.

Gunnar went into the forge and examined the metal table. He didn't have much for Anna. He fished out two ashtrays – that was all he had, and it wouldn't make him rich… *But you* are *rich*, the nagging thought reminded him, and he gently put the ashtrays back on his table. He picked up the rose, forgotten on the anvil, and turned it around in his blackened hand. Anna would be pleased to see it finished. But Gunnar no longer felt the need to please Anna and he put the unfinished rose back where he found it.

As Karl trotted towards Klettafjörður, Gunnar indulged in thoughts about the ring. It sounded like some sort of treasure someone might kill or die for. Maybe the exciting bit was finally coming. The blacksmith started designing the delicate ring in his head, even though he liked his fires big, his hammers heavy, and his metal thick. He didn't even notice his hand automatically reaching for the flask until he had actually taken a sip of the liquor – how did that happen? He hadn't intended to… Gunnar put it back and tried to go back to the image of the ring, but his mind was already imagining the conversation in the store. His stomach slowly clenched, cheeks warmed in a way he was so familiar with. Gunnar allowed himself one more sip, a very small one, firm in his decision not to drink another drop. He smacked his lips, examining the flask in his hand as if he had never seen it before. But before returning the flask to his pocket he quickly uncorked it again and poured a good half of its contents down his throat. It wasn't his fault. Anybody would feel like this having to deal with those two. It was medicinal. He was already starting to feel better.

In Klettafjörður, Anna locked the door of the store and turned back to Brynhildur, whose make-up was now smudged with tears.

"You have completely ruined this dress," Anna snapped. "You're stupid, irresponsible, and you have no idea what you're doing. I thought you could at least sew. What *were* you even doing? Oh, no need to tell me, it's all about your bosoms, isn't it? You think they will somehow fix the problem? Look at your sister! Think about it, silly girl," Anna said, then scowled again, as at the age of thirty-two Brynhildur was hardly a girl even if she acted like one. "Why do you think she is married and you aren't? Give me this dress. I'll fix it for you. We can't afford to buy new clothes, since we hardly sell any!"

"Ásta is a traitor," burst out Brynhildur, holding on to the dress, knowing what it would look like once Anna fixed it. "You said it yourself. She's sleeping with the enemy…"

"Stop speaking ill about your sister," huffed Anna. "She is always welcome here. She treats her mother with love and respect, unlike you!"

Brynhildur gave her a wounded look. "I am *sorry*, Mother. I just want everything to be alright…" She sniffled again, then wiped her nose with the ruined dress.

"Mark my words," said Anna. "This is never going to help you accomplish anything. It is not the dress that's the problem and it's not the make-up or whatever it is that you have done to make your hair so shiny. You're doing it all wrong."

Brynhildur threw the remnants of the dress on the floor as two more angry tears flew down her face, smudging the eyeliner further. "What am I supposed to do then?! Tell me, Mother, how did *you* catch Father? What did you or Ásta do that I am not doing? Tell me!"

To Brynhildur's surprise, Anna blushed, then crossed her arms, pursed her lips and gave Brynhildur a long, hard stare. She didn't answer.

"What? What did I say now?"

"You must have respect for your par–" started Anna, but Brynhildur immediately interrupted. "Yes, Mother, I know. My father is dead, a horrible accident a long time ago and you don't want to talk about it, that's fine. But I'm asking how you caught him when he was still alive!"

Anna looked around, seeking escape. "Things were, umm, different back then…" she began. "Oh! I think someone's at the door."

"There's no one at the door," snapped Brynhildur, but then a shy knock followed – one that conveyed hope that the door would remain locked.

"It's our Gunnar!" beamed Anna.

"I didn't know you liked him so much," muttered Brynhildur as her mother ran to the door and opened it.

"Come in, Gunnar, it's cold," rattled Anna, grabbing his arm and pulling him inside. "So lovely to see you! Although we'd been expecting you yesterday. We worried something happened to you. Is everything going well?"

"I forgot," muttered the blacksmith. "Very busy."

She snatched the bag from his hands and looked inside. "More ashtrays, really, Gunnar? We told you to make *roses*. But it's perfectly fine, I'll just put those next to the other three. You have enough money now, we hear. Where did you get that money from?"

"Lots of work at the moment," Gunnar said, staring confusedly at the top of Brynhildur's head sticking out from behind the counter, and wondering if he perhaps he had drunk too much. "Er. How do you know…"

"Oh YES!" boomed Anna, tempted to wave her hand in front of his eyes. "You're working for Maureen, the artist. I saw her *art* and let me tell you, I am not very impressed, but who am I to judge? Anyway, I sent her your way, as I'm sure she mentioned. You're not wearing the new boots? Ásta tells me you picked out a lovely pair. They're very good for the price, although if you had let me know I would have gotten them for you much cheaper. Not that price matters to you, I guess."

"You know everything," whispered Gunnar. A muscle started to twitch in his face.

"What are you doing? Stand up," Anna quickly hissed towards her daughter, then returned to the blacksmith. "Of course we do, dear…" Her attention, however, was divided now. Brynhildur stood with her back towards Gunnar and Anna, staring at a small mirror, furiously dabbing at her face with the remains of the ruined dress. Maybe Brynhildur was undergoing some sort of very early senility because of her spinsterhood? Anna squinted, trying to keep an eye on each of them simultaneously.

"Mother," said Brynhildur without turning back. "The old papers."

"Oh yes," remembered Anna. "Anything else, dear Gunnar? You still have bread?"

"No, no, I mean – aye, the bread, the papers – I have to go. Lots and lots to do…"

"Roses, I hope," said Anna. "Whatever it is that you're doing, Brynhildur, stop right now. Here you are, Gunnar. Go wash your face. No, not you, Gunnar, don't look so alarmed. Toothbrush? Coffee? Anything exciting happening? Maybe some sugar…?"

"Is your back better?" interrupted Brynhildur.

"Oh yes," said Anna, "haven't you bought Helga's mattress because of your back…?"

Gunnar clutched the papers against his chest and bolted out of the store without paying, nearly taking the door along.

"I know exactly what to do," offered Brynhildur after a brief pause. "I'm going to bake some scones and find out how he is doing—"

"Oh no, you will *not* bake any scones for that smelly drunk, and you will *not* find out how he is doing. You will stay away from him. And for God's sake, stop ruining your clothes."

"You forgot to ask him about the one hundred kronur note," hissed Brynhildur. As far as revenge went, it was very little to get excited about, but she had nothing more. Anna gave her an icy glare, and Brynhildur decided to sulk in silence.

It was Anna herself who taught her daughters how to find answers to every question they had. And Brynhildur had many right now. Why did her mother refuse to talk about Father? Where did someone like Gunnar get a hundred kronur note? Last but not least, why did Mother work so hard to keep her spinster daughter away from an eligible bachelor who had money to spend on new boots during a recession?

### Then

Whilst Bjarni and Arnar were working on the house and Juana on mastering the language, Ingvar was busy with his career. The boys' parents would never have been able to pay for his education, but he was picked by the pastor who noticed the boy outshone all the others his age. Therefore, the Church of Iceland financed Ingvar's education, and he understood it was a once in a lifetime chance. For it wasn't just Arnar who wanted luck and fortune. Ingvar simply understood those words differently.

His fellow students didn't get much sleep, because they were busy sampling the delights of the big city. Ingvar didn't sleep much either, busy studying, reading, writing. The others boasted about their conquests. Ingvar had no idea how to even talk to girls and didn't waste time trying. The other students dropped out. Ingvar wrote better, longer papers, and eventually became known in certain social circles, those that appreciated sharp wit more than light chit-chat.

At that time, Iceland still remained under Danish rule, but a group focused around Jón Sigurðsson started to talk about independence. These were not drunken students, but serious academics and politicians. Ingvar immediately took notice and adjusted his opinions accordingly. Since then his writings were no longer popular with his Danish professors, but they opened the door for him to join the group and gain a certain degree of respect within their ranks. A few articles with his name underneath appeared in the papers. Ingvar attached copies to the letters he sent to the bishop, knowing the news would spread. There was no need to mention that his articles appeared somewhere near the last page or that he never had a chance to even speak to Jón.

"My brothers tell me how beautiful the village is," Ingvar wrote. "It fills me with sadness to hear that it is still only called 'the village'. Of course, I understand that the…" Which word to pick? "…venerable Reverend Kristófer, being as busy as he is, didn't find time to take care of that. Why would he? I know how much work he is burdened with, and it will be a great honour for me to provide him with all the help I can." Ingvar hesitated, wondering how much regret he should express over the death of the old pastor who paid for his education and treated him so well. His pen moved over the paper indecisively until Ingvar decided it was better to focus on the living than the dead. "My greatest wish is to return to my roots. If only I could become a pastor myself once my education is finished next year!"

All people needed God in their lives, agreed the bishop, both confused and excited… but why would a young politician and thinker whose career was in such ascent wish to become a mere pastor at a small fishing village? The Church had paid for his education, Ingvar responded. It was time to repay the favour, both to God and man, to step out of the lecture halls and learn the real life. The bishop found himself nodding in agreement as he read those words. He knew better than to believe Ingvar's self-effacing words. The young man used the phrases "by sheer luck" and "despite my ineptitude" way too often. Smart, hard-working, a great mind, but too modest, worried the bishop, already wondering how to help the young man realise his true potential.

Same as everyone else, the bishop was unaware that, while Arnar just grabbed whatever he wanted, Ingvar talked people into giving him what he hadn't even asked for. The bishop couldn't have been more pleased than to announce that Ingvar's dream would come true. He would get the necessary recommendation letter, and it would be an enthusiastic one. He encouraged Ingvar to be less hard on himself, reminding him of his many achievements, praising his qualities and academic knowledge.

Ingvar smiled as he read those words. He was so used to getting what he wanted that his eyes were already on a bigger prize. He didn't intend to remain a pastor for long, but he enjoyed the realisation that even though it would still take months for his education to be completed he had already secured the next step. People already knew who he was and that he was coming over. They passed the cut-outs from the papers between each other and read the articles aloud whether they understood them or not. Ingvar was becoming a rising star in Iceland despite the fact he hadn't set his foot in the country for years. The only person who wasn't excited about Ingvar's upcoming arrival was the "venerable" fifty-one-year-old Reverend Kristófer, who had no intention of sharing his power – or, God forbid, the money.

The bishop found himself feeling very ungodly towards Reverend Kristófer, whom he considered to be a charmless, dried out prune of a man. It was clear that the idea of "sharing some of his burden" didn't appeal to the Reverend at all. The bishop sighed heavily, staring sadly at his brandy, knowing it was his duty to serve as an intermediate between the two pastors. He quietly muttered a prayer, hoping to be struck by a revelation, as he stared at Ingvar's letter, and God answered! Ingvar's words could melt a glacier. Obviously, the best way to go about it would be to direct Ingvar straight to Reverend Kristófer. They would settle matters with one another, sparing the bishop the extra worry and the trip. Hallelujah! Relieved, he wrote a brief, rather dry note to Bjarni, the young pastor's brother, reminding him yet again that the church and dwelling for Ingvar needed to be ready very soon. He imagined three months should be plenty of time. Nevertheless, he added a postscript gently reminding him that sloth was one of the seven deadly sins.

Bjarni lived in a continuous state of anxiety. Each of his clients praised his work and recommended him to others, yet Bjarni kept worrying he would be discovered to be the uneducated crook that he really was. He wanted to become the best builder Iceland ever bore, yet he kept worrying that he'd find himself and his employees without work. Therefore, he never dared to say no to any request and his schedule was full even before the church was unexpectedly added to it. With so little time, all the other plans would now have to be postponed. The Bailiff's wife had been overjoyed to coordinate the fundraiser, as Reverend Kristófer was naturally too busy, and everyone living in the vicinity had put money together for this job. He knew that some of them had hardly any to spare and that he would make no profit whatsoever on the project. Worse, he had to convince his workers to work without earning a krona in the most difficult period of the year, when faint daylight only accompanied them for four or five precious hours. Bjarni spent half of his time determined to pull off the feat. He devoted the remaining hours to planning his escape to America.

He passed along the bishop's letters to Guðrún to read to the others. She was raising three children and was pregnant with a fourth, but also took care of a few sheep and ran an inn – a fancy name for four benches, two tables and many pitchers of ale. Her husband worked away from home, which added to their income and meant she was one of the lucky few who didn't have to travel to provide for her family. She and Juana were the only two people who actually spent all their time in the village, and owning an inn gave Guðrún the pleasant feeling of being an informal leader of the community.

There was nothing of interest in the bishop's note, and it was swiftly dismissed. They could now move on to the main attraction: the first letter in years that Ingvar sent to his brothers. "Dearest Bjarni and Arnar," Guðrún read, and Bjarni winced even though he had read the letter ten times before bringing it over. "First, let me express my deepest gratitude to everyone for receiving me so warmly. I couldn't be happier, nor could I feel more humble being able to serve God in a place as beautiful as you describe–"

"What did you describe?" interrupted Niels, a fisherman known mostly for his clumsiness and complete lack of manners.

"I said it was a fishing village," said Bjarni.

"Please don't feel like you must build anything special," continued the innkeeper, "all I require is an office to write in and a bed to sleep in–"

"And a church," interrupted Niels again, "could be useful."

"If you can't keep quiet, get out of here," barked Arnar. Niels worked Arnar's last nerve whenever they had to spend more than two minutes in the same room. Juana gently squeezed Arnar's arm and he relaxed, although he was still resentful of the fact that Ingvar's letters were addressed to Bjarni and that their future pastor hadn't asked for *his* opinion on the village.

"I hope he brings a lot of books with him," said bearish Magnús, the fishermen's captain, dreamily. Unlike the others, who were snuff users, he preferred a pipe. He felt it fit his personality better, same as his neatly trimmed beard. Even when he accidentally set his moustache on fire, he refused to switch to snuff. "God knows we could do with some new books."

"He is a member of the Independence movement," exclaimed Niels, who ironically enough was the only fisherman who wasn't independent, and his share of the fish caught went to a farmer nearby. "I hear he is the best friend of *the* Jón Sigurðsson!"

"Nonsense," said Guðrún, raising her eyes from the letter. "Jón is dead."

"But they worked together!"

"Still–"

"And he writes books and has them published!"

"Will you please shut up?" Arnar was tensing again, Juana sensed.

"And he will be nicer than Reverend Kristófer," piped Elísabet, the eldest daughter of Guðrún.

"His books will probably all be about politics," said Bjarni.

"By now I am ready to read about politics too," said Magnús, puffing on his pipe, only to discover it had gone out again. "Anything but the damned Bible. I mean… I've heard The Sagas so many times I don't need to read them anymore, I could recite them all myself. In fact, I might have written a few extra ones."

"Now, now," said his wife, Fríða. Most of the women stayed away from the inn – except, of course, on special evenings like this one – but she spent most of the day cleaning fish, gutting fish, drying fish, cooking fish and felt she deserved peaceful evenings with a drink or two. "Don't you fancy yourself a new Snorri, writing your 'extra Sagas'. All you write is your diary."

"That's not true! I write poems as well."

"Oh yes," said Guðrún. "Haven't we heard them. You should only be allowed to read them when everyone is drunk and the kids are asleep… Put your brother to sleep, Elísabet," she commanded, suddenly reminded of the existence of her children. "Now," she added before Elísabet had a chance to protest. "The rest of you be quiet and listen to the letter."

"He will need a parsonage as well," Niels declared and spat on the floor. "Do we have to build everything by ourselves?"

Arnar ground his teeth, and Bjarni felt an acidic taste in his throat and mouth.

"Quiet," said Guðrún again, but by now everyone was already expressing their opinions about what the right thing to do was.

"*Afsakið,*" said Juana. Voices immediately died down, all eyes on her for a moment.

Guðrún threw her a quick, grateful smile, then turned to Niels with a frown. "I have no idea where I finished. Why don't you go on, Nilli?"

Bjarni swallowed the rest of the beer, trying to get the bile filling his throat back down into his stomach. He knew exactly where Guðrún had finished. "He's coming in early spring," he muttered. "Sends us the best of wishes and greetings. Cannot wait. And so on."

The ale didn't help, and Bjarni felt sick now. They had three months, maybe three and a half, as Ingvar hadn't provided an exact date. Three months of scarce daylight and generous amounts of snow, sleet, and heavy winds… "I've got an idea," he said. "It will spare us both time and money. We'll make the church and the parsonage one building."

"Isn't that unusual?"

*Exactly*, thought Bjarni. "Trust me," he said. "I've got enough experience. It will all be well in the end." Those words would later come back to haunt him. But for now, all he could think of was that they would save time and build a church like no other. Even Ingvar, whose expectations seemed to be low, would have to be amazed by such a feat. And Bjarni would prove his true worth, to others and to himself.

"Fishing season is going to start," muttered Magnús.

"It hasn't yet. In the meantime we can all work on the church," snapped Arnar. He was tense and anxious this evening and didn't know why. He would remember this feeling later, and wonder if somehow he'd had a premonition of imminent disaster. He freed his arm from Juana's hand to reach for his pitcher, but drinking didn't seem to help him either. Arnar knew he'd end up doing the lion's share of the work, but that had never troubled him before. Something else felt wrong.

Juana, on the other hand, felt that all was right with the world. She understood she would see even less of her husband, but she also knew something he didn't. Juana's and Fríða's eyes met, and Juana smiled. Fríða responded with a nervous smirk, then quickly averted her gaze. Nothing could upset Juana on that particular evening. Tonight was the time her husband – married in front of God or not – would hear even more exciting news.

Upon their return home Arnar was tipsy, happy, and Juana knew he would be in the mood to make love. They kissed and his hands wandered under her clothes. He started to tickle her and Juana giggled.

"I love it when you're so happy," laughed Arnar. "Any particular reason?"

"Oh yes," she said, "but I don't know exactly yet."

"What do you mean?"

"Well… it could be a boy or a girl."

Arnar stopped breathing for a split second until understanding brightened his face, immediately replaced with ecstatic joy. "This… is… perfect!" he exclaimed. "By God, Juana, my love, you couldn't bring me better news! I can't believe it!" They laughed and quibbled over names, each more ridiculous than the next. Juana suggested long and elaborate American names, and Arnar tried to come up with double entendres.

They laughed and teased each other, but secretly both were thinking about other things. Juana was relieved by his reaction, as she hadn't been sure if he would be happy. But she was also worried about God's judgement now more than ever. Maybe the new pastor could marry them, she hoped. Arnar may have laughed, but on the inside he was feeling on edge. He was thinking about money.

Arnar loved the idea of his wife being a princess, like her American mother who commanded servants and never seemed to actually do any dirty work. But they were running low on money. Her "dowry" had paid for the house, furniture, ring, all necessary knick-knacks, and there was a bit left. But his earnings were just a bit lower than their spending. A lot of the villagers bartered, but Juana didn't seem to possess that art. Now he would have no choice but to break the news to her. She had to start working, really working, like the Icelandic women she thought so plain. There was no money to be earned from building the church, and no way Arnar could extricate himself from the job.

"I love you," he whispered into her ear. "We are going to have a beautiful baby together, in our beautiful house." He'd find a way for her to work somewhere nearby, he was already thinking. His precious, one-of-a-kind wife would not go to work for a grumpy farmer on the other side of the country. She definitely wouldn't be allowed to work for any single man, in fact for any man at all. They would need to sit and talk about it, but not now, now was the time to bicker good-humouredly about whether "Engelbert" would be a good name for an Icelandic boy. Then, to Juana's surprise, Arnar suddenly changed the topic.

"Why don't you start going to the winter-gatherings?" he asked. "You could learn a lot, make more friends…"

"But… you always said I would stand out too much and that I wouldn't enjoy them…"

"It's time for you to become a real Icelander, so you know how to raise one," said Arnar, who realised the men, including himself, would be too busy to attend. It was safe to let her go, and she might even learn something. She would spend time with other women, their children, listen to the readings, watch them spin wool and perhaps even join… "You will love it," he said, and that was it.

The initial reaction to Juana's appearance at a winter-gathering was silent shock. It took the women and children a few minutes to stop gawking at her. Fríða, who was hosting the gathering, forced herself to start behaving correctly and soon voices filled the air, even if the conversation felt stilted. Juana sat in a corner, trying her best to look relaxed, not daring to join the chit-chat. Talking and listening to Icelandic was still work for her, and multiple people talking at once made it nearly impossible for her to understand anything. So she tuned them out and sat quietly with an enigmatic smile, hoping nobody was going to ask her any questions.

Once enough inquiries about the health of cows, sheep, and children were exchanged, Katrín, Fríða's older daughter, started to read. From what Juana could understand, it was a Saga. She couldn't focus on listening, because Fríða was simultaneously attempting to teach her how to spin wool. Juana became completely confused, unable to hear the quick, whispered instructions over Katrín's unwavering voice.

"Mother," exclaimed Jórunn, Katrín's younger sister, who was watching the two women. "She's useless. She doesn't know how to do anything. Why do you talk to her?"

"Shh, child," hissed Fríða. "It's not like you learned everything in one evening either."

"But I can't listen to the story like this," complained the girl.

"Now I can't either because you keep talking. Be quiet." Fríða smiled apologetically, but Juana, hunched over the spindle, didn't even notice. Her hands faltered.

Katrín's voice broke as she was reading. She had some sympathy for Juana, but not enough to stand up for her, not in her family's presence. She would put a spider in Jórunn's bed, Katrín promised herself, even though she felt somewhat puzzled. Spinning wool was so easy that she could do it while reading the Catechism…

"You missed half a page," said Jórunn, who was way too smart for her age. Two spiders, Katrín decided.

Fríða gave up on teaching Juana to spin wool. It was much faster just to do it herself, and she could do it without paying attention to what she was doing. Juana stared blankly, feeling like the light from the candles and lamps stopped just before reaching the spot where she sat, leaving her in a dark hole. The only thing left for her to do was pay attention to the Saga, but it was long and meandering, filled with words she'd never heard before. After an hour or so she excused herself politely. Both reading and wool-spinning immediately ceased.

"She really is a princess," said Sigurveig, who was a new addition to the village. Her husband Valdimar had replaced a fisherman who drowned and was forgotten as soon as his widow left to return to her family in the countryside. "Doesn't she do anything?"

"Well, well," said Fríða, "let's have some coffee with brandy. No, not you, Jórunn. Take your little sister and go play outside."

"It's winter," responded the girl.

"Then play under the table," barked Katrín, who still had to find two spiders once the conversation was over.

"Juana is a nice woman," said Guðrún. "She does everything around the house. They have a nice garden. Helps me with the sheep sometimes." Then she stopped, because there was nothing else to add.

"Big deal," said Sigurveig. "Everybody does that."

"Brandy?" asked Fríða. Sigurveig waved her away. "She's pregnant now," she said. "I bet now she won't even do anything around the house."

"They brought money from America," explained Guðrún. "She doesn't have to do anything."

"Nobody has to do anything, but doesn't she get bored? What *does* she do all day?"

"She goes to the hot springs," informed Katrín. "To do the laundry."

Sigurveig threw her a disdainful look. "I see. Too good to boil it in urine like everyone else. I'd like to know how rich they are. What is that house like?"

The women looked at each other. None of them had ever visited. "Large," said Guðrún.

"Why don't you ask Arnar?"

"Niels will ask," said Guðrún. The others looked at her, and she smirked. "Trust me," she said, "he will."

Fríða licked her lips. "Coffee, anyone? Brandy?" she asked, and Guðrún relented, warm, relaxed. She knew how easy it would be to wind up Niels. A pitcher of ale on the house, a remark thrown into the air as if muttering to herself, and Nilli would ensure no question would go unanswered. He had no tact or patience and could be counted on to ask the most unsuitable questions. As usual, Guðrún was right.

When Arnar joined the other patrons, Niels was already finishing his second ale. "Why did you return from America?" he asked between quick swigs, as if worried Guðrún was going to change her mind and take his pitcher away.

"And a good evening to you," answered Arnar, immediately irritated.

"Manners," huffed Guðrún. "So, Arnar… would you like some brandy whilst you're telling us about it? On the house."

Arnar looked around, as if seeking escape, only to find five pairs of eyes glued curiously to his face. Bjarni's stare was the most intense, the taste in his mouth bitter. He, too, was ready to hear why anybody would return from the New World to live in a fishing village without a name. A year before Arnar's escapade Bjarni tried to join the others who went to America. He failed. When his brother's attempt not only worked but turned out to be such an enormous success, Bjarni took it personally. As he was still putting together basic cabinets and digging shacks in the hills, Arnar was earning a lot of money and courting the most beautiful woman in the world. It would have been an easier pill to swallow if Arnar had stayed there and never returned.

"If only you knew," sighed Arnar. "Thank you, Guðrún. America isn't what people describe in their letters and articles. It's an awful place to live. Aye, if you're smart, strong and hard-working, like me, you can succeed. Just look at my wife and my house," he said proudly, before returning to his gloomy tone. "But living there to stay? A whole different story. People who do not return are simply failures who can't save enough money to make it back here. They have to lie to pretend they are better than they really are."

Doubtful looks were exchanged.

"It's nothing like here. Imagine that someone takes all this away," Arnar waved his hand around. "All the farms, the valleys, the sheep, the huts, the skies, the coast…"

"I wouldn't mind that at all if it got me rich," said Valdimar.

"The weather is unbearable. In the summer it's too hot to breathe. In the winter you get so much snow your door won't open. But can you take a break from working? No. Do they have winter-gatherings? Maybe they do, but I wouldn't know because Icelanders are not invited. Not unless they want to show off that they can afford one. Like a pet. Remember the powdered sugar, Bjarni?"

His brother muttered something and shifted uncomfortably on the bench.

"What about powdered sugar?" asked Niels immediately.

"I don't want to talk about it," said Bjarni quietly.

"Well, we want to know," said Niels. It was easy to be brave around Bjarni. If he got upset the worst he would do was leave the inn in a huff.

"Someone get my brother another ale, he'll need it," laughed Arnar. "This was a year before I left. Hallgrímur, a friend of ours, came back to visit his family and Bjarni invited him over to listen to his stories. Hallgrímur told us that in America raisins grew in the earth like grass grows here in Iceland, so people did raisin-making like they would do hay-making at home. Then Hallgrímur said they would get blizzards in America, but it wouldn't melt, because icing sugar fell from the sky instead of snow. So, when you had a wife – and it is very easy to marry in America, I can tell you that's true – she would love sweeping the porch to save the icing sugar for later."

Bjarni was staring at his pitcher, his face purple.

"So, this will come as a surprise to all of you, but it wasn't true. There were no raisins and no powdered sugar waiting. Just a lot of work for people who made fun of you. Weird people you couldn't even understand. Some had black skin – they were born at night, that's why." He wagged his finger threateningly. "That is what happens there. Your friends who went to America, why do you think so many of them never return? They are too ashamed. If you ever go there, do as I have: take the Americans' money, take their women, and run…"

"Isn't that illegal?" interrupted Niels. "How did you manage to get a permit?"

"You don't need a permit there."

"So you didn't even ask her parents' permission?" Magnús was dumbfounded.

"Of course not! We made a plan, took all we needed, then went straight to the boat and came here."

"I don't know if I believe you," said Bjarni, his voice finally back and his face slowly returning to its normal colour. "So many people wrote letters, and I've read it in the papers as well. I don't think you're telling the truth."

"I swear to God," answered Arnar, then grinned at his brother. "If you don't believe me, go and find out. Bring back some raisins and powdered sugar." He got Bjarni another ale to soften the impact of the joke. "It's not worth dreaming about," he whispered into his brother's reddened ear. "You're doing just fine here. If you went there you'd be yet another pet Icelander working for somebody else. Here you're an independent man who hires others. You have *me* working for you, that's how well you are doing. Trust me, brother. There's nothing for you in America. I swear to God," Arnar repeated, then smiled. He had no intention to remain Bjarni's employee for long.

# Saturday, March 13, 1920

"Today is the thirteenth," announced Sigurd. "Don't forget to knock on wood."

*Eight,* encouraged the darkness, *seventy-two, one hundred sixty-four.*

"Nobody asked you," said Gunnar. Rarely did his days get bad so early in the morning.

"Just letting you know… I mean… I'm sorry, I forgot."

The blacksmith didn't bother answering. They were sitting in the kitchen now, with the old man placed on one of the chairs at a well-lit spot where he could read. Gunnar wordlessly stared at the window, his fingers drumming on the table, then he suddenly brightened up. "Say, you probably won't be taking your mattress when you leave, aye? That would be a lot of hassle. I think you should leave it here."

"Of course I'll leave it here," said Sigurd grumpily. "Along with the pillows and bedding." Gunnar's beard moved up, which meant he was smiling. Sigurd tried to turn and see what Gunnar was staring at so intently, but the only thing he noticed was that there were no curtains in the window behind him. Which meant he was visible from the outside. Sigurd shifted in the chair uncomfortably. "Say… do your customers visit you here at home?"

"Nobody ever visits me. They knock on the forge door. If it's open, then it's open, and if it isn't, then it isn't."

"Ah," breathed Sigurd politely. "Can they see me from there?"

"No. Tell me more about America. How long have you been living there?"

"Do you know, it's been so long I can't even remember. Fifteen years, twenty?"

"And it was so horrible the whole time?"

Sigurd smiled, tried to lean back on the chair, and almost slid off it. "Remember, Arnar went there a very long time ago. Also, it's just a story. In any case, it was a very different place then, and most people stayed together, worked together. He was lucky to be hired by that family but also unlucky because he ended up on his own. Everyone who lives there has their own story. Don't forget the money I gave you came from America."

"Did you have any black children that were born at night?"

The smile disappeared from Sigurd's face. "See," he said, "this is where you stop asking questions and go to work."

Gunnar frowned. "Then kill someone finally. Someone I don't know. Not Juana, I like her. And maybe not the brothers. Come up with something."

## Then

There was one project Bjarni absolutely couldn't postpone, because he had already been paid for it. His team was in the middle of building a house for an old woman who had moved into the village. There was nothing unusual about someone new moving in or out, but Gullveig, for that was her name, soon replaced Juana as the black sheep of the village. She was some distant relative of Niels, which would usually dictate that she should stay with him. Instead she rented a room from Guðrún. Niels, who didn't want Gullveig under his leaky roof, kept his relief to himself. Nevertheless, worried he'd be blamed, he made sure that everybody knew how shocked he was by *certain people* having no respect for family bonds anymore. Within a few days people started warning each other about getting cornered by Nilli. He had never been particularly popular, but now conversations ended even more quickly. This, too, was Gullveig's fault, he decided.

Despite the fact that it was wintertime, Gullveig convinced Bjarni to build her a house by offering to double his normal price and pay half upfront. But, when Bjarni found out that all his resources needed to be allocated to the church, he had to tell all his clients that no work would be done in the coming months. Gullveig was the last to be informed.

"I see," she said, nodding. "You must be feeling unwell under so much pressure." That alone was more than she said to most people.

Bjarni gave her a pained look, but said nothing.

"Would it help if I pay the rest upfront? So that you have a bit of financial security," she said, nodding again, answering her own question. It was as if she could read his mind. Bjarni's biggest problem regarding the church was the money. Time was a precious commodity, but his was no longer the only construction team around, and he couldn't afford to lose the members of his team by forcing them to work without pay for months. Gullveig nodded encouragingly and waited for his inevitable decision.

Once he reluctantly agreed, she fished a wrapped package from one of her many pockets. It just so happened to be the right amount of money.

Bjarni swallowed loudly, and Gullveig looked at him with sympathy. "If you can get dried ginger," she said, "grind it to powder and mix a spoonful in a mug of hot water." Then she waved him away with a royal gesture, rendering Bjarni so disoriented that he wasn't sure if he'd heard her correctly. He left, his hat wrapped around the money, confusion in his eyes. Instead of ginger tea, he settled for a beer downstairs in Guðrún's kitchen and shared the news with her. Bjarni's voice was slurring slightly when he finished his litany of problems and complaints, and he felt guilty for only talking about himself.

"How come your husband is never around?" he asked.

"Oh… he's here often enough. Where do you think little Ísabella came from? Expect another one a year from now."

"Don't you ever feel lonely? Are you happy?"

Guðrún shrugged. "With this bunch around I have no time to feel lonely. What about your wife?"

"What? I don't have one."

"Exactly. Why is that?"

"You know," Bjarni started reluctantly, staring into the empty pitcher, then burped loudly and grimaced in pain. He wondered if he could get dried ginger in town, as Guðrún had none. "I never really stay long anywhere. When I'm back here, I work and sleep. I don't get to meet… ladies."

"Oh, I could introduce you to some ladies. You've got money, a good job, you're not half-bad looking. Don't tell me you haven't met anyone in town."

"Ah, her," said Bjarni, looking away. "She talked too much."

"Aha," answered Guðrún, who had no idea who he was talking about. "And the other one?" she risked.

"Aye… she was too pretty for me. And walked funny…"

Guðrún shook her head in disbelief. "Bjarni," she started, "a good woman would take so much weight off your shoulders, help you, bear your children…"

A loud thump interrupted them, immediately followed by one of the most irritating sounds in the world – a crying baby. This provided Bjarni with an opportunity to excuse himself, and relieved Guðrún from continuing the conversation. She had no time to figure out who was guilty of what, so she shouted at every child in sight. At this age the older ones should either be taking care of younger ones or they should leave home and start working.

"Hello?" asked Niels, who had let himself in without knocking.

Guðrún nearly cried out in surprise. "Are you not working?" she asked, incredulous. It was relatively early in the day, and neither the builders nor the fishermen could have possibly returned yet. "It's not open. I'm making dinner, and no, you aren't getting any."

"Broken wrist," muttered Niels. He raised his hand, which was wrapped in a bandage. "Give me a break. And a beer."

"It's not my business," she said, pouring him one, "but I heard that your finances aren't so good. Maybe you shouldn't spend money on beer."

"Aye, it's not your business," he answered and turned his attention to the pitcher. He seemed unusually quiet and rather subdued, nursing his wrist lovingly. She frowned. Niels was definitely on Guðrún's dislike list, but today he got a refill that he didn't have to pay for, followed by another. His puppy-like gratitude earned him a poorly-masked disdainful glance from her. "So, Nilli, my boy," she said gaily, when Niels seemed to be inebriated just enough. "Tell me about Gullveig."

He immediately livened up. "She has no respect for family—"

"Yes, so I hear, frequently," interrupted Guðrún, rolling her eyes. "Lower your voice, she's upstairs. Who is she?"

"I'm not sure," answered Niels. He was staring at the ceiling, his eyes jumping around as if to make sure that there was no hole through which the old woman could be listening. He lowered his voice to a theatrical whisper. "She's my aunt's aunt, or grand-aunt, something like that. I don't think even my mother remembers who she is."

"Send her a letter and ask," said Guðrún. "So, she's not your grandmother? Where does she get all the money from?"

"I don't know," said Niels, "but she sure as hell ain't giving any to me. I remember times when family meant something—"

"She's decades older than you. If you remember those times, she does as well."

"She's always been old," he said. "Wearing those black dresses. She never even talked to me. They say blood is thicker than water, but…"

He wouldn't be getting another beer even if he paid, Guðrún decided and stopped listening.

A few days later Juana miscarried…

## *Now*

"Wait," interrupted Gunnar. "That's not what I meant."

"Why? I killed someone you didn't know. Nobody knew that baby yet." Sigurd smiled. "It's normal," he added, unsure how much the blacksmith knew about human reproduction. "Happens all the time."

The blacksmith muttered something dirty. "Then no more killing for a while. Some fights. Between grown-ups."


## *Then*

Juana wouldn't let go of the sadness. Arnar consoled her for a few nights, but soon returned to his regular life and work. It was his unborn child as well, but nobody saw him tearing up about it. Guðrún, in goodwill, visited to tell Juana all about her own miscarriages.

"I feel like a spark of life was in me," whispered Juana, "and it is gone now, and it's just some ash and smoke…"

"Nonsense! It's just some blood, you'll get pregnant again," Guðrún quickly interrupted. "Don't worry. It happens to many of us. It happened to me a few times and now look at me! Three… actually four terrible children ruining my life! Everything will be fine. It's normal. No need to be so sad." She stroked Juana's cheek, saw imminent tears and quickly excused herself, thinking that this would have gone better had she not brought little Ísabella along. On the plus side, she now knew what the house looked like from the inside and couldn't wait to share it at the next gathering.

Life in the village continued as usual. Sigurveig's brother, Ásgeir, moved in with her and her husband, Valdimar. Ásgeir's intention was to become a fisherman, but he found himself joining the construction team instead. He didn't complain too much even when he was told that he'd be paid in food and beer for the coming few weeks. It wasn't like he had much choice either. In the race between the builders and time, time was winning, but nobody was willing to concede that or give up.

Ásgeir was a man of few words. He'd spend evenings in the inn slowly draining his ale, listening to others and only rarely adding a word or two. He gave equal inattention to conversations, jokes, verbal fights, and women gawking at him. His indifference seemed to attract them all even more. As far as Arnar was concerned, Ásgeir looked like a hungry weasel, yet his rodent-like features somehow also made him irresistible to women. Even Guðrún found herself losing track of conversations, entranced by the sight of her favourite patron. Katrín unexpectedly visited the building site just in case there was something Ásgeir, and of course any of the others, might have needed. But when Magnús found out that Fríða suggested the workers needed to take a lunch break so that she could visit and bring them some "tasty treats", Ásgeir nearly made his first enemy. Fríða was subsequently forbidden from visiting either the building site or the inn. Attempting to prove that all was good in his household and marriage, Magnús became ostentatiously friendly towards Ásgeir, fooling no one but himself. Magnús had a short temper and a strong punch, so the anecdote was declared a secret. This meant that it took a while before each dweller of the village had a chance to hear it – right after promising that it would never be shared with anybody else.

Guðrún personally delivered the news to Juana. "Tas-aty treats," giggled Juana, and it was the first time since the miscarriage that she emerged from her sad grey cloud. Guðrún smiled too, relieved and pleased, then corrected her pronunciation.

"Is he that… tas-ty?" asked Juana with a little wicked glimmer in her eye. *Girnlegur,* she repeated under her breath.

"Well," said Guðrún, actually blushing a little, "let me just say that Fríða now drinks her morning coffee with brandy to get over her dismay…"

Juana laughed. "How do you even know that? Is nothing a secret?"

"Oh," said the innkeeper, "a bit of harmless gossip never hurt anyone!"

When Arnar arrived home he was very pleased to find his wife out of bed, colour on her face, and a hot meal waiting for him. He was just tipsy enough to laugh with her, at the same time watching his words carefully. He didn't want to risk sending her back into the gloomy silence, and so listened to her instead, as Juana related Guðrún's visit.

"*R-n-l-g,*" she said all of a sudden, confusing Arnar.

"G… what?"

"Is the new *tasty* guy really so *tasty*?" asked Juana. She loved the new word and elongated it with gusto.

"What tasty guy are you talking about?"

"Guðrún says that this *gir-n-legur* Ásgeir got Fríða in trouble. Or maybe the other way round. Anyway," she continued, oblivious to the sudden change of expression on Arnar's face, "I just thought this was funny. But you're very tasty, too."

Arnar didn't find any of this funny, especially not the word "too". Juana continued to chatter, throwing the word "tasty" into every other sentence, but he wasn't listening anymore, his eyes darkened, forehead wrinkled in thought. Perhaps a little chat with the weasel-man was in order.

The next evening Ásgeir arrived at the inn with a black eye, Arnar with a split lip, and they sat at opposite ends of the short bench, refusing to acknowledge each other's existence. After a few minutes Arnar pushed away his pitcher, spat on the floor, stood up and left before Guðrún had the time to tell him off. Ásgeir stared into space for a minute, then got up, threw a coin on the table, and walked out as well. Guðrún looked at Bjarni questioningly.

"They had accidents," he said. "Both of them at the same time, apparently. Nobody saw anything."

"Accidents," said the innkeeper. "How very interesting. I hope you don't mind me asking, but is the church going to be ready on time? With all the accidents?"

In the last few days a corrugated iron roof had been installed, a task that took four men three days to complete. Bjarni had joked that it would be good if some rain fell, so they could check the roof for leaks. Overnight a hurricane-force wind struck. The roof that he had personally declared safe and sound had been torn off, landing metres away, iron bent as though it were paper. Bjarni was already used to the acidic taste of bile in his mouth and throat, but this was the first time he actually threw up upon his arrival at the building site. He raised his hand to his mouth now and belched. He didn't answer her question, looking away in shame.

"Don't worry," encouraged Guðrún. "I hear the other job is finished. It will all be over soon."

"Yes," he agreed, his lips pale, "it probably will be." Indeed, the finishing touches to Gullveig's house had been put in place today, ten days before the agreed date. The building hadn't suffered as much as a dent, despite the hurricane.

"Bjarni, dear," said Guðrún softly, observing his pained expression and the way he pressed his hand to his chest, "please don't take this the wrong way, but you might try drinking less ale and more warm milk. Just for your own health."

Even if Gullveig had asked for help moving into her new house, nobody would have been available. Guðrún later swore she never even noticed the old woman's departure. One day she was living in the guest room at the inn, keeping to herself, and the next day she was gone.

Juana waited for Arnar's return from work to ask his permission to work for Gullveig. Apparently the old woman just so happened to be passing by, and surprised Juana with a job offer. It seemed completely innocuous – she needed help around the house due to her back problems. When Arnar heard how much Gullveig was willing to pay he granted his approval much faster than he would have liked. He worked seven days a week, no matter the weather, and the closer Ingvar's arrival loomed, the longer his days became. But Arnar wasn't making any money, so there was no way to shield his princess from working anymore. He told himself the old woman was harmless. She lived nearby, maybe a fifteen-minute brisk walk away, and judging by all Arnar had heard so far, Gullveig seemed to be swimming in money. It was time to put his suspicions aside, he told himself. Just an old woman like any other.

Gullveig was very easy to work for, Juana reported. All she apparently owned were a few identical black dresses, some shoes and coats, thick books in matching covers without titles or authors on the side, and basic cooking utensils. Unless the Holy Bible was hidden somewhere, Juana hadn't seen one, nor had she noticed a cross. The bedroom was equally sparse: a bed under a slanted roof, a tiny window, a chair, and a chest with spare bedding and an extra pillow that never got used. Gullveig seemed to spend most of the time in her bed, due to her back problems. Juana did all the chores, but there wasn't much to do, as one woman couldn't eat a lot or make the house dirty on daily basis. Her favourite part of the job was taking Gullveig's dresses out to wash them in the hot spring, which gave her an opportunity to take long baths without feeling guilty. If only Gullveig dirtied her dresses more often!

As Arnar listened, his resentment towards Gullveig grew. The pay was *too* good. How was the old crone who did literally nothing able to pay twice the price for a house that was larger and nicer than his own? Why was she throwing money at Juana? The fact that their livelihood depended on Juana's wages felt like an extra slap in the face. Arnar needed the church to be finished, so he could get paid work again. His princess was supposed to be spoiled rotten with happiness and material goods, not to be the sole breadwinner. The only consolation was that this state was temporary. From then on, though, when Juana talked about Gullveig, Arnar's smile was stiff and forced, and he almost missed something that seemed very interesting.

When Gullveig wasn't resting in bed, she often retreated to the other room, its door painted black. Juana, curious to see what was hiding inside, walked around the house twice until she realised the room must have no windows. She didn't dare ask, nor did she try to enter the room. Gullveig didn't enforce many rules, but she had been very stern when Juana innocently asked if the room needed a bit of sweeping. That was the only interesting thing that she had to share, but it sounded excitedly ominous.

The mention of a windowless room with a black painted door excited the villagers. In connection with the black books and black dresses, the mysterious chamber was immediately christened The Black Room, which made it sound even more sinister. Of course the construction team were aware that they had built that room, same as everything else, but they hadn't given it much thought until now. How odd to have a room without a window, the inn's patrons muttered, how would one breathe in there? What would one *do* in there?

Later, when the deeds were done, nobody could remember who said it first, who used the word "curse". The church was cursed. An old, black-clad, strangely rich woman arrived in the village. She had a Black Room that had no windows and no Holy Bible. Everything was going perfectly well until her arrival. Was that really a coincidence?

The seed had been sown, and it started to grow fast.

"You must find out what she's doing in that Black Room," Arnar said to Juana, as they lay in bed. "It's very important."

"Why is it important?" she asked, yawning. She felt unusually tired.

Arnar lowered his voice, even though they were at home with the doors and windows closed. "We think she really is a witch," he confessed, making the sign of a cross. "You must be very, very careful."

"Nonsense. She barely moves." Juana snuffed out the candle.

"She moves in that room," he pointed out. "Find out."

Juana didn't answer, already asleep. Arnar lay in bed for hours, staring at the ceiling.

When Juana arrived at Gullveig's house the next day she found a basket on the doorstep. It contained some flowers, freshly baked bread, a chunk of cheese, two eggs – a rarity in the village – and a card. Bewildered, Juana brought it inside. She offered to read the card, but Gullveig lifted herself from the bed, walked over in a way that seemed more energetic than usual, and read it herself, squinting. "Ah," she said with a mysterious smile. She disappeared into The Black Room, taking the card with her. She stayed there only for a minute or two, then emerged, locked the door, and returned to bed. Juana swept the perfectly clean floor two more times in case Gullveig felt the need to share something, then ran to the inn. Guðrún was the only person who didn't work at this time of day, and the news had to be discussed immediately.

"The eggs come from Sigurveig," said Guðrún. "She's the only one with a hen. Ásgeir will ask her."

"But why would Sigurveig bring a basket of food to Gullveig?"

"Payment for something magical," answered Guðrún in the confident tone of someone well-versed in matters of sorcery.

"Something good or bad?"

"Only you can find out. If there is another basket, you must look at the card."

Guðrún was excited by the conversation, and impatiently waited for the men to arrive after work to share in the news, but they seemed disinterested and very quiet. Ásgeir accepted the free pitcher of ale, reluctantly agreed to question his sister, then sipped the beer as usual without saying another word. Grey-faced Bjarni hunched over his mug of warm milk, even though Guðrún had added a splash of brandy to it to cheer him up. Only Arnar found her words interesting, and Guðrún had a disconcerting thought: why was he finding out from her and not from his wife, who had discovered the information in the first place? Had they no chance to talk about it before he came to the inn? In fact, did he go home at all? No matter who came to the inn on a given evening, Arnar was always present. Married men, like Magnús, visited maybe once a week. Bjarni and Ásgeir, both single and stuck in the village until the church was ready, had nothing better to do. But Arnar was there every evening, without fail. She gave Arnar a contemptuous look but didn't say a word.

Had Guðrún asked, Arnar would have told her that his wife's moods and feelings both endeared him to her and frightened him. There were unexpected kisses, whispers, smiles, embraces, and the way she looked at him, making him feel like the king of the world. He had never known a woman who behaved like this. But there were also times when she'd sit silently and stare at that damn family photo. Besides, since the miscarriage, she'd fallen into anguish the likes of which he had never seen before. He never knew which Juana would await him when he reached home.

No matter what, he had to be the strong arm she needed, had to never budge when she laughed about "tasty" men, had to keep on smiling through everything life threw at him.

Unbeknownst to him and everybody else, the worst was still to come.

# Sunday, March 14, 1920

*Seven,* said the darkness the moment Gunnar opened his eyes. *Seventy-one, one hundred sixty-three.*

"My ankle is getting better," announced Sigurd cheerfully, once the blacksmith placed him on the chair. "Thanks for the books, by the way. It's very interesting to read Wilde and Shakespeare in Icelandic."

"Good. If you're done with your story before you go, you can give me a summary."

"Gladly," said Sigurd, enthusiastically. "*Romeo and Juliet* is a play about a young man and a young woman who fall in love, despite many obstac–"

"Aye. Love it. Eat faster, I gotta work."

"But it's Sunday… ah. Of course. Look, could I stay in the kitchen today? There's more light."

"And how are you going to use your chamber pot? What if you want to lie down? Not going to carry you around all the time. You're going back to bed. Hurry up."

"You sound upset. Did something happen? Do you want to talk?"

"Just eat faster," repeated Gunnar, his fingers impatiently drumming on the table. Sigurd didn't dare utter another word.

Gunnar slammed the forge door shut with such force that he almost cut Ragnar in half. The alarmed dog yelped, but, unusually, the blacksmith paid him no attention. Gunnar fished the unfinished rose from the other rubbish on the table, turned it between his blackened fingers, then placed it in the recess of the anvil again. Looking at it didn't make him feel anything in particular. This should have been worrisome, but he couldn't manage to feel worried either. The forerunner of darkness was the big nothing, a Gunnar-shaped gap in the world.

With bottle in hand, he stepped outside. Overnight the ground had turned into mud, and so, seemingly, had the musty and immobile air. Heavy, dark clouds covered the sky. Everything seemed grey and motionless, including Gunnar himself. The weather would get worse before it got even worse.

Ragnar let out a small, concerned whine. He knew where Gunnar was going. The blacksmith wasn't dressed for a walk, but he had the medication to keep him warm. As he was passing by the shed he stopped, opened the door, and squinted, trying to count the bottles in the feeble light. His heart started to beat faster, and he counted them all again. There should have been more, Gunnar was sure of that. He shivered at the mental image of running out. He'd have to start on the next batch as soon as possible. But not now. Now Gunnar and the darkness were taking a walk. Ragnar followed, wagging his tail every now and then, always hoping for the best, always disappointed, but never giving up. They walked towards the other cliff, which faced the farm of Gunnar's nearest neighbour, Hallgrímur. This cliff was safe, and no fence was necessary. Gunnar sat down on the edge, opened the bottle and took a good swig, then examined the level of liquid with some concern.

Hallgrímur was yet another sheep-herder. They would meet every now and then, about once every three months. Hallgrímur's younger children made a lot of noise during those visits, excited to show off their latest tricks to the guest. Hallgrímur and his wife chided the kids and apologised to Gunnar. They'd have coffee, none of them would say much, and everyone but the children would feel relieved when Gunnar went home, feeling that his neighbourly duties had been fulfilled. The blacksmith didn't understand how so many people managed to cope with each other, especially in the winter when they were stuck together under one roof with little to do. Stranger still, they seemed to enjoy it.

*You're broken,* the darkness taunted him. *You don't know how to live like normal people. No wonder nobody loves you. When you die nobody will remember you. That will be your legacy,* said the darkness, its disembodied voice filled with fake pity.

"I'm not going to die," said Gunnar weakly. But his limbs were getting heavier, as though someone were putting layer after layer of chainmail armour on him. His legs were first, then arms, torso. A visor of an invisible helmet obscured his view until the greyness surrounding him shrunk to a point. The bottle in his hand seemed to weigh twice, then three times as much as usual. His fingers opened, and the bottle rolled away, some of the liquid spilling on the grass. It didn't matter. The darkness might have always left before, but this time he knew it wouldn't. He *was* going to die this time. Gunnar closed his eyes and allowed his body to fall back. Ragnar wailed pleadingly, then started licking Gunnar's face.

The blacksmith barely felt the sensation, as though the nerves in his skin had died. A rock was digging painfully into the small of his back, and Gunnar wanted to move away from it, but his body stopped responding to his commands. Juana, he thought. Trapped in her bed, unable to "let go of her sadness", waiting for her own darkness to subside. She, too, carried a festering wound inside. At least she had someone who loved her. Gunnar didn't.

The anniversary of his mother's death would arrive in *seventy-one* days. The darkness habitually brought back the memory of the day when he found his mother's body in bed. She died in her sleep, Father had said. Sóley's face was contorted in terror, eyes bulging and open wide, as if she were unexpectedly struck by an opponent a hundred times bigger than her. Karl, Gunnar's father, held him in a strong embrace as the boy sobbed. "Twenty-fourth of May," he said. "She may be gone now, but we will never forget her." As the years passed, Gunnar forgot Sóley's facial features, her hair colour, but he never forgot the terror in her dead eyes. Or the date.

Every year on the twenty-fourth of May they would light a candle for her spirit. Father and son would drink ale together and reminisce. The boy was always quiet at first, but livened up as the pitchers emptied. On the other hand, Karl's mood seemed to darken as the hours passed. Still, they retold the same anecdotes, made sure the stories would never disappear, and sometimes it felt as though Sóley would come into the kitchen any moment to tell them off for drinking too much. The blankets she knitted were still used every day, Karl still wore the *lopapeysa* she made. He was wearing it on the day he failed to get out of bed in the morning. He laughed it off – a little cold, he explained. Gunnar was shocked at the sight of his father's shrunken body, grey skin, the woollen sweater hanging from Karl's shoulders. The changes were so gradual he had failed to notice them until now.

"I'm just having a cold," muttered Karl. "Stop with the morbid talk and get to work. The forge won't build itself." He continued to command from his bed, but his voice became quieter and weaker. Gunnar had heard about a young doctor fresh out of medical school, who had recently moved into Klettafjörður, and shyly suggested bringing him over. Karl refused to let a charlatan set foot inside his house, and repeated that he would get well soon, all he needed was a bit more rest. Gunnar didn't dare oppose his father, so he watched the big bear of a man turn into a skeletal figure repeating, in a voice barely louder than a whisper, that he just needed some rest. That was, until he started saying other things, scary things.

"I have sinned," wheezed Karl one night. "I deserve all of this, all the pain." He had never mentioned pain before.

"Please let me get the doctor," pleaded Gunnar.

"I am going to die... and that's good. Everyone's... time comes. My time is now."

Gunnar took one last look at the emaciated face, then bolted out of the house.

He returned with the doctor an hour later. Brynjólf found it difficult to understand Gunnar's half-cried explanations and repeated calmly that he needed to see the patient. Gunnar let the doctor in, then closed the door and sat outside. It was the twenty-fourth of August, exactly three months since his mother's death anniversary. He heard the cuckoo clock in the kitchen – one, two... nine times, as he stared at the red fire of the sun setting on the horizon.

The door opened behind him, and the young doctor sat next to him on the stairs. Gunnar's mind seemed full of tar, his stomach clenched in fear. He didn't want to ask any questions because he feared the answers.

Finally, the doctor spoke. "I'm sorry," he said, then put his arm around Gunnar's shoulders and sighed. "Reverend Guðmundur should have been here instead of me. He's gone... I'm sorry for your loss. There was nothing I could have done. I should have been notified months ago. I can't believe you let this progress so long... He didn't like doctors, am I right?"

"Nay," mumbled Gunnar. His lips barely moved, as though they were made of iron. "He said you... *they* were charlatans." Brynjólf didn't budge, looking away as the boy cried soundlessly.

The doctor told Gunnar to burn everything that belonged to his father. The memoirs and poems his father wrote, his clothes, shoes, all the books including the Bible, and his bedding. Everything that couldn't be cleaned with alcohol had to go, said the doctor, handing Gunnar a large bottle of rectified spirit. Don't drink it, he warned, it will poison you. He gave Gunnar another, smaller bottle: whisky. It helped get through the blinding pain of erasing traces of Karl's life, and when the bottle was empty the young smith bought another one. Gunnar isolated himself from the world, missing all the talk about prohibition until the law went into effect. When Anna told him in secret that it was possible to obtain alcohol from doctors as medication, Gunnar gathered all his courage to ask for some. He got what he requested, and returned the next week to ask for more, then still more. With every visit Brynjólf's face seemed more concerned than before, and his sighs grew deeper, but the doctor never refused a prescription.

*It's the fourteenth of March today,* said the darkness thoughtfully. *Seems to be a nice day to die. You're at a cliff. Why not jump off?*

"Because it's not high enough," answered Gunnar out loud. For something so powerful, darkness could be really stupid sometimes. He sat up, huffing angrily. "Am I right or am I right?" he asked Ragnar, who answered with ecstatic barks. Unlike Gunnar himself, the dog firmly believed his master would always return from wherever it was that he went.

The blacksmith looked at the plains of Hallgrímur's farm again, then at the mountains. The deep blue sky contrasted with the snow on the peaks, and the sun painted the clouds with a warm tint like fresh cow milk. The mountains would be purple soon, covered by lupines. The white walls of the buildings, tiny in the distance, shone surrounded by the muddy soil. In a few weeks spring would really arrive. Grass would wake up and paint the ground green, as long as the frost of the winter didn't return. Gunnar lowered his eyes, lifted himself up with a groan, and started walking home. A moment later he stopped in his tracks, and his gaze anxiously scanned around until he found the bottle. He picked it up very carefully, avoiding wasting another drop.

*Seven,* reminded the darkness, and a chill climbed down his spine. The battle was won, but one day, sooner or later, he would lose the war.

"I don't feel like working," Gunnar announced when he returned home. "We'll eat, then you can go on with the story." He poured himself a mug of coffee, then offered another one to Sigurd, who seemed taken aback. "What?"

"You're drinking coffee?"

"So?"

"With… nothing?"

"So what?"

"But… surely not because it's Sunday?"

Gunnar shrugged. "I just don't feel like it."

Sigurd shook his head, bewildered. "You just don't feel like drinking?"

"Stop sticking your nose where it doesn't belong. I don't ask you questions."

"Okay, okay," muttered Sigurd. "So tomorrow you will go to Reykjavík, is that right?"

"Aye. Make a list or something. Not going to go there every day. It's two hours there, another two back. Takes all day. The cleaning woman is coming. I don't like being home when she's here."

"Oh… yes… the cleaning woman. How long does it take her to do… the things she does?"

"A while. I'll tell her my cousin is here. She'll bring you some food. She's harmless."

Sigurd produced an unconvincing, sour smile. He could feel his heartbeat in his temples. "Have you ever had a cousin stay here?"

"There has to be a first time."

"We don't look alike," muttered the old man. He raised his hand to scratch his itchy, stubbly chin in a gesture he had learnt quite recently.

"Who cares? Like she'll notice. She's got mush for brains. She can't even talk. Just whine." Gunnar demonstrated the sounds and laughed out loud when Ragnar's ears jumped and the dog whined back. His master put his unfinished plate of food on the floor, and Ragnar enthusiastically wolfed it down. Sigurd's fork stopped on the way to his mouth. The sight took him back to his youth without any warning. He put the fork down a bit louder than necessary, looked at it, then at Gunnar's black hands…

"Do you ever wash your clothes?" he blurted out.

Gunnar glared at him. "If you're done eating, you can start with the story. That was hardly a fight. And there were no magical spells."

"It's called a build-up," pointed out Sigurd. "It's for dramatic effect."

"I don't care for no build-up. Make them fight properly. They don't have to die yet."

### Then

Every night Ingvar knelt by his bed and asked God to provide him with patience, gratitude, modesty, courage, and power. He was ready to take the next step upwards.

The first impression needed to be prepared meticulously. Ingvar wouldn't send a messenger to ensure a grand welcome. Instead, he would show up unannounced, blinking in the spring's sunshine, overwhelmed by the beauty of everything. His hand would go up to cover his open mouth at the sight of the church and dwelling, even if it was nothing but a painted shed. His passion and modesty would be noticed and praised despite his insistence that he was just one of God's many servants. Trusted, loved, admired, the young Reverend would lead by example.

Ingvar did not share those thoughts with the bishop, who welcomed him with open arms. Unfortunately, apologised the bishop, he would not be able to personally introduce the young pastor to Reverend Kristófer. Ingvar assured him that there was no need to worry, and that he couldn't wait to meet his future mentor and friend. But as he would find out the day after, Reverend Kristófer was forced to undertake a sudden trip to the country. It was impossible to tell when he would return, said the grumpy housekeeper, shutting the door in his face without as much as saying "God bless". Anger rolled through Ingvar, but his polite smile didn't waver. He had overcome bigger obstacles before. The old pastor's reluctance towards the inevitable was a mere inconvenience. And Ingvar's self-control was legendary.

He was assured that he couldn't possibly get lost on his way to the village-without-a-name. All he had to do was follow a path between the hills. But the horse pulling the cart was quite old, and the journey seemed to take forever. As the sun started to go down, Ingvar realised it would have been a good idea to either have waited or hurried. He had to quickly rethink his first impression – perhaps the best course of events, after all, was to knock on the door of the nearest house he encountered, politely asking for some food and a corner to sleep in. In the shed or a stable, he quickly corrected himself. But the first thing he saw was a building site, and he had to rethink his plans again. There was a man standing in front of the site, staring at it, too deep in thought to notice the sound of the cart. Before deciding whether to introduce himself as the new pastor or simply as a weary traveller, Ingvar noticed a cross already installed on the roof of the building. How strange to build two churches so near to each other, he mused, then produced a warm smile when the man finally noticed the approaching cart and turned, seemingly alarmed.

"Excuse me, good man," said Ingvar cheerfully, descending from the cart. The man's eyes widened, and he covered his mouth with his hand. Ingvar's warm smile remained intact. He took a step forward. The man took a step back. The setting sun turned him into a black silhouette, blinding the young pastor. "Are you alright?" Ingvar asked, covering his eyes, trying to take a closer look.

"I," said Bjarni, dropping his hand to hold on to his stomach, "eh, I must, eh." Then he quickly retreated, to Ingvar's bewilderment.

The sight of his brother made Bjarni realise his mistake, his many mistakes, including the fact that he wasn't on a ship headed for America.

He should have alerted the bishop about the problems. The bishop could have sent a letter to Ingvar, or Bjarni could have done it himself. A messenger could have told Ingvar to stay in town a bit longer. It seemed so clear now. But until the very last moment, until literally seconds ago, Bjarni kept deluding himself and convincing others that they would somehow manage to finish on time. Here stood the ultimate proof that he was nothing but an impostor, pretending he knew what he was doing. If only he hadn't insisted on something unusual, if only the wind hadn't torn the roof off, if only…

"Hello?" shouted Ingvar. He was hungry, tired, and becoming impatient. Even if he had arrived in the wrong place, this seemed to be an extremely unusual reaction. Where can I be then, he wondered, examining the building again. Then he felt the blood drain from his face. No. He *must* have lost his way…

Someone emerged from the building, and Ingvar squinted against the sun again. Without a word the man whistled, then continued to gawk. Another man joined him, wiping sweat from his forehead, then froze with his hand still raised, also staring without a word.

"What is going on?" demanded Ingvar, failing to keep the polite smile on his face and the anger out of his voice. "Who are you?"

Someone shyly tugged at his sleeve.

"It's, it's… It's me, Bjarni," squealed a man, whose face took on a greenish hue despite the red flames of the sun. "I am so sorry, brother, I didn't think, I thought I– we would, I'm so sorry, I promise…" His voice died out as he saw Ingvar's eyes narrow. Sunlight illuminated the pastor's pale face – skin tight over his cheekbones – thinner, more refined features than Arnar's – Adam's apple moving up and down – the tightness of his jaw – lips pressed so hard now that they formed a line. Everyone stopped breathing, waiting for Ingvar's reaction. Bjarni would have run away had he been able to move.

"Remind me," Ingvar said, his voice quiet, polite, cold. "Who is the person responsible for this?"

Bjarni's chest felt too tight for his heart. "Me," he whimpered.

As Bjarni watched his brother exchange a handshake with Ásgeir, then a bear hug with Arnar, his mind churned out thoughts of escaping. To America, to Denmark, to a coffin six-feet under, jumping into the ocean… The twins laughed, and Bjarni shivered. Ingvar patted Arnar's back, waved Ásgeir goodbye, then turned towards Bjarni again. As he slowly approached, Bjarni watched him the way a mouse watches a hungry cat.

"Is there a place I could stay?" the pastor asked.

"Of course, of course," Bjarni answered feverishly. "A guest room at the inn…"

"I don't think it would be suitable for a pastor to stay at an inn," answered Ingvar. His voice was strained, but still quiet and polite. He paused, seemingly for hours, and Bjarni winced, preparing for the worst. "My good man," Ingvar finally said, his tone dripping with disdain. Then he averted his gaze just as the sun finally disappeared behind the horizon, and the air instantly chilled.

Bjarni faltered. *I have a name,* he thought. *I hardly slept for months. I can't eat. I'm in constant pain. I am your* brother. But he, too, was disgusted with himself, and did not voice any of those thoughts. He would have preferred a yell, a slap, something that would alleviate at least a tiny sliver of the shame consuming his insides.

"So!" said Arnar, approaching with a big grin, wiping his hands on a rag, then throwing it on the ground. "The three, finally united as one! Hey, Ingvar, I have a great idea. Why don't you stay with us? My wife will be delighted to have you around!" He put his hand on Ingvar's shoulder. "She doesn't speak Icelandic well yet, so maybe you can help her with the language," continued Arnar, "and we will work night and day to make sure all is ready for you as soon as possib—"

With one swift movement, Ingvar pushed Arnar's hand off. "What the hell are you talking about?" he barked through clenched teeth.

"But… why… I'm just…"

"This is the welcome I get? No church? Nowhere for me to live? What am I supposed to do?"

"Your dwelling will be a part of the…"

"Shut up! I don't care if it will be a part of a royal palace! The important thing is that right now it is nothing and nowhere! You had *months* for this," spat Ingvar. "Multiple letters have been sent! A fundraiser has been performed! You have no excuses. Why did no one alert me? What do you think I am going to do at your house, with your wife who needs help with the language? Should I wash the dishes, gut the fish?! Or am I supposed to build a little altar by the privy to bless your shits?!" Drops of saliva hit Arnar's face.

The furious outburst stopped as unexpectedly as it had started. Ingvar's eyes closed. His lips moved silently, his fists unclenched, scowl disappeared, forehead smoothened. "Now," he said in a soft, kind voice.

"No need to get upset. Of course, sometimes things just d-don't work out the way we expect. The Lord works in mysterious ways. I am sure that everything is going to be just fine. Thank you for the invite, Arnar. Let's go, I am absolutely starving, and I am sure you are too after a full day of work." He looked at the building again. "Assuming that's what you've been doing today. Why don't you get in the cart, Arnar? Take the reins, I don't know the way. I'm looking forward to meeting your lovely wife. Does she speak *any* language at all?"

*What about me?* Bjarni wanted to ask, but didn't dare. The cart started to roll. He saw Arnar turn, sneak a quick look at him, his face a pale mask in the moonlight. *My good man*, Bjarni's mind echoed, and his throat filled with bile. *I am your brother. I have a name.* He fell to his knees, overwhelmed by shame, anger, hunger, nausea. He dry-heaved, but nothing came out. Perhaps this was exactly what he deserved. "My good man" was still better than "you utter and complete failure", which was what he felt he was.

Bjarni couldn't remember the last time he managed to eat a full meal and keep it down. If God saw it fit to strike him with thunder right at this moment, he would have welcomed it, but the sky remained cloudless. Moonshine illuminated walls of the church beautifully, the black holes where stained glass windows were supposed to be, the gleaming cross on the roof. Bjarni only realised he was biting the inside of his cheek when he tasted blood. The breeze on his clammy skin made him shiver violently, as though he were ill, which he could well have been, too tired to stand straight. Home seemed hundreds of miles away. Guðrún lived even further. There was no way he would follow the cart to Arnar's house. Ásgeir and Sigurveig lived at the other side of the village, an hour's walk even when he felt fit…

Gullveig, remembered Bjarni. She lived nearby. She mentioned, what was it… powdered ginger? Bjarni had never seen ginger before, but perhaps she had some at home. The sun had set, aye, but it wasn't that late… As he began to trudge, he couldn't tell for sure whether he was still hearing the squeaking of the cart wheels, or whether it was just his feverish imagination.

Arnar held on to the reins as though they could save him from Ingvar's wrath. He wished he could make the wheels squeak more quietly, or that he could come up with something to say.

"I'm sorry about that outburst, brother," said Ingvar unexpectedly. Arnar flinched, as though expecting a punch, nearly falling off the cart.

Ingvar, mortified, raised his hand to his mouth. "Good God. Please d-don't react like this. I didn't know I… could be like that. My behaviour was unacceptable, and I shall repent." *Stutter time*, he thought.

"It's understandable," muttered Arnar, "I… *we* failed you…"

"Oh no! You can't blame yourself for this. I had expected… well… I d-d-don't know. Just…" Ingvar swallowed. "I would be grateful if you didn't tell people about this… I should never have said those things." He swallowed again, as the cart rolled slowly in the moonlight, looking for words, rubbing his eyes. "I'm so very tired, you know? This was a very long trip…"

"Bjarni thought… we all thought we would manage. It was all bad luck. We would have gotten it done in time, had it not been for the cur– the bad luck. Really, I've been working in construction for years, and I have never seen so many things go wrong. But this I swear, we will work day and night to…"

"It's absolutely fine," said Ingvar reassuringly. There were benefits that could be gained from misfortune, he thought, already busy planning. "If this is what God decided, then that's what it is. I am s-s-sorry about what I said, and that's really all that matters. I missed you, brother."

"I missed you too," said Arnar. "There," he pointed, his tone inadvertently proud. "This is where we live."

As Arnar predicted, Juana accepted the new development without a fuss. The pastor was a gentle, educated man with kind eyes and a shy smile, and she enjoyed his company. He was very graceful about the delay, yet when Guðrún suggested that the guest room at the inn could be temporarily adapted for him to improvise a mass, Ingvar firmly refused. It wouldn't have been appropriate, he softly explained, and Guðrún hung her head in shame.

"Don't worry," said Ingvar with a kind smile. "I know you're trying to help, and I am grateful. Perhaps it would be possible to use your guest room to take confessions?"

Guðrún's face lit as if sun had risen inside her. "Of course," she gasped in excitement. Oh, the things she could find out…!

"We will just have to ensure that no sound can escape," he continued, nodding politely, watching her smile wane. "There are things on which I can't budge, and this is one of them. Everything that is said in confession is said in absolute confidence. I'm sure you know that. I mean, you wouldn't want your own s-s-secrets to be known by everyone."

Guðrún's throat felt very dry now, and she coughed. "Of course I wouldn't," she said. Ingvar smiled and thanked her. The more people would confess, the more he would be able to learn about the village and relationships between its inhabitants. He politely refused her offer of an ale. He didn't drink, he explained, and for a moment she felt ashamed again, as if she had done something wrong. But the pastor accepted a cup of coffee, thanked her again so profusely and so eloquently that she nearly had to ask him to stop, then questioned Guðrún about her children and family life. As he was leaving, she found herself already looking forward to talking to him again. It was rare that she felt so safe, understood, and listened to...

Her thoughts were interrupted by a loud thud, followed by a child's screaming. Guðrún shook her head. Why would Juana, or anybody else for that matter, want to have children?

Each day brought more daylight, so Bjarni and Arnar worked longer hours. "We need to be done with this as soon as possible," Bjarni insisted one night. Despite the thick woollen mittens, his calloused hands seemed to be bleeding, the wool painfully rubbed his skin. Even with torches stuck into the half-frozen ground they couldn't go on. "I need to start making money again."

"Me too," nodded Arnar in agreement. "Do you know," he said, "I love Ingvar a lot."

"Aye," said Bjarni, looking away. "So do I, so do I."

"But I just can't wait to be alone with my wife again, you know?"

"Uhum."

"It's not that I think anything is happening there... I mean... he's a pastor. And I trust him, and her, too. It's just that... people get thoughts? You know?"

Bjarni, who had no idea what Arnar was talking about, nodded. *My good man*, he heard over and over again, Ingvar's voice echoing in his skull. "I just want to be done," he said out loud. "Get rid of this damned place..."

"Careful," whispered Arnar, "it's a church."

Bjarni made the sign of the cross before continuing. "I want to be done, and once I am, I will never set a foot in here again."

"Really?" asked his brother after a pause.

"Really," nodded Bjarni. *Remind me. Who is the person responsible for this?*

"We won't get anything more done today," said Arnar. "It's too dark. Let's go."

"To the inn?"

Arnar didn't answer for a moment. "Home," he finally said. "You do what you want, I'm going home. To my wife."

"Goodnight," said Bjarni. "I'll just make sure all is good here." He watched his brother depart, then pulled one of the torches out of the ground. He fought the impulse to throw it at the unfinished building site and watch everything burn. Instead, he started to walk towards Gullveig's house. She didn't ask for any payment, but Bjarni knew the custom. He briefly wondered what she did with the empty baskets.

As Arnar walked home, his thoughts wandered towards Juana, and he scowled. They never had time for themselves anymore. When he returned from work she was either asleep or they had to endure the company of Ingvar. Arnar chided himself. There were households where ten people lived under one roof. It's just that none of them was a pastor…

Arnar hadn't been able to get intimate with his own wife for weeks now, and she didn't seem too upset about it. No, he thought, he was just making things up, he was tired, he was stupid. Perhaps it was a spell of Gullveig's… of course it was, he realised, walking a bit faster through the cool, foggy night. It was clear as day that she had cast a spell on the church. At the same time, every krona Arnar and Juana spent came from the witch's hands. It couldn't go on, but it *had* to, because he wasn't making money, and he wasn't making money because the witch made it impossible to complete the church! The fishermen went back to fishing, and he couldn't blame them for doing so. Dumb Niels injured himself, and so was completely useless for any sort of work. At least the "tasty" Ásgeir came over for some hours, even though he always left early…

Tasty.

Sigurveig and Valdimar were both away. Ásgeir had the house to himself. Perhaps not just to himself… Why did he always leave early?

Arnar stopped in his tracks. He hit his forehead with an open palm, then let out a furious cry. How could he have ever suspected his own brother? A pastor? How stupid could he have been? Juana's voice repeating the word "tasty" reverberated over and over in his head. It was clear as day! He started to walk faster, then broke into a run. In his imagination Arnar could already see his fist breaking the weasel-man's jaw, he could hear the ugly snap of bones. The first lesson clearly wasn't enough for Ásgeir to know his place.

The next morning, as Arnar walked towards the church, he was limping slightly, but there was a new spring in his step. He waved happily towards his brother, who had been waiting, quietly boiling inside, for at least half an hour.

"What have you done to Ásgeir?!" shouted Bjarni, then punched Arnar's shoulder. "Tell me!"

"Ow!" laughed Arnar. "No need to hit me! It was an accident."

"Hell no! How did he have an accident at night?"

"Ssshhh, you don't know who might hear us. It probably happened when he was working here yesterday…"

"We both saw him leave yesterday, you idiot!" yelled Bjarni and raised his hand, but not fast enough. Arnar grabbed Bjarni's wrist and twisted his arm behind his back.

"Let me go, and stop bloody laughing, you big cretin!"

"Don't worry," said Arnar, still holding his brother's arm, still chuckling. "Stop acting like a fool, I promise I won't let anybody know."

"Okay," hissed Bjarni, "but what won't you let anybody know?"

"Ásgeir left in the afternoon. Correct?"

"Aye."

"And you're saying he seemed fine?"

"What kind of stupid–"

"And he isn't here today due to an accident," continued Arnar, then let out an involuntary chuckle.

"There's nothing funny about it!"

"No, no," said Arnar, composing himself, then let go of Bjarni's wrist. "Just tell me one thing. He went home, you went home, now you're here, he is not. How did you find out he had an accident?"

Bjarni's face reddened, then paled. He did not answer.

"Perhaps you were just passing by on your way home, late at night, and you felt like paying him a friendly visit? Just in case he had an accident? Perhaps someone saw you coming?"

"It's– it's not your business what I do at night–"

"You have no idea what a relief this is," said Arnar, then locked his brother in a bear hug. "I can't believe how stupid I was! Tasty, indeed!"

"The hell," muttered Bjarni, trying to extricate himself from the embrace. "What does tasting have to do with anything…"

"Hey," interrupted Arnar, serious again. "Let's get that church finished. Let's show the witch her curse can't split us, it can't stop us. We'll get it done. Just don't beat me up again, because I'm all sore already. Your friend knows how to punch back when an accident hits him."

Arnar brightened up, as did the sky. Clearly, Ásgeir was no threat to his marriage. Neither was Ingvar – since the initial outburst, which Arnar now thought of as completely justifiable, the pastor had never given him a reason to suspect him of so much as a sinful thought. But he couldn't stop obsessing over the fact that he and Juana were financially dependent on Gullveig, a person he feared and despised.

"Can you believe," rattled Juana excitedly when they finally found themselves alone. "Reverend Kristófer is ab-so-lutely unhelpful, and poor Ingvar has to…"

"You must stop working for the witch," he interrupted. "Even if it means we have to go into the country. Her curses are no longer working for now, and the work on the church is going very well, but mark my words, she will try again…"

"What are you talking about? She's nice. I never heard her curse even once."

"She put a curse on the church, then she tried to make me fight with Ásgeir and Bjarni."

"You've gone crazy," Juana said, shaking her head. "You're overworked. And I need to go out for a bit, breathe some fresh air. I'm too hot."

"What?" Arnar was immediately concerned. Not once since their arrival did Juana complain about feeling too hot. The summer may have officially begun, but that didn't stop the soil from freezing at night.

"I must have eaten something," she said, then smiled heroically, massaging her tummy. Both of them stepped outside, but a minute later Juana announced she needed to sit down. Arnar, worried sick, caressed her hair and promised himself to work *even* harder, so that he could have his wife and his house for himself again as soon as possible. But all of his muscles hurt, his knuckles were scraped to the bone, and a tempting thought came: he could take a day or two off to rest… The thought immediately left him when Ingvar let himself in without so much as knocking. Arnar smiled sourly. "Good evening," he said. *You have to go*, he thought.

Ten days later as Bjarni finished painting the window grille on the back of Ingvar's house, then wiped sweat off his forehead smearing it with paint instead, he saw Magnús, Arnar and Ásgeir standing next to each other, hands in their pockets.

"What?" he demanded, his face red again. Thanks to Gullveig's help he no longer suffered from heartburn, but the smallest things could still make him shake with fury. "Have you got nothing to do?"

"No," said Arnar, "we don't."

The brush and can of black paint fell to the ground, staining Bjarni's shoes.

This was the biggest, most difficult job he had ever undertaken. The more things went wrong, the less progress he noticed, until he became convinced that the church would never be ready. He obsessed over tiny details, no longer able to see the bigger picture, too blinded by the botched paint job to notice everything else. Bjarni sat on the ground, then lay down, breathing deeply. There was no relief, no fulfilment. Only exhaustion, sadness, never-ending repetitions of the words "who is responsible for this?" in Bjarni's head. It was his fault and nobody else's. He was responsible, he was the failure, he was found out. He didn't need to look at the others to know they pitied him, the *good man* who failed them all.

The time has come to own up to it and do the right thing. Arnar seemed to be a natural leader, good-humoured, calmer, more able to keep his composure... mostly. Under his command the church would probably have been ready a long time ago. Yes, decided Bjarni, he would break the news to his brother soon, perhaps tomorrow. But now they hugged, then went their separate ways.

Arnar didn't feel like celebrating at the inn. He wanted to go home, inform Ingvar that his dwelling was ready to move into and his church ready to preach in. He was happy. They would now say goodbye to the pastor, to his belongings. They would have time for themselves again. Arnar could now take a break, a short one since they desperately needed money, but...

Despite the fact it was the middle of the day, the window shutters were closed, and a bad feeling came over him. He nearly tore the door out, then blinked, trying to see. The inside was only lit by one flickering candle and the little light that managed to squeeze between the shutters.

"What... what's going on?"

As his eyes slowly got used to the darkness, he could make out more and more details. Ingvar sat next to Juana, his arm around her shoulder. Juana's hands were tightly wrapped around her stomach. Arnar's heart beat so hard it felt like a crazed bird trying to escape a cage.

"There was so much blood," the pastor muttered. "I'm so sorry. I didn't know what to do. It's all over now."

A million thoughts immediately ran through Arnar's head. How did he not know anything? Had Ingvar done anything to help? Had he done anything to harm Juana? Was Gullveig's money cursed? *Who was the father?* He stood, mouth agape, watching his wife – motionless, soundless, curled up in the darkness.

Ingvar stood up and smiled sympathetically. "I'm going to leave you two alone," he whispered, touching his brother's shoulder in passing as he left. His words echoed in Arnar's mind. *It's all over now.* If only that were true.

Life went on – as it had to. Juana did not receive a lot of attention this time. The village was busy taking care of everything that had been postponed for months as they worked on the church. The busiest person turned out to be Ingvar.

In the previous weeks he had been lulled into a certain sense of calm laziness. Sometimes he took a stroll to the building site, nodding wisely, commenting politely on the developments. Guðrún's guest room remained empty, as nobody seemed to have any sins to confess. Ingvar tried to figure out the directions in which to go to visit the other villages, but never actually got around to doing so. He also failed to pin down Reverend Kristófer. Requests for copies of documents were never answered. Surprise visits always ended with the housekeeper sternly informing Ingvar that the Reverend was busy elsewhere, and the date of his return was unknown.

Clearly, those were signs that his tenure hadn't started yet, and he should relax, focusing on getting to know the people around him. The rest would be taken care of later. Ingvar had, however, missed a crucial detail. Now that the time had come, and the bishop officially consecrated the building, Ingvar's duties officially started. Each and every one of them at once.

A regular trickle of visitors, sometimes three or four at a time, bringing presents, started immediately. All those people required at least half an hour of his attention and none of them announced their arrival in advance. It was still the honeymoon period, when every word or gesture would contribute to the impression he made. A side effect of the visits was that he now had enough brandy and coffee to last him a few lifetimes. Ingvar had given up explaining that he didn't drink alcohol, passing the bottles to everyone who wanted them. Bjarni refused to accept anything, and the pastor didn't insist. Even thinking about Bjarni made Ingvar tense with irritation. It was beyond him why anybody would give such an unreliable man any important position when Arnar was clearly the natural leader.

Ingvar was also constantly pestered by children. It didn't matter whether he stayed in or not. On a daily basis he would be asked solemnly, "Reverend Ingvar, are you coming over soon for our exams?" Ingvar smiled, knowing this excitement would only last until his first visit. But the children also tore him away from work.

His first sermon attracted so many people that half of them couldn't fit in the church. Those fortunate enough to hear repeated his words to those in the back. Someone, whose name he missed, shyly asked for a typed copy, and that was the moment when Ingvar realised he couldn't continue without help. He needed a list of the children and their ages, all the names and addresses, kept up to date. Someone needed to help him start a book society, then keep track of the books' whereabouts, pick up his mail, take care of the paperwork, the chores, welcome the guests... He made his pick after a chat with Guðrún. Katrín, the eldest of Magnús and Fríða's children, was now fourteen years old. She wrote in beautiful cursive and adored both her jobs: working for the pastor, which consumed most of her day, and bringing all the gossip to the inn in the evening.

"He's so busy," worried Katrín. "He doesn't get much sleep. He has all this work that needs to be done. I wish I could do more to help."

"Oh yeah?" asked Niels from the back.

"Shut up," said Katrín, without so much as turning her head. "I'm talking to Guðrún only."

"No, you're not. He's our pastor too, and we need to know everything."

"Take care of your beer, Nilli," barked Guðrún. "Your *last* beer."

Bjarni sat in his corner, again looking as though a little dark cloud hung over his head. Every chuckle he heard was probably aimed at him, and God only knew what was being said behind his back. *Remind me,* Ingvar's voice asked in his head over and over again, *who is the person responsible for this?* The answer never changed. He was the failure that his clients must have been talking about. Was it just his imagination, or were there fewer of them now? It seemed clear that Arnar should take over, but perhaps Bjarni was just chickening out from responsibilities?

Nobody noticed his misery. Ásgeir was busy staring at his fingernails. Niels and Guðrún were now bickering about customers' rights versus private property laws. Katrín was sulking, as she wasn't done with her musings about how lovely the pastor's clothes smelled, or how polite he was. Magnús emitted a loud snore, startling himself into waking up and returning to his pipe. He dropped it a moment later, when Arnar opened the door and stumbled inside.

"Brandy," he said.

Katrín shivered. She knew that tone of voice, gruff, stilted. She hadn't forgotten the days when Fríða was still allowed at the inn, when Magnús and she drank as much as they could, when they returned home and fought, then noisily made love. Since then, Magnús had mellowed considerably, as had her mother – subdued and quiet now, no longer rambling about tasty treats to wind her husband up. But relief at the changes was constantly undermined by anxiety that they were temporary, and seeing Arnar hunched over the table made Katrín's skin break out in goosebumps.

"I have to go," she exclaimed nervously. "Work. And stuff." She looked at her father pleadingly.

"Aye," muttered Magnús. "We'll go together. It's dark."

"So what?" asked Nilli, confused. "Aw! Don't kick me! Aye, I guess I have work at home too." Before departing, he quickly lifted the pitcher to his mouth, hoping one last drop still hid inside. Ásgeir simply stood up without a word, nodded at Guðrún and Bjarni, then followed the others.

Guðrún sat next to Arnar and poured some brandy into a mug. He drained it without a word.

"You're welcome," she said. "Sorry you couldn't slam the door. I haven't oiled the hinges since last year."

"I'm not in the mood for this."

"What's going on?"

His fist landed on the table with a loud thump. "I said, I'm not in the mood!"

"This is my inn, and my house," pointed out Guðrún. "Bjarni, talk to him, or get him out."

Bjarni looked at his brother uncertainly. "Um…" he started.

"Go away," said Arnar wearily, and his shoulders dropped as if he deflated. "Can I have more brandy? Please?"

"You can," said Guðrún, "as long as you tell me – I mean, *Bjarni* – what's going on."

"It's the witch," muttered Arnar. "She poisoned my wife."

"No," gasped Bjarni. Everyone knew that Juana had miscarried again, and everyone knew not to talk about it.

"I come home today," continued his brother, "and she's measuring some drops. I ask, what's this. She says, the witch came by and brought those drops; she said they would help. I throw the bottle away, and Juana gets angry, she screams at me. I say that it's the witch who killed our baby with those drops. Juana says that she only just got the drops today, the witch never gave her anything else before. Then she calls me a fool." He stopped, lifted the mug, smelling the brandy instead of drinking it.

"And then?" asked Guðrún impatiently.

"And then I'm here, and I don't know what to do," he stammered, then swallowed the drink, grimacing as if it were some sort of bitter medicine.

"Maybe slow down a bit," said Guðrún. "What were those drops?"

Arnar looked at her with bloodshot eyes. "I don't know. Witchery. Poison."

"You hate Gullveig, don't you?"

"What do you think? She killed my child!"

After a moment of consideration, Guðrún put her arm around Arnar's big shoulders. "How?"

"How would I know?" roared Arnar, slamming the cup on the table again, scattering drops of alcohol. "I don't know anything about spells or potions!"

"I think you should go home," Guðrún said, withdrawing her arm.

"You go home," he retorted, "and talk to my wife, who barely spoke to me for weeks, hardly does anything around the house, but has time for the witch, drinks her potions..."

"Gullveig pays her," said Bjarni. Arnar and Guðrún both turned to look at him as if they had forgotten that he was even there. "It's Juana's job to spend time with her. You gave her your permission, too..." His brother's eyes narrowed into slits, and Bjarni abruptly stopped.

"How's that business of yours?"

"You need to sleep," said Guðrún icily, taking away the empty mug. "Talk to Juana, or don't. You're right, it isn't our business. Whatever it is you're going to do, you won't be doing it here. Go home."

"I'll go too," said Bjarni, pulling himself from behind the table. "Guðrún, how much do I...?"

"Tomorrow."

"I don't want to go home..." Arnar's voice broke, and his shoulders shook. Bjarni and Guðrún exchanged worried looks, not knowing what to expect next. He could fall under the table as easily as break it in two.

"Let's go for a walk, then," offered Bjarni. "Let's talk. You can spend the night in my spare bed if you like."

"I can't leave her alone. She's in danger, don't you understand?"

"Arnar, I can see things are very, very wrong with you…"

"You don't see anything, Bjarni." Their eyes met. Arnar's eyes were red, his gaze empty. "You've never even slept with a woman. You've never loved a woman more than everything else. You've never seen her bleed from down there and heard her scream. You haven't lost a child you didn't even know about. And you've never had her push you away every time you tried to touch her. You're right. I'll go home, close the doors and pretend everything is fine."

Two pairs of eyes watched his departure.

"I don't know," said Bjarni, shaking his head. "What should we do? You always know, Guðrún." He looked at her hopefully, and she turned her face away from him.

"We have to tell Ingvar," she reluctantly said.

He nodded, relieved. "We have to tell Ingvar."

Even as they were saying those very words, they knew that they wouldn't. It wasn't done. Arnar was the master of his house and it was up to the master of the house to solve the household's problems behind closed doors, just like everyone else.

### Now

Gunnar was snoring on his chair again, and Sigurd's eyes had closed. The warmth of the fire and the late hour made him doze off into a half-dream. The fire turned into a glowing blur, a back drop for a group of people. They were fighting. Yelling. A clay mug broke hitting the wall. A fist flew towards him–

Sigurd woke up with a start, then rubbed his eyes. Gunnar was slumped on the chair, his hands hanging freely, but even asleep he held his coffee mug in such a way so as not to spill a drop. It was the same clay mug that Sigurd just saw in his dream, and it took him a second to compose himself and remember what was real and what wasn't. He took a deep breath.

"GUNNAR!!!" he shouted, and the blacksmith nearly jumped out of his skin. The mug fell on the ground and broke. "Put me in bed!"

# Monday, March 15, 1920

Sigurd instinctively pulled the sheepskin up to cover his face when he heard a tiny, alarmed squeak.

"You," he heard. "My cousin's in there. I'm letting you know so you don't faint or something. Give him some food before you leave. He's ill. Leave him alone. Clean the pot under his bed. Here's an extra krona for that."

A grunt.

"Cook me meat soup."

Protesting whine.

"I don't care there's no meat. Go back to town and buy some. Here's another extra krona." Sigurd scowled – this was too much money. "Stop bringing me goat cheese. I hate it. Told you twenty times. You can take it home with you. Anyway. I'm going to Reykjavík." At the sound of the door shutting Sigurd quickly dove between the sheepskins, leaving just enough of a gap to look through and to breathe. He wanted to piss, but the pot was almost full already. He felt that the moment he'd emerge from under the covers the woman would enter the room, and he *had* to see her first.

She seemed to be taking hours in the kitchen, and Sigurd drifted away into a restless nap. He awoke to see a hand in front of his face, and barely stifled a surprised yelp. The fingers were stiff and unnaturally twisted. She was kneeling by the bed, removing the pot from underneath, clumsily lifting herself back up bit by bit. Sigurd now saw her other, seemingly normal hand, the pot itself dangerously tilting, then her knees. He listened as she dragged one of her feet behind the other. Sshhh, tap, sshhh, tap, sshhh, tap… He felt sorry for her for a second, then took a sharp intake of breath, his eyes wide open under the smelly sheepskin. Would this be his fate, too? What if after all those years this was how things would really end?

The woman returned, placed the pot under the bed again, and started sweeping the floor. Sigurd tried to catch a glimpse of his moving target. Her hair wasn't grey yet, but that was all he could tell. The day was cloudy, and the window wasn't letting enough light in. It was impossible not to notice that she wasn't doing a very good job – which was understandable given her condition. She didn't utter a single sound. Sigurd watched the cleaning woman, hidden in his sheepskin fort, until he fell asleep again.

When he woke up the house was quiet, and a bowl of meat soup had been placed next to the bed. It wasn't hot anymore, but warm enough, and it smelled great. Most importantly it wasn't burnt. He still didn't know who the woman was, but she was gone for now, which meant he was safe. With enough luck he would depart before her next visit. Sshhh, tap… Sigurd quietly prayed for luck, as he would need all he could get.

A slam of the door made him start. Sigurd straightened and prepared a polite smile, which disappeared the moment Gunnar barged into the room.

"Look at my coat," enthused Gunnar. "It's got a fur-lined hood. Never had a coat like that. Do you think I look good in brown? I think I look good in brown." He caressed the coat, grinning, failing to notice Sigurd's pursed lips. "And the sleeves are just right." Gunnar raised one of his arms to demonstrate. "Can you see, or do you need more light?" He flipped the switch, then in one swift motion stuck his wrist right under Sigurd's nose. The old man backed away, hitting the wall with the back of his head. "What do you think those buttons are made of?"

"Celluloid. Stop spending the damn money."

"It's my money now. I bought you three books. Just said I want books for a cousin of mine, who reads a lot. Something new and popular. I'm hungry."

"We're not finished talking about your clothes."

Gunnar bared his white teeth in a happy grin. "I know, right…?"

"You can't wear them," barked Sigurd. "It will be noticed. How are you going to explain all this?"

"I thought about it on my way home," answered the blacksmith proudly. "I've had a good year. Lots of clients."

"If you bothered to read the papers you'd know we're in a recession. How much have you earned this year so far? How much did this coat alone cost you? You told me about this Brynhildur who asks questions, what do you think she will say?" Gunnar's lips were moving in quiet calculations, his grin melting until there was nothing left of it, the proud stance fading into his normal slumped posture.

The sight was miserable, and Sigurd nearly felt sorry. "I suggest you wear your old coat a bit longer," he said. "Introduce one item every few weeks…"

Gunnar turned and left the room without waiting for the sentence to end. He flipped the light switch on his way out. Sigurd heard the forge door slam and was alone again, with his three new books and no light to read them by.

The blacksmith automatically swept the clean anvil with one move of his hand, then sat on the anvil. He had to be careful not to make the coat dirty, because he would be returning it. Along with the sweater he wore underneath and the new steel-toed boots. He lifted himself back up, and slowly, reluctantly slid off the coat. Gunnar didn't know what the lining was, but it was shiny, and just the right amount of slippery for him not to have to fight the garment to get it off. He hung it on the hook by the door, then started unbuttoning the *lopapeysa*, still staring miserably at the coat. No matter what Sigurd thought, he was certain he looked good in brown. Once the garments were off, he felt cold. There were two things that never failed to warm him up, and since Gunnar wasn't drinking at the moment, he lit a fire. The coal was taking a while to catch, and thick white-grey smoke rose up. It seemed to be getting in his eyes, and Gunnar raised his hand to rub the smoke out…

"Oh, stop pitying yourself," he heard. "Just don't let Brynhildur see you in the coat. Problem solved."

The blacksmith stilled mid-movement. His head slowly turned towards the corner the voice had come from. It was his scrap metal pile. There was no one to be found there. It wasn't the all-too-familiar voice of the darkness either.

"Who is this?"

No answer.

"Anybody there?" asked Gunnar, louder. His stomach started its familiar twist.

"You are not aloooooone…" sung a voice, followed by a chuckle.

I haven't touched a drop, realised the blacksmith with a startle. He backed towards the door, blindly feeling behind his back for the light switch. The pale light revealed that he was, in fact, alone. Gunnar squinted and stared at his scrap pile, which had apparently become sentient.

"You won't see me until I want you to see me," explained the voice.

"Hell and all devils! I refuse to go crazy!"

"You're not crazy. Well, maybe just a bit." Laughter.

"I can't hear anything," said Gunnar loudly, walking out of the forge. He locked the door, then leaned upon it.

"All good?" Sigurd called out. "Done already?"

"Taking a break," Gunnar shouted back. He sat on the kitchen chair and hid his face in his hands. Ragnar, concerned, tried to push his muzzle between his legs. Gunnar patted the dog's head half-heartedly, then gently pushed him away. Somewhat offended, Ragnar gave up, whining before going back to his usual spot.

"You're very quiet," Sigurd observed from behind the rag. Gunnar didn't respond. "Um, should I be quiet too?"

"Aye!" Going crazy would be the end of everything. Gunnar had seen a crazy woman once in town, many years ago. He'd clung to his father's leg, terrified, as the woman passed him by, arguing passionately with the air. Two older boys – who scared him as well – pointed and laughed at her. He never saw her again and never bothered wondering about her further fate, not until now. She probably ended up on the parish, but they would never take on a mad heathen.

"Don't worry," said the kettle reassuringly. "You're not crazy, not yet, at least."

The blacksmith jumped to his feet. So did Ragnar, wagging his tail, excited at the possibility of a walk. "Stay in the forge," threatened Gunnar. Ragnar tilted his head questioningly. The kettle didn't respond.

"What?" shouted Sigurd, but all he heard was roar of wind. Gunnar pulled the door open and the rain and wind hit him in the face with such a force that he almost fell back inside. Ragnar whimpered and swiftly returned to his blanket, but even a blizzard couldn't stop Gunnar now. Fighting the wind, shaking from both cold and fear, the blacksmith reached his shed. He grabbed one of the bottles and drank a good quarter without stopping for breath. As fear continued to consume his insides, Gunnar walked outside and stood there, bottle in his hand, wind and rain flogging him. He forced himself to endure both the icy cold that reached his bones and the burning in his mouth and throat. Crazy or not, his mind could still overrule his body's strongest instincts… but the darkness could overrule his mind when it felt like it, and now the kettle had started to talk…

No. As long as it was his house, he'd be the one to decide who was allowed to live in it, and disembodied voices had to go. The blacksmith took another swig, the wind rapidly changed direction and the leather apron suddenly became a sail. Gunnar stumbled, trying not to fall on his face. The only choices he had were staying in the shed or returning home, and he couldn't stay in the shed forever. Besides, there was no guarantee the copper still he used to produce his medicine wouldn't start talking… He dragged his feet despite the cold rain. It seemed strangely familiar, exactly a week ago (*six*, remarked the darkness) Gunnar went to pick up some medication from his shed, but what he brought home instead was his unwanted lodger…

Was it a horse's whinny?

"I can't hear anything," he said out loud, but still wiped his eyes with his sleeve. Something much worse than a hallucination seemed to be approaching. Gunnar could see the unmistakable beauty of a mare that was Stjarna, and there was a powerful female figure perched on top, which meant... With a wail Gunnar broke into a run, hoping to get home first and lock the door, for as much good that could do now. He nearly made it.

"Hello, Gunnar," shouted Brynhildur. "What the hell are you doing outside in this weather? Get inside and make yourself comfortable. I'm going to put Stjarna in the stable, and I'll be with you in a moment. Where is the stable?"

"Sure, aye, of course, no problem, there at the back, take your time." The blacksmith hid the bottle behind his back and looked up with a stiff grin, trying to look natural and carefree, only to be blinded by the rain.

"Take my time? In this weather? You've gone crazy!" Brynhildur tried to jump off the side-saddle gracefully, but her foot slipped, and she nearly fell in the mud. As she was still collecting herself, muttering unladylike words under her breath, Gunnar ran inside and slammed the door shut.

"You," he shouted. "Hide!"

"What? Where?"

"I don't care! Brynhildur is here!"

"Why?"

"Jesus Christ! We have no time, just *hide* somewhere!" He opened the cupboard, threw the moonshine bottle in, slammed the cupboard door shut, grabbed his new clothes, looked around in panic, ran towards the living area, threw everything inside, ran back into the kitchen and noticed the whisky bottle displayed on the table at exactly the moment Brynhildur let herself in.

Ragnar started barking. "Quiet," she said sharply, and the dog immediately stopped. "Phew." She pulled off her wet hat and looked around curiously. "Good to be inside. Why don't you take my coat, then show me—"

"No, no, the fire is not lit and it's very cold in the room. Let's stay here in the kitchen, I will make us coffee, give me your coat" – Gunnar practically ripped it off her and hung it by the door. Brynhildur, who said nothing about the room or the fire, noted the panic and filed it away for later use. She stopped resisting, curious what Gunnar would do next.

"There," panted the blacksmith, "sit by the stove." Brynhildur let him pull her away from the doorway, push her around the table, then onto the chair. He stopped right in front of her, bent forward, hands on his legs, panting. The wet leather hung heavily off his neck, water dripped off his hair and beard, and he blinked when a few drops found their way into his wide-open eyes. As hard as Brynhildur was trying, she couldn't imagine the crazy-eyed, dirty, wet man as her potential husband. She let out a quiet sigh.

"Why don't you change into something dry?"

"Oh no," exclaimed Gunnar, backing off a bit. "It will dry faster if I keep it on."

"At least take that apron off. Don't get pneumonia. Sit there," commanded Brynhildur pointing at a chair on the other side of the table. She leaned forward and steepled her fingers, then produced a concerned smile, a facial expression she had learned from Brynjólf. Gunnar was unable to stop casting quick, distracted looks towards the doorframe, and Brynhildur bent her neck to see it, too. All she could see from her spot was some tattered, ancient curtain. Her neck started to ache, and Brynhildur moved her gaze to the coat rack by the door.

"How interesting," she said. "I never saw you wearing that coat. My, have you got a lot of new things, and none from our store." Her forehead wrinkled. "Isn't it way too small for you?"

"No, no, I mean aye, it's not mine, it's– aye, would you like some coffee?"

Brynhildur licked her chapped lips. "I would, actually." Her braid weighed a ton, as wet as Gunnar's beard. She removed the wet, chafing woollen shawl, then pulled away the neckline of her dress and blew between her breasts. Whoever invented the modern brassiere was just as cruel as the person who had come up with corsets, no matter what *The Women's Paper* had to say. Brynhildur cast a quick look at Gunnar, who had just burned his hand on one of the stove's hotplates, muttering something very rude. Now that the shawl was no longer biting into her delicate skin, she was too cold. Maybe Mother was right… this one time. Brynhildur gave up fighting with her clothes and busied herself with the interesting looking bottle.

"I'm going to light a lamp," she said gaily, "because I can't read the label." She looked around. "Matches? Ah, I can see them, thank you. Really, Gunnar, you should put a tablecloth on this, I almost got a splinter. We could get you something really nice at very reasonable price. Why don't you make a fire in the room, as you suggested?"

"Nonononono…! That, we couldn't– the room's very messy, not good at all for… ladies, it's not, we can't–"

Brynhildur put a finger to her lips, and Gunnar stopped both moving and speaking. "Funny that it would be messy," she said sweetly, "wasn't Halldóra here today?"

Sigurd, who could hear every single word, took a sharp intake of breath. Gunnar just stared at Brynhildur questioningly. "Who?" he finally asked.

"Halldóra," repeated Brynhildur. She put the bottle down a bit harder than necessary. Gunnar's eyes followed, then jumped almost imperceptibly towards the ragged curtain and back. Via her powers of deduction, Brynhildur realised that this must have been where he was making his moonshine. At no point did the blacksmith look at her, and she had to wave her hand to attract his attention. "Hello? The lady who cleans your house and cooks for you? Every week for years now? Her name is Halldóra, how can you possibly not know that? How do you address her then?"

"Cleaning woman," muttered Gunnar. "Why are you here?"

"Oh, ahaha," said Brynhildur. "Just a friendly visit. I thought you must be so very lonely in here. I'm just being nice. Try to be nice, too. Focus, Gunnar! Coffee!"

The distracted blacksmith's movements were automatic. The coffee smelled lovely, and Brynhildur began to salivate. Gunnar had enough manners to fill her mug first, she noticed, then – as if in a trance – he filled his own halfway, topped it up with whisky from the bottle, and only when he took the first greedy swig did his wandering gaze land on her face again. The blacksmith started coughing, some of the coffee spilling on the table. Brynhildur watched with her lips pursed.

"Gunnar," she said austerely, before reminding herself to remain warm and friendly. "We are worried about you. We are very worried."

"Who's we?" His throat was still constricted, and another little hiccup-like cough escaped.

"Your friends. My mother, me, my sister, Brynjólf and…"

"What friends…?"

Brynhildur helped herself to the large glass sugar bowl on the windowsill, then stirred noisily the way her mother would in order to make a point. "We care for you," she repeated, "we know you're very lonely here and someone should take care of you." She leaned forward again, her face the living embodiment of loving concern. Gunnar withdrew, shielding himself with the mug he held in both hands. Brynhildur, large and imposing in the light of the oil lamp, seemed to tower over him, even though she was sitting.

"No need to care," he protested. "I'm very happy."

"No," Brynhildur assured him, "you are not. It is a widely known fact that a woman can survive without a man, but a man cannot survive without a woman." She stopped for a split second, unsure whether the article didn't have it the other way round. "Stop being difficult, Gunnar. You can clearly afford to get married. All you need is the right woman. Someone who likes you, who would straighten your ways, give you children…"

"I don't want no wife or children." He demonstratively drained his mug in one go, started coughing again, and some of the liquid emerged through his nose.

"Very well," Brynhildur said coldly, leaning back and crossing her arms. "Then the only thing that can be done is to report you to the Sheriff for breaking the prohibition laws." She paused. "Of course, none of your *friends* would ever do that, even though we all know you make moonshine here. My mother knows, I know, Brynjólf knows. But since we are your *friends*, we don't want to get you in trouble and we know that things are going to get better for you once you get married."

No response came.

"And of course," she continued with gusto, pretending to admire the mug, "someone needs to take care of your spending…"

"What care is that now…?"

"We don't want you to spend all your money at once, do we? Do you know, you forgot to tell me where you got it all from. Surely not from that artist, or from what my mother sells at the store…" Brynhildur paused and looked at her watch. Anna had seemed very suspicious when her daughter announced that she was going for a ride to catch some fresh air in the pouring rain. "That reminds me – we owe you three kronur. Anyway, we came up with a plan for you."

"What plan?" wailed the blacksmith. The lamp flickered, and the dancing shadows behind Brynhildur's back looked like a ghost army itching to attack.

"We sat together and talked about you. All of your *friends*, who care about you. It hurts all of us to see you like this, my sweet Gunnar. We know how upset you were when your father died, but that was many years ago. Shh, don't say a word. You may soon become a father yourself… Have you ever kissed a girl, dear Gunnar?" Her eyelashes fluttered, an encouraging smile lit her face. Gunnar's chair creaked in protest. He was now closer to the forge door than he was to the table.

"Please," he said, desperately, "just leave me alone. I am having a really bad day. It's... I'll be... some other time. Please. I beg you."

"Good," nodded Brynhildur. "Tomorrow, then."

"What, no... why tomorrow?"

"Just relax. Have a drink, if you must," she sighed. "Because tomorrow you are getting visitors and I will join as well, to make sure everything goes according to plan."

"Am I getting visitors?"

"Is there an echo in here?" She raised her hand to her ear and chuckled gaily. Gunnar didn't join in, his gaze fixed on the kettle. "They call themselves the Conservative Women of Iceland. Seriously! There are only two of them. Thóra and Laufey. Thóra is the fat one with the weirdest hats. You must have seen her hats! Laufey is a bit... well, she's kind of dumb. Um, of course I mean that in a nice way. You might call her a quiet person filled with warm presence. You'll know which one is which, because Thóra will do all the talking. You don't have to listen to her, just nod. Don't tell them I said that."

"Why," wailed Gunnar. "What have I done?"

"It's for your own good, my dearest! They are harmless, mostly. What you need to see is that it's not just your friends like me who are worrying about you. Other people are taking notice too, although of course we assure them everything is perfectly fine. But only when they ask. Still, we can't have an unconfirmed heathen here, living on his own without a wife and children. I mean, it's just not *done*."

Gunnar shivered. He was fiddling with the mug in a way which, if it had been one of Doctor Brynjólf's wife's tiny porcelain pieces, he would have ground it to dust by now.

"It can be helped," Brynhildur continued. "Very easily. So people aren't scared of you anymore."

"What? Are people scared of me?"

She cackled with laughter. "Don't worry, it's just children. Mostly. Their mothers tell them that if they don't study Catechism like they should, they will turn into a heathen, like you. Anyway, the Conservative Women want to make sure you get confirmed. They will want you to study the Bible."

"I studied the Bible," muttered the blacksmith, staring longingly at the reflections of light on the bottle. "Unless they added something new."

"Gunnar! Those are exactly the kind of remarks you are not allowed to make!" She raised her wrist, and tapped a fingernail on the watch, inadvertently reminding herself she had to go. "They are coming here tomorrow at six o'clock. I will come over at six-thirty to rescue you. Hide your bottles and try to look presentable." She bent over and fished a little red can from her bag. "Those are breath mints. Won't hurt to chew a few of them. If you manage to get to a barber, tomorrow is a good day for that. Get a tablecloth. What else…?" She twisted her neck again, cast a look at the doorway, and clucked her tongue. "This dirty thing must go before they see it. Throw it out. We'll give you a nice dis—"

The blacksmith bared his teeth and growled, which surprised her so much that she stopped talking. He stood up so rapidly the chair fell to the floor, and suddenly he seemed scary rather than scared. "Get out," he growled, leaning forward, his fists clenched. Brynhildur's eyes opened wide. She had never realised how large and imposing the blacksmith was compared to her. "Out," urged Gunnar. He crossed his arms on his chest and glared at her.

"I," she squeaked, then cleared her throat. "Yes, I have to go." So, this was what alcohol did to men, thought Brynhildur. Even men like Gunnar. She got dressed without another word, shivering from contact with the awful shawl and cold lining of her wet coat. Neither of them bothered with goodbyes.

Once the door shut behind her, all of Gunnar's emotions erupted in a high-pitched, tearful cry. He hid his face in the dirty rag, trying to stop the tears. He remained like this for a minute or so before resorting to preparing two sorts of coffee, one for Sigurd, one for himself.

"So that was Brynhildur," Sigurd said, accepting his mug. "Very impressive."

"I am doomed," groaned the blacksmith.

"Not at all! Just engaged and blackmailed. Sit down and breathe deeply."

"Doomed."

"Oh, come on, you big baby! Be a man and stand up to her, or you'll have a perfect family in no—"

"I don't want to talk about this," snarled the blacksmith.

Sigurd smiled – a lopsided, slightly mocking grin. "How's the work?"

"Good. Aye. Been thinking about making something for you."

"For me? I don't need anything."

"Then no crutches for you."

"Crutches?!" The rapid movement caused Sigurd's ankle to protest half-heartedly.

"So you can try walking. Been over a week. Surely you feel better."

Sigurd shook his head sadly. "I don't think I can do it yet, even with crutches."

Gunnar shrugged. "If you can't, then you can't." He scratched his chin, found something in his beard, examined it closely, then threw it into the fire. Sigurd's patchy stubble immediately began to itch. "Say, do they have prohibition in Denmark?"

"What? I have no idea. What does Denmark have to do with anything?"

"I'm emigrating."

Sigurd nearly choked on his coffee. "You can't be serious. Because of the Constipated Women of Iceland?"

"They know everything," exclaimed Gunnar, shifting on the chair and nearly slipping to the floor. He was more drunk than he thought, but with a talking kettle and a Brynhildur in the kitchen everybody would... "I just want to live my life in peace. What's wrong with that?"

"But you will live your life. It will just be different."

"I don't want it to be different." The blacksmith paused. "Maybe a bit different. But not with... her being here all the time. Made up my mind. I'm emigrating."

"Calm down," said Sigurd. "We'll brainstorm about that, but for now, take this piece of advice: you can only hide something in two ways – either in plain sight, or so well that nobody will know there is something to find. Obviously, it's too late for you to take the first option."

"Emigrating," moaned Gunnar, trying to remember what other countries there were. America, Denmark, Germany, Spain... A muscle in his face twitched.

"There are other options, other women, ones that don't talk so much. Don't you think it would be much more difficult to leave for a whole different country, a different language, a different culture?"

"Worked for Juana," muttered Gunnar. "Sort of. I'm going to bed."

"No story tonight?"

"No. I've heard too many words today." The blacksmith went to the kitchen, returned with an almost empty bottle, and started climbing up the ladder. "Goodnight."

Sigurd was enjoying both the coffee and the situation enough not to realise that he was in Gunnar's good chair, by the fire, comfortable, relaxed, warm, and that he'd have to get back to bed by himself.

"Sit," said Gunnar. "You will watch the blacksmith at work."

"Excellent! I always wanted–"

"Quietly," stipulated Gunnar. "And be careful of sparks."

"How can I be careful if I can't move?"

"Not my problem."

It took Sigurd about ten minutes to lose interest. All Gunnar did was stick pieces of metal in the fire, wait, briskly pull them out, hit them with a hammer until the yellow glow turned red, then return them back to the fire. Sigurd couldn't make sense of the blacksmith's movements, nor could he see any pattern in them. The acrid, sour stink of burning coal made him feel sick. At least the forge looked better than it smelled. The tongs hung in a row, arranged by size and shape. Hammers hung from special hooks on the wall, also neatly arranged. The moment Gunnar switched to another, smaller hammer, the former was returned to its place. Even the floor was surprisingly clean, except for the small pieces of coal or iron that flew around when Gunnar hit the hot metal. The scrap pile in a corner was the only thing that didn't look neat.

Sigurd stared into the fire, wondering why the space was so cold with flames so high. His eyes began to shut out of boredom, and he had to force himself not to doze off despite the deafening noise. He found himself wishing that Gunnar hadn't interrupted him in the middle of the "What Season Actually Suits Your Personality?" quiz in *The Women's Paper*, and he stopped paying attention until sparks flew in front of his face. Sigurd squealed in surprise, and his hand jumped to cover his eyes.

"I told you to be careful," Gunnar said. His face looked serious, but there was a hint of barely contained laughter in his voice, and Sigurd guessed it was a setup. He ground his teeth. There was only one end of jokes he liked to be on.

"I think I've seen enough. Can you get me back in the kitchen?"

"You scared?"

Sigurd had to admit, reluctantly, that he was indeed a bit scared. He now understood the leather apron, holes burned in sweaters and trousers, Gunnar's callused, scarred hands. He preferred to be in his chair in the kitchen, equipped with books and a fresh mug of coffee. Gunnar returned to the forge, where he stuck the crutch into the fire again, pushed the lever regulating airflow, pulled it back, pulled the metal – still black – out of the fire, then stuck it back in and pushed the lever again. His hand automatically extended towards a half-full bottle on the table, and he only noticed the movement when his warm hand wrapped around the cold glass. He couldn't drink today, he remembered, so he put the bottle back on the table, but when he tried to let go his fingers wouldn't listen. Gunnar's mouth was dry. Maybe the bottle was less than half-full. It was also really, really small. Nobody would notice, and he would feel just a tiny bit better. Besides, the breath mints would almost certainly kill the smell…

"No," he exclaimed loudly, withdrawing his hand. He turned back towards the fire and pulled out the metal. Yellow heat – not quite hot enough, but he couldn't wait – just one small drink to soothe his nerves – but he had never managed to have just one, he'd tried way too many times – although he could stop any time he wanted, of course, it's just that the time was never right – time! What time could it have been by now? It was still light, but how much longer – his hands were trembling, why were they trembling? The hot iron slipped out of the tongs and fell to the floor. Gunnar automatically reached for it and roared a curse. All five fingers!

"Just put your hand in the water," advised a voice from the corner.

"I know what to do," barked the blacksmith, submerging his hand in the water tank. "Hell and all devils! Last thing I needed!"

"That's enough. You can take it out."

"It's not enough! Let me tell you, I've had burns before–"

"Take it out and look at it," sniggered the disembodied voice.

Gunnar reluctantly removed his hand from the dirty water. There was no pain, and his skin looked just like it always had. Bewildered, he looked at the hand again, then at the other one just in case. "Did you do that? How?"

"Who knows? Maybe I did," mused the voice, "maybe I didn't."

"Enough! I want to know what's going on, or, or…"

Something materialised in the corner, then stepped into the dim light. It was, undeniably, a man. Red-haired, red-bearded, rather thin and wiry, dressed fully in cowhide leather. His eyes shone emerald green, even though hardly any light reached his face. He was approximately as tall as a small child. Gunnar blinked rapidly, then rubbed his eyes. The creature bowed, then cackled in laughter.

"The hell are you?"

"Oh, I am an elf."

"Nonsense! Elves are beautiful, carefree, they sing and dance… and they don't exist!" The blacksmith covered his eyes with his hand, then opened his fingers just enough – the creature still stood in the corner, but now with its arms crossed on its chest. Gunnar's hand was trembling again.

"Are you suggesting I am not beautiful?"

"Aye, I mean nay," confirmed the blacksmith hurriedly, unwilling to argue with supernatural beings. "Extremely beautiful."

"Good," said the ginger man, cackling again. "Be more careful when you're working."

Sigurd could hear Gunnar's gruff voice through the door and became simultaneously intrigued and worried – there must be a client visiting. Suppose Gunnar would invite the client in for a cup of coffee… Sigurd quickly grabbed *The Picture of Dorian Gray*, opened it to a random page, and hid his face behind it. He could still hear Gunnar's voice, but the forge door remained closed. Sigurd slowly lowered the book, peeking over it, only now realising he was holding the book upside down.

"I am very careful," Gunnar shouted at the elf, "when no trolls interrupt me without warning!"

"How am I supposed to let you know? Say: knock, knock? Hey, hey, I see what you're doing, put those tongs down. You can't hit me anyway, I'm incorporeal. Just go on working, and I'll check on you later. Enjoy your day." A cackle followed, then the elf stepped back into the scrap pile. He clearly had no problem with the that fact its legs were now one with shards of iron.

"Wait! Who are you?"

The elf turned to look at the blacksmith critically. "I'm not telling you my name, Gunnar. Names have more power than you think. Just call me an elf."

"Hell no. You're not a bloody elf. You're some nasty troll. Nay, you're not a troll, you don't exist! I'm going insane." The blacksmith tried to rub his eyes, forgetting about the tongs and hitting himself in the forehead. "Hell and all devils!"

"I told you to be careful. Devils don't exist. I, on the other hand, do. Maybe," said the small man. "Just come up with a name for me."

"How about ginger minge?"

"A *respectful* name."

Gunnar muttered something very disrespectful.

"If you really need a name, call me Grendel. Does that help?"

The blacksmith stared wordlessly at the smiling creature. "Your name is *so* not Grendel."

"Of course it isn't. Grendel or an elf. Your choice."

"Aye. Go away, Grendel, I am trying to work here."

To his surprise, the elf took a bow. "I'll be back," he said and disappeared, not bothering with the blurring anymore.

"Wha– when?"

Silence. Gunnar blinked, then closed his eyes and rubbed his temples. Even if he didn't have a headache yet, one must have been near with all this stress. There was an easy way to deal with it, right here, literally within reach of his hand...

"No drinking," scolded the scrap pile. "Not before the hags go away. Then you can feast as much as you like."

The blacksmith switched off the blower and marched out.

"Was there a client?" asked Sigurd. "Who was it?"

"Nobody. I was talking to Ragnar." Gunnar locked the door, put the key in his pocket, then leaned against the door and closed his eyes.

"Really," said the old man. "Because Ragnar is here in the corner." The dog tried to cosy up to Sigurd, having resigned himself to the thought that the new person was here to stay. He began his advances by playfully prodding the broken ankle with his muzzle. It didn't go well.

"Then I was talking to myself." Gunnar unglued himself from the door, then walked to the stove and started lighting a fire with shaky hands. Sigurd kept staring. Gunnar turned, the match burning in his hand. "Why don't you make yourself useful? Pour me a small drink. Just don't let me have more than one..." The flame reached his fingers, and the blacksmith just blew it out without so much as a frown.

"I'm not pouring you anything," huffed Sigurd. "If you want to kill yourself, do it on your own. When they're gone. Brew some coffee. Is there more of that *kjötsúpa* I had yesterday? It was delicious."

Gunnar finally shut the door of the stove, looked out the window, and winced nervously, which made Sigurd wince as well. "It's dark," gasped Gunnar. "They're coming. You're going in the forge."

"Good God," said Sigurd, twisting his head to take a look outside. "Nobody's there, and it's not dark. It's just cloudy. Time doesn't go by that fast. Breathe. You've got hours. I'll tell you some more of the story once we've finished eating."

Gunnar closed his eyes and took a deep breath. His lips trembled slightly as he counted to ten, then he opened his eyes and studied the window again. "It looks dark to me," he announced.

Sigurd rolled his eyes. "We got up maybe four hours ago. There's tons of time... I meant to say, maybe stir the soup..."

"It's not even warm yet. After we eat, you're going in the forge, and that's the end of it."

"Will you light a fire at least...? Some light, so I can read?"

"Hell no. They could see something. You'll manage. I'll give you blankets."

"An oil lamp," begged Sigurd, "they won't see the light of an oil lamp...! Don't put me in there for hours in the dark and cold!"

"I'll make you some coffee." Gunnar wrinkled his nose, and Sigurd sniffed the air, concerned. Gunnar moved the ladle in the pan once, back and forth. "This is going to be the worst..."

"Nonsense. Two old hags are coming to tell you to study the Bible. You nod, then send them away. Done. If worst comes to worst, Brynhildur will save you from being saved by the Constipated Women." He chuckled. "You can't tell me this isn't at least a bit funny."

"It isn't," muttered Gunnar. "I think it's really getting dark. Maybe there's no time for you to eat."

Sigurd's grin disappeared. Gunnar scratched his chin, staring at the ladle sticking out of the pot. "I have a great idea," he announced, cheering up as he reached for the ladle and stirred. "I'm going to hide in the forge, too. They'll never find me." The blacksmith waved the ladle in the air triumphantly, spraying drops of soup.

"Oh, they will," said Sigurd, cleaning his forehead with his sleeve. "Just later. When you are not prepared. Act like a man and get ready. Do you even have a tablecloth? And take this thing off the doorframe, hang a prop–" Gunnar's snarl stopped him mid-word. Sigurd recoiled from the hand holding the ladle. "I'm sorry! But tell me what for! What did I say again?"

"My mother made this," grunted Gunnar. "It's going anywhere over my dead body."

"I'm so sorry," said Sigurd, hurriedly. The first time he saw Gunnar he had thought of the devil. Now the blacksmith looked like an angry werewolf. With a ladle. "I had no idea. My sincere apologies. Just... um... if I may suggest... just so nobody touches it. Especially that awful Brynhildur. You know she's going to try something."

Gunnar reached towards the rag. It was a miserable sight – soot-coloured, torn, hardly recognisable as the woollen curtain it was once made to be. "Aye," he said reluctantly. "You're right." His brows furrowed. "What am I supposed to do?"

*Stir the soup*, Sigurd begged in his thoughts. "Best put it upstairs, next to your bed."

Gunnar slowly wrapped his hand around the rag, then hesitated. He let go of it and looked at the ladle in his other hand, as though surprised by it. "I… can't." He swallowed. "I don't have anything else anymore."

"I understand," said Sigurd, softly. "I know this comforts you. But Gunnar, surely it's been many yea– Dear Lord. I'm so sorry, I'm really trying…"

"It's fine," murmured Gunnar. He petted the rag lovingly. "Twenty-three years, nine months, twenty-one days."

Sigurd found himself at a loss for words.

"Not taking it down. I just won't let them in." He turned back towards the stove and, to Sigurd's great relief, stirred the soup. "Problem solved."

"It isn't, Gunnar. They will return as many times as it takes. Remember in the story, when Ingvar is trying to see the old Reverend? The only thing that stops him is the housekeeper. You don't have a housekeeper. They won't only get you, they'll get you by surprise." He softened his voice. "Take it down. Put it in a safe place. Let them come in, do their thing, send them away. Everything will be as though they've never been here. I'll tell you a bit of the story to pass the time."

"I hope Ingvar never gets to that old Reverend," muttered Gunnar vengefully.

### Then

Juana avoided Gullveig's uncharacteristically curious gaze, hoping the old woman would remain silent, like she did most of the time. And she did, but Juana snapped anyway.

"He says he will change," she burst out, "and I trust him. It was just this one time. It will not happen again. We are truly married now," she said, inadvertently lowering her voice to a whisper. "In front of God. Ingvar married us. Everything is going to start anew. Arnar is a changed man."

Gullveig's doubtful expression was getting on her nerves…

## Now

"Wait," interrupted Gunnar. "I have no idea what you are talking about."

Sigurd raised his eyebrows. "What do you mean?"

"What was 'just this one time'? How are they now married? Ingvar married them?"

The old man said nothing. He just sat in his spot, looking at Gunnar with a polite expression, saying nothing.

The blacksmith blushed and looked down. "Sorry," he murmured. "I probably fell asleep. Or forgot. I forget things…"

Sigurd still said nothing.

"Go on," said Gunnar. He was inadvertently drumming his fingers on the table, cursing his bad memory. If only there was medication for that.

## Then

"My husband is different," Juana continued. "He really is. I wouldn't love him otherwise." She knew from the books she'd read that the only thing men needed in order to change their ways was the love of a good woman. And God knew that she loved her *husband* with all her heart. "It's a new beginning, don't you understand?" she pleaded. No reaction. "Say something, Gullveig, I know I'm just a servant for you, but can't you even pretend to be happy for me?"

The old woman sighed. "I'm going to show you something." She disappeared into The Black Room, returning with a worn-out leather bag. "Those are rune stones. You can ask them questions, and sometimes they answer."

"Talking stones? With runes? Isn't that a fairy tale?"

Gullveig frowned disapprovingly, but her tone didn't change. "The very same ones, aye. Except they are not a fairy tale. Think about a question. I suggest you make it as specific as possible. Don't ask 'what's going to happen', ask as clearly as you can, as long as it's not a 'yes/no' question. For instance, 'what is my marriage to Arnar going to be like?' or even 'what is the coming year with Arnar going to be like?'. Think about it, repeat the question in your head, then pull two runes out of the bag."

The only thing Juana could think of was telling Guðrún as soon as possible that Gullveig's Black Room contained magical rocks with runes on them. She pulled two of them out of the bag: an I, then an N, and examined them curiously. They were blue, polished, with golden vein-like lines running through them. They reminded her of auroras, and Juana rolled them in her hand, fascinated by the smooth surfaces, until she remembered the important bit were the carvings. "They are so pretty," she said. "So, what do they say? 'In'?"

Gullveig stared silently into her eyes before answering. "Whatever it is that you thought about, it's the worst idea you could possibly have. What they are saying is – get off the ship and swim home before the storm attacks."

"Silly," laughed Juana. "A real fortune-teller would say we will be very happy and have many children."

Gullveig frowned. "What was your question?"

"I didn't ask one," admitted Juana with a chuckle. She returned the rune stones into the bag, ignoring Gullveig's pursed lips, then admired the ring on her finger. The gold was scratched. Such was nature of gold, Arnar explained. But the rock burned red like it had since the first time she saw it. It all fitted. Juana and Arnar were not so young and untouched by worries anymore, but still precious to each other, and the passion between them still burned like a bright fire. If it were possible, Juana would have loved to shout it from the mountain top, but it would mean admitting they'd repeatedly sinned in the face of God. Perhaps even telling Gullveig was a mistake. The only people who knew anything had changed were the witnesses and Ingvar. Arnar assured her that Bjarni and Ásgeir each had a secret of their own – he did not reveal what it was, but he seemed certain they wouldn't talk.

What neither she nor Arnar knew was that they had already been found out. Ingvar had made a mistake. Exhausted, as he always was these days, weeks, months, he left the marriage certificate for Katrín to deal with, along with all the other paperwork. Then he went to sleep and was gone before the wick of the candle stopped smoking.

Katrín looked at the pile of paper waiting for her like every morning, and immediately noticed the sheet on top. It announced that Arnar and Juana married this Sunday – yesterday. She rubbed her eyes – she was obviously seeing things. But the text stood there, black on white, written with Ingvar's elaborate cursive, rounded s's and a's. Signatures of the witnesses: Bjarni and Ásgeir. She checked the date again. It was definitely this Sunday. But… how was that even possible? Did they remarry? Was the American wedding not legal in Iceland? But then… why such a long wait?

Katrín put the marriage certificate to the side, deciding she would deal with it later. She then flipped through the rest of the papers and sighed.

In her first weeks, opening the mail felt very exciting and important. She read the letters and summarised them for the pastor, who would then smile and thank her. But no matter how nicely Katrín tried to put it, the tone of the letters was changing. With a sense of dread she opened a letter from the newspaper for which Ingvar wrote a monthly column. The latest instalment had not arrived on time, and they wondered if it was lost in the post. Perhaps, they suggested, he could send them a copy as soon as possible. She knew no such column had been written, because she would have been the one to type it out. If there was a way to soften the message, Katrín didn't know how, so she just wrote a short sentence on Ingvar's to-do list. A lot of things were added to the list, but very few were crossed out, she noted with concern. Katrín wasn't concerned about her own to-do list, even though it was just as long as his. She was used to hard work. But the pastor needed rest, she thought, he needed love, a warm embrace in the arms of...

Her own thought caught her by surprise. The chair she was rocking on wobbled backwards, and Katrín grabbed the desk to stop herself from falling. She succeeded, but the sudden pull had caused the inkwell to fall. Cursing under her breath, she quickly put it up again, barely stopped herself before wiping her fingers on her dress, then assessed the damage. The doily was ruined, but she never liked the thing anyway. The letter from the editor was completely illegible now and some ink was still dripping over the edge of the desk. Katrín grabbed some paper and threw it on the stain before noticing what it was. Paralysed, she watched, helpless, as the ink soaked through the marriage certificate, obscuring Ingvar's beautiful cursive. For a moment she thought about cutting out the ruined middle, as most of the paper was still legible, but of course the idea was ridiculous. Unable to make any decision she watched the ink stains slowly spread on the sheet of paper.

The pastor couldn't find out about it. He would never marry her then, Katrín thought, and felt goosebumps covering her skin. Where did *that* thought suddenly come from...? From seeing a marriage certificate...? Not that there was much left to look at. The letter from the editor didn't matter, there was nothing Katrín could do about the column, but the certificate had to disappear if she were to keep her job and... have Ingvar all for herself.

There was a new, determined expression on her face as she watched the papers burn, then threw the doily in as well before washing her hands and splashing cold water over her face…

## *Now*

"Go on," urged Gunnar when Sigurd stopped.

"It *is* getting dark now," said Sigurd, twisting his neck uncomfortably to look out the window. "Perhaps you really should hide me in the forge."

"Blanket," muttered Gunnar, carrying Sigurd into the cold forge with much less care than Sigurd would have liked. "Change clothes… lock the door… my medicine…"

"No," said Sigurd sharply. "Not before they leave."

Gunnar dropped him on a chair. "I meant hiding it."

"Ah, good. Don't forget to give me a lamp, and some coffee. And my books."

"Breath mints," muttered the blacksmith. The forge door was locked, bottles stored away, a somewhat more presentable blanket hung from the doorframe. Gunnar tried to wash his hands. Disappointed, he bit his nails short, then used a knife to pick some dirt from under them. Last, he popped a breath mint in his mouth. A moment later cold sweat covered his forehead, his eyes popped out, then the blacksmith spat the thing out, coughing. He was already suffering, and they were not even here yet. He ran into the room to ensure everything looked good. Fire was made, the bed remade to look unused. Doubtfully, he tried to smell his own breath, then decided to give another mint a try, even if it was going to kill him. It tasted like etching acid, mould, and poison. Gunnar's fingers started drumming on the table again. He looked at the cupboard above the window…

"It's going to be fine," encouraged Grendel, sitting on a hotplate on the stove, dangling his legs. "You've got half an hour before they come. Read that book, or something."

"Please stop doing this," panted Gunnar, clutching at his chest. "I changed my mind. Say 'knock, knock' first. How are your trousers not on fire?"

"I'm immaterial," reminded the elf, crossing his legs. Ragnar, who was observing Grendel from his safe corner, jumped to his feet and readied for attack, tail tucked, ears back, teeth bared, emitting a sinister growl.

The elf tsk-tsked. "Poor thing. Tell him I'm nice. Speaking of your stove, I wouldn't—"

"Go burn in hell where you came from."

"I'm just trying to help. Speaking of burning—"

"Go. Away."

"They're going to ask—"

"Go away!"

Ragnar lowered his body, ready to attack. His courage was increased by the fact that a table divided him from the elf.

"Very good," pouted affronted Grendel. "As you wish. Don't say I didn't try to warn you." Even his disappearance somehow conveyed disapproval.

"About what?" demanded Gunnar. "God damn you all!" Ragnar whimpered, moving backwards into his corner, staring at his master in search of an answer. Their eyes met. "I don't know either," said the blacksmith. "I don't know anything anymore." He rubbed his eyes, then looked dubiously at the dog. "Don't *you* start talking now." To his relief Ragnar didn't answer, and they sat in silence, man and dog, waiting for the hammer to fall. Gunnar examined the situation again. The kettle was currently silent, slowly heating up. The two nicest soup bowls he owned stood on the table, in case the Conservative Women of Iceland were hungry...

An abrupt knock kicked every single thought out of Gunnar's head. He stared at the door in terror. He should have hidden in the forge, why did he allow Sigurd to talk him out of it? As another impatient, firm *knock-knock-knock* shook the door, Gunnar suddenly noticed his many mistakes and omissions. There was no tablecloth, so conservative elbows were now exposed to splinters. There were bowls, but no spoons, he forgot...

"Anybody in there?!"

He forgot he had to let them in.

The first thing he saw as he opened the door – slowly and carefully – was a round, misshapen, crimson-purple object. *Cow's heart*, he thought in confusion. Then the person underneath the hat raised her head and cast him a look so evil that Gunnar took a startled step back. His hand shot towards his heart, looking for the flask that wasn't there. The Conservative Lady was a good twenty centimetres shorter than him, but the hat seemed to double her height. He was gawking, unable to think of a single thing to say or do.

"Well?" inquired the hat owner. "Are we going to stand here forever?"

"Oh," he gasped. "Aye. Uh... come in."

"And God bless you too," hissed the woman. Gunnar flattened himself against the wall and nearly knocked the coat rack over as she rolled past him. Without looking, she extended a white-gloved hand and held out a dripping umbrella. Gunnar took it without a word, then turned to close the door. Only now did he notice there was indeed another Conservative Woman. She was standing a step away from the door, hunched, clutching a massive leather bag.

"I'm so sorry, may I?" she panted, and produced an uncertain, tight-lipped smile. She had no hat, only a pale green scarf wrapped around her head, the same colour as her bulging eyes.

"Of course, um, God bless," he said.

"Thank you. Laufey is my name. God bless this house and its tenants."

"That's just me," he explained. Laufey shook her pale pink coat off. She started to thank Gunnar before he had a chance to take it from her but didn't get far before a loud grunt interrupted them. The other Conservative Woman already sat herself down at the warmest spot by the stove. Gunnar and Laufey watched as she very demonstratively slid her finger on the underside of the table. She then examined the dark, sooty stain on her white glove. Laufey's sympathetic gaze met Gunnar's horror-stricken one.

"*Just* as I expected," the Woman said to nobody in particular. "A pigsty." She rubbed the index finger against her thumb, which spread the stain further. The corners of her mouth naturally pointed down at all times, but her frown still deepened. With her gloved hand still in the air, she turned towards Gunnar. "My name is Thóra Guðmundsdóttir. I am the daughter of *the* late Reverend Guðmundur." Her sizeable body was positioned in such a way that she was not touching anything but the chair. Her bag, the same colour as the hat, remained in her lap. She hadn't even opened the top button of her coat.

"…Aye?" said Gunnar.

Thóra emitted an elongated sigh. "We shall be *much* obliged if you found it in your heathen soul to offer us coffee." She inadvertently rested her elbow against the table, then quickly raised it, and tried to contort her arm to check the coat for stains.

Laufey wrung the handles of her bag the way Gunnar would have been wringing his hat, had he been holding it. Gunnar's hand inadvertently budged towards his chest again. He stood in the middle of the kitchen, unsure whether he had permission to sit, waiting for Thóra to give him a clue. He cast a pleading look towards Laufey, but her eyes were fixed on the bag she kept in her lap. Ragnar, who hadn't emitted a single sound so far, curled himself on the blanket trying to take the smallest amount of space possible.

Thóra's gloved fingers continued rubbing against each other. She impatiently nodded towards the stove.

"Coffee," Gunnar ruckled. His throat was very dry. "Almost ready." Thóra didn't seem to blink, and he started to perspire realising he would have to step closer towards her in order to reach the kettle. "Maybe," he tried bravely, "something to eat would be nice…"

"Oh, gladly," said Laufey gratefully. Thóra's stare turned her way, and Laufey's pale skin paled a bit further.

"I have *kjötsúpa*," whispered Gunnar, "freshly made, especially for the C-c-con…" His voice faltered, then stopped.

"Really," said Thóra. "*Meat* soup. *This* is what you consider suitable for Christians who bring the word of Our Lord into your heathen house."

Gunnar froze, close to tears. "Aye?" he finally squealed.

"It's Lent," quickly explained Laufey. "We don't eat meat during Lent…"

"*I* shall proceed with the conversation, if it does not upset you, Laufey dear. It *is* Lent indeed. Not that *certain* people are expected to possess awareness of that."

Ragnar let out a quiet cry and crawled under his blanket.

"We *shall* settle for coffee," Thóra nobly relented. "I do *not* expect you to possess the ability nor the common sense to prepare *lummur*."

Laufey's stomach growled loudly under the bag in her lap. "Dried fish would have been appropriate as well," she whispered. "With butter…"

"Never *mind, never* mind," interrupted Thóra, rolling her eyes, continuing to inadvertently rub her fingers. Her glove was no longer white. "*Do* consider yourself informed for the next visit. What did you say your name was?"

"Gunnar," said Gunnar and Laufey in unison.

Thóra pursed her lips and repositioned her large self on the chair. "Laufey dear," she finally said. "*Do* please present the gifts."

"Oh yes!" Laufey started wrestling with her handbag, her hands shaking. "Ah!" she exclaimed, and a hint of a smile appeared on her face. "Here is the Good Book…"

"Yes, I shall take that." Thóra grabbed the proffered tome, then dropped it on the table from a safe height. "Here is the Good Book, Gunnar dear."

"And here are the Psalms…"

"Yes, here are the Psalms, Gunnar *dear*." *Thump*. Thóra might have been sitting in the warmest spot, but her voice and stare remained cold.

Laufey's smile faded into an expression of terror as she continued rummaging through her bag. "I don't think I brought the cross," she reported in a whisper, her lips pale.

"I *shan't* say I am surprised, Laufey," sighed Thóra. "You will bring it next time."

"Why?" cried Gunnar. "Why next time?"

"I beg your pardon?"

"Brynhildur didn't say anything about next time…!"

"And what does *Brynhildur* have to do with our visit?" The snap of Thóra's voice reminded Gunnar of the sound ice made when it wasn't thick enough to walk on safely. When the kettle started to whistle Gunnar was so startled it took him a moment to realise what was happening. Before he had so much as moved, Laufey was already noisily making the coffee. She cast him a strangely guilty look from her safe spot behind Thóra's back. At the last moment Gunnar managed to curse silently rather than loudly.

"I heard that," Thóra informed him. "Please *do* answer my inquiry."

A memory he didn't know he had flashed through his mind: Reverend Guðmundur, not yet old, bending his massive figure over little Gunnar to examine him before straightening and uttering, from an enormous height, the words "Please remove this adolescent from my vicinity".

"Nay!" he burst out, "I will not answer, I don't know any inquiries, I don't want no cross or nothing, please just– just go, leave me alone! I have people in here all the time, I haven't had a moment to myself for days, don't you ever– I don't want– this is, I, just go, I…"

A mug fell to the floor and broke. Gunnar's words died. Thóra didn't even budge.

"As ever, as ever," she declared. "Laufey dear, I can *not* for the love of our Lord understand why you must always be so clumsy."

"Sorry," said Laufey. She didn't sound like she meant it. Thóra huffed again, then cleared her throat to attract Gunnar's attention. The blacksmith didn't react, completely paralysed. A quiet whine arose from under the blanket in the corner.

"Unacceptable," Thóra decreed. "We are clearly not welcome here."

A sliver of hope arose in Gunnar's heart, and an uncertain smile almost appeared on his face.

"God, however," she continued, "is welcome anywhere. And He has chosen us, His humble servants, to carry His words into *this* home. There is no point in resisting the Lord's will, young man. This discussion might be over for now... *Do* leave those utensils alone, Laufey dear, we are departing... but it shall be continued."

"But I was just m– of course, yes, we are dep-departing."

"It is my promise that we will return as often as necessary, until you let our Lord's unconditional love, happiness, and joy into your heathen heart. Umbrella, Laufey. Don't forget your coat."

"I won't," promised Laufey, casting a regretful look towards the stove.

"You *were* supposed to remember the cross too, Laufey dear," said Thóra. Then her unblinking gaze returned to the glove. "Ruined. *Do* consider ensuring the cleanliness of your dwelling before our future visit. Cleanliness is next to godliness."

Gunnar flattened himself against the wall again as Thóra sailed past, followed by Laufey's toddle.

"I'll bring you a new mug," whispered Laufey confidentially. "My apologies."

"Stop apologising for yourself, Laufey," barked Thóra. "It's not your fault you're all thumbs. Show some assertiveness. Open the door for me, I'm not touching anything else in here." She turned and took everything in one more time. "Pitiful. God *bless*." Laufey squeezed past, grabbed the handle and opened the door, revealing Brynhildur with her hand raised to knock.

"Oooo..." said Brynhildur, before quickly composing herself. "*Blessuð*, ladies. I didn't expect you to be leaving so fast! I brought some *lummur* along."

"We are removing ourselves from the premises, girl, and so shall you."

"I am not actually on the premises yet, Thóra. Please let me pass."

"You shall *not* pass anywhere. You're not welcome here, attempting to lure this man with your feminine wiles. I know exactly what you're doing."

"Oh good," perked up Brynhildur, "I was worried I was being too subtle."

"How dare you! Depart immediately!"

"Gunnar!" shouted Brynhildur. "Tell them you're expecting me! We're going to study the Good Book!"

Gunnar's eyes widened. He covered his mouth with both hands to avoid making as much as a peep.

"No, you are not. Vacate the premises... vacate the *stairs*, girl." he heard.

"I'm a guest here! Just to study the… Gunnar, help me! Say something, Laufey, don't let her tell you what to do! Ow! Not the umbrella…!"

The door slammed shut.

"Knock, knock." Gunnar turned rapidly, only to see Grendel lounging on the chair Thóra freed moments ago. The elf rubbed his fingers against each other, then snorted. "Oooh, what a horrible pigsty, such a shame!"

"Leave me alone," muttered Gunnar. "Are they really gone?"

"Let me check," said the elf, jumping to the floor, then walking through the door without opening it. A protesting groan was heard from under the blanket, which seemed to be shivering.

"Jesus Christ," bellowed the blacksmith.

"Yes," reported Grendel, returning the same way he left, "they are gone. Stop Jesusing at me."

"Then perhaps you could stop this," said Gunnar weakly. "I would be *most* grateful." He tumbled towards a chair and fell on it, finally able to hide his face in his hands.

"Stop talking like Thóra. Especially as she doesn't understand half of the words she's using." The elf shook his head. "Next time don't interrupt when I'm talking to you. I was going to tell you to put your *kjötsúpa* away. More for you. I know you don't celebrate their holidays, but they do, in their way, and it's just simpler not to irritate them."

"Does Thóra dislike Brynhildur?"

Grendel sighed and sat on the stove again. Gunnar flinched slightly. "Some secrets are not mine to tell."

"I've had enough of today. Just tell me."

The elf put a finger on his lips, then listened intently. "Oh bugger," he whispered. "See you later." He disappeared a moment before very assertive knocking shook the door. Brynhildur let herself in before Gunnar managed to even blink in surprise.

"Why don't you come in," he said weakly, pouring himself some of the coffee Laufey had made.

"That was appalling," screeched Brynhildur. "She jabbed me with that umbrella! How rude! She wanted me to walk home with them, even though I was with Stjarna. Thóra says walking in the rain pleases God. I keep telling Laufey that she has to be more independent and stop listening to others all the time, but it's like she doesn't hear what I'm saying. Anyway, I told them I was rushing back home to Mother, and then took a quick detour, so I can't stay long. Thóra will check, believe me."

Gunnar believed her.

"I don't understand why neither Mother nor those two seem to accept our love," confided Brynhildur, causing the blacksmith to choke on the coffee. "I thought Mother wanted my independence, but she is smothering me with her possessiveness instead."

"Emigrate," mumbled the blacksmith. "I mean... go home. It's very late."

"Do you know," observed Brynhildur, "I wish you would stop sweating like this. It's very unattractive in a man."

Gunnar's stare was fixed on the Good Book and the Psalms.

"You're right," she said, following his gaze. "They can't tell me off for studying God's words with you. This way we will be able to spend more time together!"

## Then

Married life suited both Juana and Arnar well. There was a new spring in Juana's step, a smile on her face, songs she whistled while dancing with the broom. The sadness and anger in Arnar's eyes disappeared, replaced by renewed energy, a willingness to help others, convincing unhappy customers who'd had to wait for months that Bjarni's team was still the best choice to build their houses. Bjarni himself spent more and more time alone, trying and failing to stop ruminating over his failure. *Who is the person responsible for this?* asked Ingvar, who had never thanked his brother for months of unpaid work. *Me,* thought Bjarni, drowning in self-pity.

"We're worried," said Arnar, who came unannounced on a sunny evening. Days were getting long again, and darkness was scarce. "The guys have been talking. Are you ill? Can I help?"

"I wish," sighed Bjarni. "But you know best. We've lost good men because of this... job. They went to work elsewhere, to feed their families. I can't blame them. Why would they return? They know I'm a failure. You should take over, Arnar."

"I don't know what you mean."

"Aye, you do." Bjarni shook his head. "I'm not fit to do it, I never was. You talk to people, you arrange new jobs, you get things done. I'm useless."

"Maybe you should just take some time off...?"

Bjarni put a finger to his lips and his brother stopped talking. "I've decided," he said. "That's the end of it."

Arnar looked at him questioningly. "But you will be... well?"

"In the end."

"Take some time off? You promise?"

"Aye. I'll take some time off."

The brothers hugged, then moved on to other topics. But when Arnar left, Bjarni's resentment towards him had already begun to sprout. In the rare moments when he wasn't blaming himself, he blamed Ingvar. Until his arrival everything was going perfectly well. Now, however, he felt that it would have been nicer if Arnar didn't look so happy. His heartburn was back, and Gullveig spread her arms, helpless. There was nothing she could do, she said. Bjarni felt she could have tried harder too.

Juana's feelings towards Gullveig were similar. Now that everything was going so well, Gullveig practically stopped talking to Juana.

"I thought we were friends! Can't you at least try to be nice? At least pretend you're a bit happy for me?" Juana burst out.

Gullveig, unusually animated, walked around the house, in and out of The Black Room, not once acknowledging Juana's presence. She now stopped, turned, and gave Juana a long stare. "Yes," she muttered, "I am *exceedingly* happy for you."

Juana didn't know that particular Icelandic word and felt that the old woman used it on purpose. She ground her teeth, looking at Gullveig, who seemed done with the conversation. "You're being jealous," Juana burst out. "Because, I'll have you know, I am pregnant and it's going well this time!"

The moment the words left her mouth, Juana regretted saying them, but Gullveig didn't seem upset. She looked at the girl with sympathy and slowly shook her head. She said nothing.

The apologies on Juana's lips died before they had a chance to become alive. "What?" she demanded.

"Congratulations," Gullveig said.

Juana's hand seemed to have a mind of its own as she reached and grabbed the old woman's arm. "Why don't we ask your runes? I'm sure they'll have nicer things to say than you do!"

Gullveig didn't react. She just waited.

Juana's grip on the bony arm relaxed, then her hand dropped. "I'm sorry," she whispered. "I am so, so sorry. I will not come here anymore. I just want you to know… I am so scared, I don't know what to do or who to talk to. You are the only person who knows. I haven't told him."

The old woman nodded but said nothing.

"I tell myself it will go well," continued Juana. "Everyone told me last time that it was normal, but I feel like God is angry with me. I've sinned so many times. I deserve to be punished." She hung her head. "Thank you for all that you have done for—"

"If anybody punishes you," interrupted Gullveig, "it won't be the God you speak of. Is there blood? Problems sleeping? Pain, or itching... down there? Headaches?"

Juana paled somewhat. "How do you know?"

"Sit down," commanded Gullveig. "I'll make you coffee."

"But that's my job."

"From now on, you will come three times a week, and no more than that. I will pay you the same as I do now. I'll give you some drops to take before bedtime with sugar – they're very bitter. If things get worse, especially the blood or pain, let me know immediately." She waved away Juana's apologies and words of gratitude.

"Magical potions don't belong in this house," said Arnar angrily later that evening, as Juana tried to ignore him, counting out the drops, careful not to spill the sugar. "Throw them out. That woman needs to leave us alone."

"Don't interrupt me," muttered Juana, squinting. "She's helping me, and she doesn't ask for anything in return."

"Really," said Arnar with a smirk. "And how is she helping you?"

"Stop!" Juana turned abruptly, spilling the sugar over the table. "Look what you've done! Now I have to start again."

He grabbed both the bottle and the spoon from her hands, opened the door, and threw them as far as he could.

"What is wrong with you?" she cried. Her shoulders started to shake. "Why can't anybody just be happy for me? For us? Not even you? Do you want this child? What is it that you want?"

"You're pregnant," Arnar whispered. He knelt in front of her and held her hands. "Happiness," he said, quietly. "I want us, all three of us, to be happy. That is all I want. I will not let anybody get between us. I don't care how much she pays you. She will not split us."

"She warned me that you—" Juana started, then paused.

Arnar stopped breathing.

"No," said Juana quickly, "I... misspoke. I meant... she is... very happy for us and wishes us all the best." But she was no longer looking into Arnar's eyes, and he let her hands slip from his. "Let me sleep," she murmured. "We'll talk tomorrow. Goodnight."

"Tell me," he whispered. "Did she feed you, or give you anything to drink?"

"Arnar, please. I drank coffee, that's all, and I watched her prepare it. Go to sleep."

She lay in bed motionless, breathing regularly, but Arnar knew she wasn't asleep. Neither was he, consumed by dread. It seemed he couldn't do anything right. But was it really his fault? It was Gullveig who sabotaged the church long enough to ruin Ingvar's relationship with his brothers, corrupting the good pastor the moment he arrived. Gullveig destroyed Bjarni's self-confidence, pride, source of income. Gullveig stood next to the bed, huge, spreading her crow-like wings, each of her giant claws holding a little bottle, her face replaced with a grimacing skull…

"Arnar," Juana said, her voice tense, strangled. He didn't react. "Arnar," she repeated, grabbing his arm. "Wake up. You must go get her, now."

"What are you talking about…?" he mumbled. "It was just a dream."

"It's not a dream," she rasped. "You must get Gullveig over here and fast! Please!"

Arnar sat up, then pulled off the duvet in one swift motion. The ever-present summer sunlight was peeking through the shutters, and he saw the terribly familiar black stain. He stilled and stared at the stain. It was slowly growing.

"Why aren't you doing anything?" shrieked Juana. "Help me!"

"Oh, my love," he said, trying to embrace her, but Juana pushed him away, screaming, begging for the potion he threw away, cursing, scratching at his face. "Stop," he said, first quietly, then with more desperation, "I love you, stop, stop, we can get through this!" She wriggled out of his embrace, tried to get out of bed, nearly falling on the floor until he pulled her back into bed, trying to avoid her fists, nails, not knowing what to do, there was more blood, her voice got weaker as he lay on top of her, whispering, crying, holding her wrists, avoiding her teeth – she bit his chin, but he wouldn't give up holding on to her, repeating "I love you", trying not to hear the yells, wails, cries, curses, each of which stabbed his heart, but there was nothing they could do, it was the coffee, must have been the coffee, the drops were but the last step, the witch murdered again, she had to be stopped, Juana's cries were turning into sobs, her body becoming limp, her fists relaxing until she let out a cry so piercing and desperate Arnar's heart broke in two.

The church now stood proudly, withstanding any wind or storm. It was a proof that the crone could be defeated. Arnar had waited too long, he had let it get way too far. Not one more day would be wasted.

The next evening some of the inn's patrons were kindly, but firmly, asked not to be in attendance. Magnús, Bjarni, and Ásgeir squeezed onto one small bench, with Arnar and Niels opposite them. Arnar's hand held Niels's wrist like an iron shackle.

"Tell them," said Arnar in a voice that sounded like thunder.

"Um…" started Nilli, then hesitated.

"Give him an ale," ordered Arnar, and Guðrún, for once, immediately obeyed. "Talk. Tell them what you told me."

Niels took a swig, then looked around for an escape. The iron grip on his wrist tightened, and his face contorted in pain. "She's…" He stopped. "I'm… I don't know…"

"I think it would be easy to break your wrist again," suggested Arnar.

"Stop!" yelled Niels. "Let go!" The grip relaxed. "I don't know who she is! She's just always been around in the family, then she would disappear and return. She's always been old, and always wore those black dresses. I don't know whether she has children, a husband, I don't know anything but what I said. I don't know where the money comes from, but let me tell you she definitely doesn't– nooo, let go!"

"Good," said Arnar. He let go of Nilli's wrist, leaving shapes of his fingers behind. They'd turn into bruises tomorrow. "Drink your beer." He then turned to Bjarni. "Your turn. Tell them about The Black Room."

"Idiocy," huffed Bjarni. "The door is painted black, because I had no other paint left."

"What about windows?"

"You know damn well it doesn't have windows. Arnar, you worked on that house."

"I curse every moment! All her potions, poisons, it all happens in there, all the evil! That's where she keeps her magical stones! She stole pieces from the sky, and, and…" He ran out of words, red-faced, breathing heavily.

"That's true," said Guðrún. "Well, the stones. Juana said they look like polished tears, or ice, they are round, blue and shiny, and there is gold in them. And they are carved with letters, but that's not what they mean."

"Runes," said Ásgeir. He tried to shrug, but there was not enough space on the bench.

"I'm sorry for your loss, Arnar, but that's ridiculous," said Magnús. "So, she's got rune stones. Big deal. Every trickster worth their salt has rune stones. They travel around, and tell you your fortune, and that fortune always has a lot of money and beautiful women in it."

The mug in Arnar's hand exploded. Had he been still holding Nilli's wrist, his fingers would have crushed it. Still, Arnar's voice remained steady even as blood started to drip from the inside of his hand. "She doesn't travel anywhere. She doesn't do tricks. She doesn't entertain for money. She has all she needs. She's a witch, not a trickster, she doesn't steal hens, she kills babies in the womb."

"You can't prove it…" started Magnús, then glanced at Arnar's hand, "…but of course I believe you."

"She's got very odd books," said Guðrún. "Juana told me. You can't see any text on them," she continued. "Probably bound in human skin. Only other witches can read them. It's clear as day."

"So?" said Bjarni. "What do you want to do about it, Arnar?"

Arnar said nothing, just opened his hand and looked at it, seemingly surprised by the blood.

"Go on," urged Bjarni. "I know you. You've got a plan. What is it?"

"Niels," muttered Arnar.

"I– well– everybody knows what to do with witches," stuttered Niels. "I mean… it's a wooden house."

"Niels, she's your *family*," said Guðrún. There wasn't much conviction in her voice.

"Aye, and much good does it do to me! Does she ever remember that family members need to support each other? She does not, let me tell you! And she murdered Arnar's child in cold blood!"

"Why are we here?" asked Ásgeir.

Silence filled the inn.

"I'll need help," Arnar said quietly.

"We'll be found out," muttered Magnús. "Someone will tell the authorities."

Arnar noticed the word "we" and he wasn't surprised. Once, on a very dark winter night Magnús told them about his grandmother. She was a very talented storyteller and knew a lot about the hidden folk, dark magic, witches. Decades later, her bedtime stories still kept the burly fisherman awake at night.

"I know exactly what you are talking about," said Bjarni in a tired voice, "and it will not happen. If nobody else, Ingvar will find out."

"An accident!" shouted Niels excitedly. "She was reading at night with the candles lit, or preparing her pentagrams or God knows what else, and then a candle fell. The house burned to the ground. The end."

"Have you no shame?" asked Bjarni, incredulously. "She is your family, for God's sake. It's your duty to go and report all this to the authorities. Nobody else is going to do—" He stopped abruptly. Magnús was examining his fingernails. Niels was admiring the ceiling. Even Ásgeir seemed to be looking for something deep inside his pitcher. Arnar's gaze was unwavering. The days of Bjarni's leadership were over, both at work and outside of it.

"Give my brother an ale, Guðrún," commanded Arnar, not taking his eyes off Bjarni's face, watching his brother shrink. "Give everyone an ale. Brandy for me. I'll tell you about my plan."

# Wednesday, March 17, 1920

Gunnar carefully opened one eye, and a headache struck him like a hammer's blow. His mouth tasted of poison, his stomach was twisted into tight knots, and the tiny amount of light coming through the small skylight made him sick. The blacksmith closed his eye again, grimacing. He lowered his hand, trying to feel for a bottle on the floor, but there didn't seem to be any. He would have to get out of bed eventually, but at this moment Gunnar felt one ill-advised movement would cause him to empty his stomach on the floor. There was no saliva in his mouth that he could swallow. Death would have been a relief.

His bed was slowly rotating – he could feel that even with his eyes closed. *The witch*, he thought, and this brought back Brynhildur's face. Her lips were moving, but no sound came out. To his horror, there were more and more Brynhildurs behind her, multiplying, moving in an odd, wave-like motion that made him feel even sicker, until Grendel appeared in his dream.

"Wake up," the elf said, snapping his fingers, and Gunnar's eyes opened.

There was no way to tell how long he had slept. One careful movement of his heavy head made it clear that no work would get done today. As Gunnar descended the ladder in slow motion, Sigurd watched him without a word. Unlike the blacksmith, he remembered the events of last night, the amount of alcohol that had been consumed, the words, then the tears and incoherent confessions that interrupted the story. This kind of deplorable behaviour was why Sigurd never drank. Gunnar's secrets were at worst pathetic; Sigurd's could get him killed. The blacksmith stumbled outside without a word, his hand withdrawing from the new blanket hanging in the doorway as though it were a spider.

A loud noise: something fell on the floor, and Sigurd winced. A whimper. Door opening, then shutting. Water from the tap. Screech of the stove door, paper being crumpled, then a match being struck. A quiet groan followed with a curse. The door again. The piercing sound of the kettle starting to whistle for about a second before it was swiftly silenced. Happy barking quickly interrupted by Gunnar's muttering. A spoon hitting something. Smell of freshly made coffee. Unmistakable gurgling of liquid being poured from a bottle.

When Gunnar handed Sigurd a large mug of coffee and a chunk of bread, Sigurd couldn't stop himself from wrinkling his nose. Something smelled horrible, but Sigurd didn't dare say a word, just watched Gunnar pull himself back up the ladder. The familiar sound upstairs, like a sack of potatoes landing, meant the blacksmith made it back to bed.

Sigurd, scowling, smelled the bread, then the coffee, but neither of them seemed to be the source of the sharp chemical smell, different from anything he had experienced here so far. There seemed to be a hint of mint to it.

Hours passed, or perhaps minutes. Sigurd's ankle hurt, and he felt cold without the fire. He closed his eyes and tried to fall asleep, but his stubborn body refused. The creaking of the wood upstairs brought him relief, and Sigurd watched the blacksmith descend the ladder again. When Gunnar squatted to lift Sigurd – still without a word – Sigurd stopped breathing to avoid the smell of the blacksmith's breath. Gunnar's eyes were bloodshot, tearful, and blank. Killing him would be an act of mercy, thought Sigurd. He, too, was dying to get out of here.

Gunnar placed him on the good chair, then got busy trying to make a fire. His hands were not cooperating. Sigurd watched him with a mixture of sympathy, interest, and disgust.

"Maybe eat something first," he suggested when the room became grey with smoke, but there were still no flames. "Drink some coffee." He coughed, trying to wave the smoke away from his face.

"Mhm."

"I would recommend adding some milk. Perhaps some fatty fish," continued Sigurd. "It would be good for your stomach…"

Gunnar grunted, then walked out of the room. He stopped for a moment to look at the blanket covering the doorframe, wishing he could kick it. He sat on a chair and stared out the window for a while. Everything looked exactly how Gunnar was feeling: black and white, with an emphasis on the dark. He poured himself some coffee, ate some fatty salmon, looked at bread with suspicion, then chewed on the crust. He drank more coffee, then stood up with a groan and dragged his feet back into the room, bringing a plate along. The grey smoke still hung in the air. Sigurd's nose was wrinkled as he tried to simultaneously breathe through his mouth and eat.

"Why not go out," muttered Gunnar. "Try your crutches."

Sigurd's facial expression immediately changed, first to excitement, then a worried frown. "I don't know if I am ready yet."

"Does it still hurt?"

"Well… not really. I can't really describe it."

"Only one way to find out," said the blacksmith gruffly. He coughed, then raised his hand to massage his temples. "I need some fresh air. You too, been too long. It's nice outside."

Sigurd looked at the window. "Isn't it icy?"

"This is not America. If you can't walk on ice, get someone to carry you around."

The walk only lasted seconds. The boot that Gunnar had cut with shears and tied around with a leather strap, the iron crutches without as much as a layer of rubber on the bottom, and the uneven concrete steps conspired to make Sigurd fall before he had even really left the house.

"Don't make noise," demanded Gunnar, "my head aches."

"This is not funny," answered Sigurd, annoyed with the blacksmith, the stairs, and himself. "I'm bleeding." The strap burst, and the boot fell off, exposing his bare foot. He rotated it, checking on the ankle, which seemed to be unhurt. A few drops of blood trickled from a cut between the top of his foot and bottom of the shin.

Gunnar rolled his eyes. "You should see the cuts I get while working. And the burns."

"Why don't you just sh—" Sigurd suddenly coughed, then cleared his throat. "Bring me back to bed, please," he continued in a very different tone. "And get me some bandages."

"You think I'm some sort of bandage factory. Want me to clean your *wound*?"

"If you mean with your medicine, I definitely don't. *That* would probably kill me. Just get me some bandages. And light a fire. Please."

Neither of the men were in a good mood. Gunnar put Sigurd back to bed, finally succeeded at making the fire, bandaged the ankle again, then left the room. Sigurd ignored the clinking sounds, staring miserably at the new bandage wrap. God was obviously enjoying trying his patience.

"So," started Gunnar upon his return, straddling his chair, warming his back by the fire. He was now properly medicated and felt much better. "Is it fine now?"

"It's bleeding," barked Sigurd, then ground his teeth and waited for the blacksmith to stop bragging again about the *real* cuts he'd sustained at the forge. "It doesn't feel safe, the ankle. I don't know how to explain it." He pulled at the sheepskins, wishing he could sit by the fire and warm his back, too.

"You can't stand on it? Even with the crutches?"

"Not on those stairs, they are too slippery. Perhaps if you could get me down to the ground first, I'd stand in the grass, maybe. And no offence, but those crutches are a bit bendy."

"Any thicker and you wouldn't be able to lift them off the ground. You need new boots."

Sigurd nodded.

"I'll go to Reykjavík and get you some."

"Why not buy them here at Klettafjörður?"

Gunnar's beard changed shape to a less friendly one.

"Let me guess. Brynhildur?"

"And her mother, and her goddamn sister who works for the merchant. Forgot last time. If I buy boots that are not my size, they will ask questions."

"Oh good," said Sigurd. "You're finally learning..."

Someone knocked on the door, and both men stilled.

"It's her," whispered Gunnar, "I am not opening the door."

"You must," hissed Sigurd, equally terrified. "I am not here. Don't let her walk in here."

"How will I stop her? I am not opening the door! I'm not home!"

"The lights are on, she knows you're home!"

Another knock sounded – a polite, modest knock.

"That's not Brynhildur," said Sigurd in a normal voice. "She'd be inside by now."

"If it's that artist..." started Gunnar, leaving the room.

Sigurd dived under the sheepskins. His ankle was hurting now, the bandage putting pressure on the wound, but he didn't dare move. *I'm a cousin*, he thought. *Visiting. My name is...is...*

"So sorry, it's just me." Laufey's lips produced a half-smile, but her eyes remained worried and anxious. Her peach-coloured flowery dress stood in stark contrast with the gloomy landscape behind her. Gunnar's eyes moved up to check for a hat, but there was none. Just a construction of hair lacquered so artfully a hurricane couldn't ruin it. She noticed the admiring stare, and nervously raised her hand to her hair. "I'm so sorry to interrupt. I brought a... cross." She tried to smile again, and Gunnar relaxed. Laufey felt so much safer than Thóra.

"Come in," said Gunnar. "God bless."

"Oh no," exclaimed Laufey, casting a worried look aside. "I'm just here for a moment." She handed a large package to Gunnar. "The cross,"

*148*

she explained, then lowered her voice confidentially. "Hang it where she can see it. It will help. You know… next time we visit."

"Thank you," said the blacksmith, then the last sentence wiped the smile off his face. "V-visit? When…?"

"I'm sorry," Laufey said. "You will need to read the Good Book."

"I've read the Good Book," muttered Gunnar. "Frequently. I don't need to reread it unless they put something new in it."

Laufey pursed her lips tightly together, but she didn't quite manage to stop the corners from turning up.

"My apologies," he said quickly, barely stopping himself from adding "…Brynhildur told me not to say that". "When I read the Good Book and hang the cross, will that be all, and you will leave me alone?"

"Definitely," answered Laufey, "right after your confirmation. But I think Brynhildur… oh! I'm so scatter-brained! I brought you a recipe for *lummur*. Of course, don't feel like you have to make them, although I definitely… Can you read my handwriting?"

Gunnar eyed her suspiciously. "*Lummur*, traditional potato pancakes," he read. "Ingredients: potatoes, baking powder, oats, eggs, butter…" He raised his eyes. "This is printed," he grumbled. "I know what you're doing. You're checking if I can read."

Laufey's face turned puce. "I am very sorry, it wasn't my– I had no choice– I'm just so sorry. But it's a great recipe, I swear…"

"I thought I could trust you," said Gunnar, bitterly. He crumpled the recipe, threw it on the ground and slammed the door in Laufey's face as she continued to apologise. Muttering curses, he tore the paper off his new crucifix. He expected it to be small, perhaps the size of his horseshoe. But this one would be easy to hang where Thóra could see it – anywhere would do. It ended between the window and the door, right above the table. It couldn't be more visible unless Gunnar painted it red. Now he felt watched by a crucified man wearing a crown made of thorns. "Nice," muttered the blacksmith. "At least it will keep the stupid elf thing away."

"Nah," said the kettle, dismissively. "I don't think so."

Gunnar sat by the table for a few minutes, nervously drumming with his fingers that inexplicably began to move a bit slower. He lifted himself from the chair, knowing it was his cue to take a walk. Ragnar reached the door a second too late to accompany him and whimpered regretfully.

The blacksmith not only had had enough of this day, but, at this moment, he'd had enough of his life, too. He clumsily positioned himself on the cliff facing Hallgrímur's farm, feeling the familiar weight building in his chest. He had no feelings, no hope, no choice. The darkness stood next to Gunnar, with her hand extended. He knew this would be their final encounter, the one that would never end. It felt as if the darkness was another person next to him, and he slowly turned his head to see. It wouldn't have surprised Gunnar if the darkness were a twin to Brynhildur. But there was nothing out of the ordinary. Perhaps the air was even more stale, the sky and grass greyer.

He looked at Hallgrímur's sheep without much interest. Little dots in the distance, some of them white, some brown. Unimportant and inconsequential.

*Like you*, the darkness remarked.

The blacksmith forestalled the fall by carefully lowering his body onto the patches of dead grass. His stare became immobile, fixed on the grey clouds. There was sun somewhere behind them, but it couldn't find a way out. And right now, neither could he.

*It's the end of everything.*

"I know," he tried to say out loud. His lips moved, but no sound came out. Every part of Gunnar's body was made of black basalt now. Still, he could feel his cheeks being pulled down by gravity, hanging as if the skin were completely loose on his face.

*This is it*, said the darkness. *You're done. Say goodbye. You've ruined everything, like you always do.*

Gunnar couldn't protest, because he knew it was true.

He'd failed his mother. He'd never even realised anything was wrong with her. But people didn't just die in their sleep like that, did they? He'd also failed to save his father, and only bothered to bring the doctor over when it was too late – months too late, Brynjólf had said. The enormity of his failures was crushing him, sitting on his chest, holding his wrists like Arnar held Juana's, only without the love or care. Aye, he'd managed to keep the farm away from the greedy hands of Uncle Theodór, but what for? The only things of value were Karl, Ragnar, the forge. There were no cattle, no grass, no vegetables. Just soil and rocks. No family.

He quietly despised Hallgrímur and everything the sheep herder had. Gunnar had no value, no story to tell. Only the medication kept him alive, and he hated everything about it: the taste, the fact he was dependent on it, the fear he felt when he was running low and the fear he felt when Brynhildur threatened to notify the Sheriff. He needed to make more, but it just didn't seem possible to perform all the required steps. It should have been easy – boiling potatoes, mashing them, mixing sugar with water… But each of those things necessitated movement. Gunnar was such a failure he couldn't even move a finger. And then, of course, he would get caught this time. Brynhildur and his "friends" would make sure of that. Gunnar didn't know what punishment he would be subjected to. He would take death if it was on offer, but his imagination presented him with endless days in a prison cell, too small to stand up inside, thick metal bars, a hole in the ground serving as the privy, the darkness as his only company.

*Thóra won't leave you alone*, reminded the darkness. *And neither will Brynhildur. You will always have company from now on. Or shall we make a deal? I'll walk with you to the cliff where you found Sigurd, and we'll jump together.*

Sigurd! The darkness had made a mistake. Gunnar not only had Ragnar and Karl to take care of, he had Sigurd who needed help to walk again, someone to feed him, ensure his well-being. Someone to rescue. This time he wouldn't fail. Gunnar's eyes opened, as though a light switch had been flipped. Maybe he could even help with Sigurd's plan. Once Sigurd was gone, he would use the money to escape Brynhildur's suffocating embraces, Thóra's white gloves, Laufey's cheap lies and pale apologies. Now he had a plan too.

Gunnar half-smiled, then groaned as he sat up. Of his various ailments, it was the headache and stomach ache that were causing him the most trouble at the moment. Drunk on the excitement of grabbing control of his life out of Brynhildur's hands, Gunnar quickly made more decisions. No more moonshine would be made, and he wouldn't fear the Sheriff ever again. Once that threat disappeared, he would be free from Brynhildur's blackmail. He would rescue Sigurd, and then himself. Freedom was in sight. This called for a celebratory drink by the fire.

He could never figure out how long the darkness managed to pin him to the ground, but somehow the golden hour had arrived. *Must be somewhere around seven*, thought Gunnar, and to his surprise the thought didn't hurt. The clouds split in two, and the sun that emerged painted Hallgrímur's farm with warm light. The roofs were red jewels encrusted with gold and the walls shone like silver. The grey grass, licked with the fire of the sun, was now amber with just a sprinkle of cinnamon. Gunnar's brow furrowed until he realised what the colours reminded him of: the colours of tempered steel, from straw brown to intense light blue. Mother Nature was not an artist that needed to have a one-of-a-kind bookshelf to feel more important.

Mother Nature didn't care about an audience. A thousand years from now every single person living in Klettafjörður would long be forgotten, their bodies not even dust anymore, but those same mountains would still tower over the same meadows.

Gunnar's beard wandered up in a smile that was half-happy, half-melancholic. For a moment the numbers that darkness never forgot to remind him of didn't matter. He didn't matter either, but there and then it made him feel free.

### Then

The plan was simple: Gullveig's house would burn in her sleep. Arnar would wait outside her door in case she tried to get out. Lamp oil was prepared in case the wood didn't set ablaze fast enough. If heavy rain made things impossible, they would wait until the night after. Juana, ashen-faced, mute yet again, hardly left her bed. Nobody else, even Bjarni, came by anymore. Gullveig's final visitor would be Niels.

He had a sharp knife, a silver cross pendant, some holy water in a small flask, and a lot of determination. If Gullveig didn't understand the value of sharing with the lesser endowed members of the family, Niels would give her a final lesson in compassion. He was worried about her magical spells, but he reminded himself that all the danger lay in The Black Room. As long as she didn't get in there, he was safe. Probably. He touched the cross pendant to make sure it was still there, but the fear didn't go away. She had, after all, cursed a church.

The shutters were open, and the large window in front had no curtains. Niels hid behind the corner, then carefully peeked inside. He could see what probably was a bedroom and a completely normal living space, but his attention was focused solely on the Black Door. It was open, and he could see some light flickering inside. Candles or lamps. One of them would fall soon and set the house alight, Niels thought with a grin. It wasn't anybody's fault that she carelessly lit fires all over the place... Suddenly Gullveig appeared in his field of vision, and Niels withdrew, barely able to contain a yelp. His heart was about to burst out of his chest, and he took a while before daring to peek inside again. She was standing in front of The Black Room, tearing out pages from a book, crumpling them, carelessly throwing them inside. What was going on? Was this how magic worked?

Niels wiped his sweaty hands on his pants, cursing the witch, waiting for her to close that damned door and go to bed, where, according to Juana, she spent so much time. Right now, however, Gullveig seemed rather animated. She walked out of his sight, then returned with another book. This was dangerous, he thought, alarmed. If all this paper caught fire… *they* were supposed to burn the house, what was she doing?

"Go to bed," he muttered, sweating in the cold, damp air. He could tell a storm was approaching. "Rest in peace, crone." As he continued to watch, Gullveig threw the cover after the crumpled pages, then turned to look out the window. Niels let out a small cry, hiding again, unsure whether he had been seen or not. Gullveig might have looked old and frail, but she was dangerous.

Niels remembered the flask of holy water. He wasn't quite sure what to do with it. After some consideration he poured some of the water into his hand, smeared it over his face and hair, then put the cork back in and retrieved the knife. He still didn't feel safe, but he gathered enough courage to peek inside one more time. Gullveig was drinking something from a small glass bottle. *A potion*, he thought, and goosebumps immediately covered every bit of his skin. She disappeared from his field of vision again, and, as Nilli bent forward trying to see whether she went to bed, the door opened right next to him.

"Hello," Gullveig said calmly, and Niels screamed. His hand instinctively shot up, and he nearly punctured his own throat with the knife. "You're early," she continued, as Niels fought with the cork on his flask, trying to get it out without dropping the knife. "I expected you at night. Can I help you with this? We don't have much time."

"Hands off me, crone," panted Niels. "Er. Why don't we have much time?"

"Because," she explained politely, "I would like to lie down."

The stubborn cork finally fell to the ground, and Niels threw the contents of the flask in Gullveig's face.

"That's not nice at all," said Gullveig, blinking, then she clucked her tongue before wiping her face. "And it should be fire, not water. You're young, you'll learn. Why don't you come inside? It's too cold to stand here."

All colour drained from Niels's face and he dropped the bottle. Her powers must be insanely strong. He wrapped his fingers convulsively around the silver cross pendant. Gullveig, observing him, just shook her head. "Help yourself to some coffee," she said, then yawned and left him outside.

Incredulous, Niels stared as she trudged towards her bedroom, one hand on the small of her back. She lay down on her bed, sighed with relief, then closed her eyes. Niels, the rightful avenger, was very close to dropping the knife and sprinting away, but she owed him money. Yes, he told himself, that's right, she *owed* him. It was greed, not courage, that made him enter the witch's lair.

Every single hair on Niels's lanky body stood up, his eyes bulging in terror, jumping from side to side in search of potential dangers. His right hand, the one holding the knife, trembled. The left held on to the pendant. Gullveig's bed creaked, and he nearly dropped everything and ran. But there was a leather bag on the table, and a few blue and gold stones next to the bag, exactly as Juana had described them. *Gold*. Niels, his eyes the size of saucers, extended the knife as far as he could and poked at one of the magical stones. Nothing happened, and he felt brave enough to lift a string hanging off the bag with the tip of the knife until the bag hovered over the table. As Niels tried to decide what to do next, the blade, which he'd just sharpened, effortlessly cut through the string. The bag fell, and the stones scattered, some of them falling on the floor. Niels shrieked in panic and shut his eyes, expecting to be struck dead.

Nothing happened. Niels leaned against the wall, breathing heavily, trying to calm himself before entering the bedroom. His gaze remained fixed on Gullveig, and he nearly tripped over one of the stones. *Protective spell!* It took him a moment to compose himself enough to remember he had spilled the rune stones all over the floor himself.

Gullveig's eyes were closed. Her hands were crossed on her belly, a hint of a smile adorned her face, and he would have taken her for dead already had her chest not moved with every slow breath. Niels couldn't explain why this, too, made his stomach clench. She looked too peaceful. It had to be a trap. *Money*, he reminded himself, once again gathering his dwindling supplies of courage. He very slowly extended his hand until the tip of the knife pierced the skin on Gullveig's neck.

A sudden sound resembling hail hitting the window startled him so much Niels let out a panicky, high-pitched cry. When he didn't die a few sharp breaths later, he dared to look. The source of the sound was hail hitting the window. *She made it happen*, thought Niels, and suddenly his fear turned to fury. Gullveig looked fast asleep, oblivious to his presence, to the droplet of blood marking the point where his knife pierced through the skin. He stood there, gawking, wondering what to do, until the sound of thunder broke through his trance.

"Wake up," he yelled, close to tears, grabbing Gullveig's arm, shaking it. "I want my money!" Niels slapped her, hard, and pried her eyes open with his fingers. He jabbed her neck with the knife harder than before, then moved to her legs, arms, hitting her with his fists, desperate to wake her up. Some more blood trickled onto the bed. Yet, every time he let go of her body it returned to the same position, the serene smile, closed eyes, steady breathing. Niels's own blood seemed to flow upwards, into his head, making his vision blurry and his cheeks so red they were nearly purple. She was trying to make his head explode! Niels lifted the knife and lowered it with a long, piercing shriek, tears rolling down his face, stabbing Gullveig's chest with all his might again and again, screaming, until he ran out of strength. The knife fell from his hand, and he dropped to his knees. There was blood everywhere now, some of it sprayed his face, hands, clothes, yet Gullveig *still* lay in the same position, her face fixed in a peaceful smile. He would have sworn she was still breathing at the same relaxed pace.

Niels withdrew from the bedroom, not taking his eyes off her body and the bloodied sheets beneath her. A blue and golden stone shot from under his foot, and Niels fell. He was crying now, whimpering like a beaten dog, but he lifted himself up again. He had to get out of here. He couldn't stay here any longer, but…

*Money.*

Nilli jerked his head around, trying to figure out where the crone's money could be hidden. Deep inside he knew, as much as he didn't want to know. The money must have been in The Black Room, the only part of the house nobody would dare enter. The knife was useless now, and Niels dropped it. The black door was ajar. Niels kicked it as hard as he could and the door struck the wall and bounced back. Within that one moment he saw something he would never be able to forget. Monstrous figures carved from wood, shelves with jars containing what must have been magical supplies, a golden chalice that Niels was certain was full of blood, and candles, candles everywhere. One of the candles fell as the door hit the wall, and he saw it mid-flight, about to land on the pile of paper. Paralysed, he stood there in front of the door until the first streaks of smoke started coming out of the room. That was the last image his brain consciously registered.

Nilli would later recall small bits of what happened. Waves of pain going through his ankle. The heat of the flames engulfing the ceiling. Dragging himself out, trying to use his nails as hooks. Pulling himself outside a moment before the roof collapsed. The ice pellets of hail beating

*155*

him mercilessly. Wetness in his crotch. A thick envelope in his hand, Juana's name inscribed on it. Nilli crawled away, crying loudly, whipped by the hail, holding on to the envelope, unable to remember how it had made its way into his hand. He landed in a puddle of mud, crying convulsively. In his vision, Gullveig continued to smile serenely even when flames started to devour her dress, then her hair.

Ingvar was shocked when the news was brought to him: an old lady whose name escaped him had burned alive in her house. Magnús, whom he knew as a well-respected community member, explained that they suspected that a candle had fallen while she was reading. Everybody felt very sorry for her, said Magnús, wrangling his hat, staring at his feet. He then emphasised that it was very important to keep the news from Juana. She was in enough pain already, and since she worked for poor old Gullveig it would have upset her beyond belief.

"Of course," agreed Ingvar, relieved to know the dead woman's name. "Juana will not be told. Will a wake be held?"

Magnús shook his head, avoiding the pastor's eyes. "Gullveig didn't really have any other, um, friends. We might have a coffee for her at the inn or something. We owe her that much, I guess." His face gradually grew redder under Ingvar's curious gaze.

"I gather she wasn't very… popular?"

"Nobody really knew her well," agreed Magnús, shuffling his feet uncomfortably. "It's a very sad thing, but unfortunately it happened, and time cannot be turned back now."

"Was it reported?"

"She was Niels's family…"

"Good God," said Ingvar. "Yes, *now* I remember. I gather he will take care of it."

"If we could just have one last request for you, to bless the, um, ashes with holy water…" Magnús made a sign of the cross. "A lot of holy water. I have to go now. Don't want to tear you away from work for too long."

"Good," said Ingvar, rubbing his eyes. He looked at his to-do list, which now stretched to two pages. He wasn't sure what the most important thing to do now was, but the ashes could definitely wait.

"Reverend," said Katrín, "I am terribly sorry to interrupt, but you need to look at this letter."

"God bless," exclaimed Magnús, already on his way out.

Ingvar reached out his hand out without looking. The letter was urging him to return some of the books he had distributed. "Can you please take care of this," he said, flatly.

Katrín put her hand on his shoulder. "Maybe you should take some more rest," she suggested. "A nap. I will try to take care of as much as possible in the meantime and give you a report when you wake up."

"I shouldn't…" said Ingvar, yawning so hard tears appeared in his eyes, blurring his vision. Seconds later he was in bed, fully dressed, already snoring.

Katrín did not bother adding Gullveig's death to his to-do list. Casting careful looks at Ingvar, listening to his snores, she carefully picked an object that had been piquing her curiosity for weeks. It was a red, leather-bound, thick book she expected to be his diary. All she wanted to know was whether he wrote anything about her, but the book only contained newspaper cut-outs: articles Ingvar had written and published. The first one, short as it was, came out in print when he was only nineteen, and she couldn't resist gently caressing the paper with her fingers. What an exceptional man he was! She then quickly flipped the pages until she found the last cut-out. It was four months old. Katrín didn't have to ask to know that this was the last one he had published, and she sighed sadly, gave the sleeping pastor one last look, then left.

On her way to the inn Katrín decided that this was information that didn't need to be shared. She hesitated before entering, hearing raised voices. She slipped inside, quickly hid in the darkest corner, and listened.

"I don't know anything," said Arnar. "We planned this for the evening."

"I tell you," shouted Niels, "she predicted everything by magic!"

"And burned herself with her own house?"

"That's exactly what she has done!"

"How do you know?" asked Guðrún. "And what happened to you this time?"

"I broke my ankle," exclaimed Niels. "Her last curse, no doubt!"

"Someone killed her," said Bjarni, "either you or someone else did, and I will find out who!"

"Nobody did it," yelled Arnar, "I'm telling you! Do you think I would keep quiet if it were me? I would be proud, I would shout it from the mountain top! I don't have any secrets!"

"Ingvar can't find out," cried Niels.

"There's nothing for him to find out because we've done nothing!" Arnar slammed his fist on the table, and Katrín let out an involuntary gasp.

"Hey hey hey... look at that. What are you doing here, pastor's girlfriend? Spying on us?"

"Arnar," said Magnús, his tone a warning.

"You heard nothing, and you will tell him nothing," continued Arnar, fixing Katrín with a fierce glare. Her back stiffened, like someone had pulled a string tighter. "Or there will be consequences. Do you understand?"

"Arnar," repeated Magnús, louder.

"I won't tell," mumbled Katrín, suddenly reduced to the scared teenage girl that she was.

"What? I can't hear you! Say it," demanded Arnar, "louder this time."

"Arnar," said Bjarni. "Stop it. What's wrong with you? You just said. You've done nothing. Nobody did. It really was an accident. There is nothing to tell."

Muttering something, Arnar swallowed the remaining brandy. Katrín noticed he was stuck between her father and a wall so tightly he had to use his left hand. He was trapped in that corner, unable to reach her no matter how hard he might try.

"I know more than you think," she said quietly.

"Just get out of here, pastor's girlfriend," said Arnar. "You make me sick."

Magnús put his hand on Arnar's shoulder. Arnar shook it off as if it were a fly.

"I know your secret," Katrín said, her voice steadier now, louder.

"I don't have secrets." He extended his mug, not even looking, and Guðrún refilled it reluctantly, casting worried looks at Katrín. "Whatever it is that you think you know, you'll keep it to yourself. Understood?"

"What do you know?" demanded Magnús.

The fear returned. "Nothing, Father, I swear. I was just..."

"Well, I want to know too," said Arnar, his voice like restrained thunder. He stood up, pushing Magnús away, leaning over the table, resting on his fists, staring at her. "Tell me my secret, little girl. Tell me what it is that you think you know."

"Calm down," muttered Magnús, but nobody heard him.

Katrín shivered. "I was kidding..." she whispered. His drunken voice made her think of her parents' fights again. "I'm going," she said, attempting to stand up, but her dress got caught between the wall and the bench. Katrín pulled at the fabric, but nothing happened. She was trapped.

"Leave her alone," said Bjarni. "Calm down. It's nothing."

"Sit down, Arnar. And you, Katrín, know what I will do to you if you don't tell," said Magnús. "You are my daughter, you live under my roof.

You will tell." He was drunk too, she could see it in his eyes, hear it in his voice.

"She'd rather live under Ingvar's roof, if she could," said Arnar. "That's hardly a secret, little girl. We all laugh about it behind your back. Now get out of here, go back to your boyfriend."

Katrín's ears were burning, and her lips started to tingle. "Tell us about your wedding in America," she said. Her own voice sounded foreign to her, as though someone else was speaking, someone brave and stupid in equal measure. "Was it lavish? What was Juana wearing?" She noticed Bjarni's sharp intake of breath. "How old was she when you two got married, I wonder? She must have been so very young." She noticed Guðrún staring at her, almost imperceptibly shaking her head. "Although," continued Katrín, a bit quieter now, "maybe she wasn't all that young anymore, and maybe there are no wedding photographs. Maybe I should ask someone else, like Bjarni, or… or Ásgeir…" Something in Arnar's eyes made her pull at the fabric of her dress harder. She felt the dress rip and hesitated, distracted by the thought that it would have to be mended…

"She told you, didn't she," Arnar exploded without a warning. "She just had to brag! But why to you?"

"No," cried Katrín. "Juana…"

"Steady, Arnar," demanded Magnús, grabbing Arnar's belt and pulling. That was the last thing Katrín registered clearly before all hell broke loose.

Someone screamed, then cried. Blood was dripping down her father's face. Arnar, already on the table, fell with a furious roar. A sudden flash of light: the blade of a knife. Guðrún dived under the bar, emerging with a shotgun. The hideous sound of someone's fist landing on someone else's jaw, the men piled on top of each other… Arnar yelled "stop" and Guðrún yelled "run" at the same moment. No longer caring about the dress, Katrín yanked the fabric free, feeling rather than hearing it rip, the sound drowned out by the screams around her mixing with one another. Arnar's gaze was still fixed on her face. Katrín couldn't see anything else but his huge, unblinking eyes until Bjarni jumped on top of Arnar, sending him to the ground again, freeing her from the trance. Her father's shirt was now soaked in blood. Someone else – Niels? – kept cursing loudly. Ásgeir calmly raised a clay pitcher, taking aim at a blur of a moving target. "Warn Juana!" yelled Guðrún before a gunshot tore through the air. Everyone froze except for Katrín, who finally bolted out from her corner, tripping as she ran out into the moonlit night. The last thing she heard was another gunshot exploding in the small space. Uncertain for a moment, she looked around, then began to run as fast as she could, cursing her dress and uncomfortable shoes. She slipped and fell into the mud before adrenalin lifted her back. She had to warn Juana, the thought beat over and over in her head like a church bell, making her deaf and blind to everything else.

Had she paused to look back, she would have seen Arnar stumbling outside of the inn. His leg, wounded by the bullet, hurt, and a blood stain was spreading over his torn trousers. Arnar was an experienced brawler and knew from experience that once adrenalin wore off the pain would become overwhelming. "Juana," he muttered as he limped. He needed her soft embrace. He had questions for her. "Juana," he groaned, dragging his useless leg, grinding his teeth to stop the tears. He'd take care of Guðrún later, after Ásgeir, Bjarni, all those traitors, especially Katrín. "Juana…!"

"He's barely moving," reported Ásgeir, who walked towards the door and calmly observed Arnar as if nothing out of the ordinary just happened. "He won't get anywhere."

Without asking, Bjarni grabbed a bottle of brandy and split it evenly between everyone. Nilli was crying, ignored by the others, even though this time his injury was genuine.

"Do you think she'll be safe?" asked Bjarni. "Perhaps I should go there?"

"There's nothing he can do, to her or anybody else," said Guðrún. "Move your head back, Magnús. Just sit like this and don't move. I know where I shot him. He won't be able to move much for a few days, if not longer. There's no way he could outrun Katrín. And if Juana decides to stay with him, it's her choice."

"She will," muttered Bjarni.

"If she's stupid enough to take him back, then there's nothing we can do," said Guðrún. "One thing I know is that I don't want to see his face ever again."

"M' n-ffer," mumbled Magnús, two bloodied chunks of fabric sticking out of his nose.

Careful what you wish for, they say, because sometimes wishes come true.

"Right," Gunnar said to Ragnar. "We're going to work." He let the excited dog inside the forge, then shut the door and looked around, uncertain. "Elf. You here?" No response. Either Grendel had decided to hide from him or he was off doing whatever it was that elves did when they were not pestering honest people.

The blacksmith needed a distraction. Once the fire was burning, he got to work on the artist's bookshelf. It was possibly the most difficult job he'd ever done, and the least rewarding. The wooden planks she wanted were not straight, nor were they planed. He had to check his drawings every five minutes, measure everything before making the bends, check them against the numbered planks, then curse a lot. In his opinion, the "artist" was simply being "modern" and "a creative soul" for no reason other than to appear more important than she was. Nobody needed a bookshelf like this, Gunnar muttered furiously, using a ball-peen hammer to spread the metal until it was no longer too short. Bookshelves were to put books on, not to take up half of the room, he muttered, carefully fixing the bend before it had a chance to cool down. He should be charging her twice as much… and with this thought, his focus disappeared, the hammer stopping mid-air.

*You're rich.* But was he?

The elf might have stolen the money. Or turned it into straw. Now nervous, the blacksmith carelessly threw the bent metal away, then lifted the anvil with a groan that turned into a surprised scream as his back exploded in pain. He still didn't drop the anvil, placing it on the ground, remembering – too late – what Doctor Brynjólf had said about his posture. He'd take care of it later. He picked up the lid, threw it aside, and grabbed the black satchel. The money was exactly as Gunnar had left it, and he sighed in relief. He crumpled some notes without bothering to count them, then put them in the back pocket of his trousers and returned the satchel to its place, then sat on the anvil, breathing heavily.

His lower back was now radiating deceptively pleasant heat, as if a hot-water bottle had been placed there. The blacksmith scowled, knowing the heat would soon disappear, only to be replaced with blunt pain. There would be no more work done for a while. Yet the anvil had to return to its place no matter what. Perhaps if he had a stiff drink it would hurt less… ah, he remembered, he had to stop, so he'd be safe from the authorities. Although, of course, he'd be emigrating soon, so perhaps… but no, it made no sense to make another batch, as he wouldn't be able to take it along.

Keeping proper posture this time, Gunnar lifted the anvil again, grinding his teeth, and the pain squeezed tears out of his eyes. Then he switched the blower off. From experience, he'd need at least a few days off forging, perhaps even a week. The warmth was already turning into pain. The blacksmith was seeing the doctor later, so he couldn't drink. But then, the doctor knew anyway, apparently everybody did. And there were some breath mints left. Maybe just one small drink, for the pain… How did Sigurd manage without any medicine? Of course it couldn't have felt nearly half as bad, it was only an ankle, yet he just wouldn't stop talking about it…

Come to think of it, thought Gunnar, he hadn't talked about it at all today. Or, in fact, about anything else. In the morning Gunnar had brought Sigurd some food, a thermos of coffee, left them by the bed, then went to the forge. He had been preoccupied with Grendel, various women forcing themselves on him, then the money, now his back, but it was unlike Sigurd to remain so quiet for so long, almost as if he…

"No," groaned Gunnar. "Oh no, no, no!" Grimacing, he stretched his back until something cracked in his spine, a white flash of pain blinded him for a moment, then he hurried out of the forge. The pain had to wait. "Sigurd," he panted, trying to free himself from the hated blanket. "You all right?"

Sigurd slowly turned his head, and Gunnar noticed the food was still there, untouched.

"I don't know… not really." Sigurd spoke slowly, elongating vowels, as if he were drunk. "My foot… swollen. Hurts so bad. It's so hot in here. Hard to breathe…"

Gunnar looked at the fireplace. He'd forgotten to make a fire this morning. Then he moved his gaze back to Sigurd, who looked as if he'd aged ten years since the day before. "Show me," he demanded. Sigurd didn't move, so Gunnar carefully lifted the sheepskin. "Hell and all devils! It's huge."

"Mhm."

"You need to see Doctor Brynjólf," announced Gunnar. "Now it's definitely gangrene. Maybe when he chops your leg off you won't care of discretion so much."

"I can't… no d-doctor…"

"Aye. Then show me how you wiggle your toes."

"For Christ's sake… Gunnar," said Sigurd, his slurring suddenly gone, voice alarmed, "I *can't* wiggle my toes…! But I just cannot… it's too dangerous."

"Doctor Brynjólf is very nice. He's not dangerous at all."

Sigurd closed his eyes. "I just need rest… too much walking all at once…"

A long time ago it was Gunnar's father looking gaunt, his forehead sweaty, breathing shallow, repeating that he just needed some rest, refusing to be disturbed by "charlatans". Discretion or not, Sigurd was going to meet Doctor Brynjólf today. But first, Gunnar needed a really stiff drink to combat the pain and get Sigurd to the cart.


The doctor was enjoying his well-deserved lunch break. He raised a cup of coffee to his lips, but his hand stopped mid-movement. Something strange was going on outside. Unsure what to do, Brynjólf put the cup back and stood up just as the door hit the wall and Gunnar entered, carrying someone over his shoulder.

"Doctor Brynjólf," puffed Gunnar, dropping Sigurd on the bed and ignoring a protesting squeal. "I've got my, um, cousin here. Very sick. Possibly dying of gangrene. Please help him."

"What happened?" asked Brynjólf, who had initially intended to say something completely different.

"He's got a broken ankle, so he stayed with me for a while," reported the blacksmith. "Now he's properly sick. You'll have to cut his foot off."

Brynjólf began with gently unwrapping the cloth Gunnar put over the leg. Then he gasped. "Who put this bandage on like that?!"

"Me," admitted Gunnar. "But it didn't look like this then."

"Hurts," whispered Sigurd.

"Of course it does! Gunnar, please stop helping people with their medical problems. Bring them to me instead."

"I told him so!" answered the blacksmith, hurt. "But he said–"

"I'm so cold," muttered Sigurd. "And hot. I don't even know anymore."

"He said–"

"Thank you, Gunnar," said the doctor. "That's enough from you. Take a seat and wait your turn. Which, by the way, is in two and half hours." He cut through the bandage. "It should already hurt less," he said.

"Nothing to worry about. It's a bacterial infection. Is that a wound I see?"

"He was walking with crutches," informed Gunnar from his chair, trying to find a position that would cause him the least pain. "And he fell…"

"Yes, Gunnar, *thank you*. What did you say your name was?"

"Uhmmm…"

"His name is Sigurd," said Gunnar.

"That's an unusual name."

"He's from America," reported the blacksmith excitedly.

Doctor Brynjólf cast a heavy look at Gunnar, then sighed pointedly before returning his attention to Sigurd's swollen leg. "The treatment isn't going to be very nice," he said. "First, I have to clean the wound really well. This is going to hurt."

"How much is it going to hurt?" inquired Gunnar, but no answer came. Sigurd remained quiet. A shiver shook his body every now and then, and his ashen face glistened with cold sweat.

"So… Sigurd. As I said, I need to clean this wound with alcohol. It will hurt. We should clean it internally, too."

Sigurd blinked a few times, trying to figure out which of the two faces floating in front of his face was real. He became nauseous and closed his eyes again. "What does that mean?"

"It means I suggest you have a large drink before I begin."

"I don't drink," muttered Sigurd.

"Of course you don't! We have prohibition here in Iceland, for the good of folk and country. But you will have to – it's medicinal."

A faint smile appeared on Sigurd's lips. "That's what Gunnar always says."

"In this case he's right." The doctor unlocked a cabinet, pulled out a bottle, and poured a generous amount into a glass. When he looked up, his gaze met Gunnar's. "Stop making that face," sighed the doctor. "I'll give you some if you promise to be quiet. Sigurd, do you need me to help you?"

"No," muttered the patient, taking a deep breath and emptying the glass with one swallow, then inadvertently licking his lips. So did the blacksmith. Doctor's orders.

"Very good," said the doctor. "Let's wait a few minutes. So – you're from America?"

"What are you going to do… to me?"

"Just lie down," answered Brynjólf. "First, I need to clean it with alcohol. But that will only be a minute. It's not as bad as it looks." He wet a bandage with cold water and carefully placed it on Sigurd's forehead.

"What happens after that?"

"You will see very soon." He sighed, then turned to Gunnar. "What have you done to your back?"

"How…?"

"I have eyes. Did you remember to keep your posture correct?"

"Aye. Nay. Sometimes."

"You shouldn't be carrying him around. Next time let me know, and I'll come over. We have a telephone, you know." There was pride in Brynjólf's voice.

"Aye, Doctor Brynjólf. But you're the only person I know with a telephone. I would have to come here to telephone you."

The doctor's concerned facial expression briefly gave way to a scowl. "Unfortunately, there isn't much I can do if you refuse to work on your posture. Sigurd, are you ready?"

"As ready as I will get," answered Sigurd. His voice was somewhat stronger, and there was a bit of colour on his face. He bit his lip but couldn't stop from crying out from the sting. Once the doctor was done, Sigurd's face was nearly green, his breaths sharp, short, and irregular.

"Maybe I should have cleaned it internally a bit more," muttered Brynjólf. "It's all done now, Sigurd. This is just iodine. You will need a lot of rest. I will come over tomorrow afternoon to see you, say, around six. I trust you will be at home, Gunnar? It would be good if you could stay away from him as much as possible. Alcoholics are more vulnerable to this in–"

"I am not an alcoholic," snapped Gunnar.

"I misspoke, my apologies," said the doctor quickly. "People in your physical condition, that's what I meant. Just try to stay away. Put him in bed. Not your bed."

"Can I catch it too?! Even if I don't scratch my foot?"

"It's a wound," muttered Sigurd weakly.

"Well, as I said, um, people who… consume drinks are in danger. But you'll be fine," assured the doctor. "Just try to keep away, that's all you need to do."

"But you *will* give me my prescription for chest pains…?" wailed the blacksmith.

"Yes, I will," said Brynjólf with another resigned sigh. "But we will have to discuss this very soon, after your cousin gets better. I don't think I've met him before. Or have I?"

"He only just came—" started Gunnar.

"Gunnar has been most helpful," interrupted Sigurd, who would have kicked the blacksmith under the table if it were possible. "What a generous man. He helped me greatly with my ankle. I fell very unluckily. Can you take a look at that?"

"I saw it already. Doesn't look great, I'm afraid. You should have come here earlier."

"He's started walking with crutches," said Gunnar. "Well, he tried. Are you sure he doesn't have gangrene? I don't want to catch gangrene."

"What an absurd! He has an infection. It's called erysipelas."

"Aaah," breathed Gunnar.

"Oh," said Sigurd.

"Don't bother memorising the name," said Brynjólf, then looked at the clock above the door. "You came in time. It might have indeed developed into gangrene if you waited too long. And now, if you excuse me…" He looked doubtfully at his unfinished lunch. Just washing his hands might not be enough. The bedding would require changing. Complications from erysipelas were both dangerous and very unpleasant, but there was no need for the two men to know that, not yet.

"Oh yes," remembered Sigurd, "I've been having a hard time sleeping… I think it might get even worse now."

"He won't take a drink," said Gunnar darkly. "That's what his problem is."

Brynjólf rolled his eyes. "I see. Sigurd, was it? I will give you sleeping pills, but be careful with them. They are very, very strong. Do not, under any circumstances, take more than one. Even if you can't sleep. If you feel unwell after the first one, give the rest back tomorrow. Do not mix them with alcohol. This is important."

"Thank you, doctor."

"You're welcome. Gunnar, be a bit more careful with your cousin, he's not a sack of potatoes. I will help you carry him back to the cart. Try to remember to watch your posture at least every now and then… I hope you can pay for all this. I am afraid I can't do it for free."

"Oh," muttered Gunnar. Under Brynjólf's fascinated gaze he pulled some money from his pocket, selected one of the notes, then packed the rest in his pocket again. He was handling the money as if it were an old handkerchief. "Is this enough?" he asked worriedly, straightening a fifty kronur note as well as he could.

The doctor needed a moment to compose himself. "My wife handles the money," he said automatically, mesmerised by the sight. Anna and Brynhildur weren't lying.

"My prescription," whined the blacksmith. He managed to haggle a double dose only because Brynjólf was too dumbfounded to argue with him.

Upon their return Sigurd immediately took one of his sleeping pills and was out cold within minutes, snoring on the bed, occasionally moaning in his sleep. Gunnar stared at him worriedly, then decided to discuss the matters with Karl and Ragnar while taking care of their well-being. None of them provided him with any useful advice, so the blacksmith made a fire, sat himself in the good chair with a bottle of whisky, shifted uncomfortably, and tried to relax. A moment later his back stiffened, but not from pain this time. Gunnar's eyes opened wide in fear. Were there germs on the chair? He remembered the doctor's instructions to clean everything with alcohol after his father died. Yet now he was in danger because he was… an alcoholic?

That was a blatant lie. He could stop any time he wanted to. He just needed to drink, it was medicinal, he got it from the doctor himself, everybody would… surely everybody *did*. Except Sigurd. And maybe except Brynhildur. But they could have been lying. When Sigurd downed his drink it clearly wasn't his first time… which reminded Gunnar that the sleeping pills and alcohol shouldn't be taken together, and he worried about that for a moment, but Sigurd's snoring was regular and sounded normal as far as the blacksmith could tell. Doctor Brynjólf would probably have said something.

Gunnar took a swig from the bottle, then looked at Sigurd, who looked as if he had aged twenty years since yesterday. A strange feeling overwhelmed the blacksmith. It was… loneliness. Less than two weeks and he'd already gotten used to having company. Perhaps he could get used to having a wife around, too. She'd do the cleaning and cooking for free. But, if he changed his mind, he wouldn't be able to get rid of her after a few weeks. Also, Brynhildur was the only woman who seemed even remotely interested. If there was a way to meet others, ones that didn't constantly talk and ask questions, Gunnar didn't know it.

Another swig.

How could he stay away from germs when he had to feed Sigurd and pass right by him to get on the ladder? Should he sleep in the forge? Was he far enough away sitting by the fire?

Another swig.

The disgusting word "alcoholic" popped into his mind again. Surely it really was a mistake. *Alcohol cleaned everything internally*, he reminded himself. He would be just fine.

Another swig.

This was what happened when you thought too much. Worrying about ridiculous things that weren't even true. Sigurd's story gave him some reprieve from the thinking, so did the medicine… the alcohol. Arnar in the story was a violent drunk, but Gunnar was never violent, and he was about to stop very soon anyway. Once the current batch was finished, he would not be making another one, he would be emigrating…

Another swig to calm the trembling of his cold, sweaty hands.

The medicine was taking too long. He wanted to forget… he forgot what he wanted to forget, but in any case… He could decide to stop thinking about these… sorts of things… This would be the last sip, he decided, then remembered again, and felt angry. What right did Doctor Brynjólf have… just because he was a doctor that didn't mean… It was bullying, that's what it was, unjust… just nasty, and Gunnar wouldn't let anyone treat him that way. If he were to stop now, he'd be admitting that Brynjólf was right. No, Gunnar made up his mind: he'd prove he was not an alcoholic by *not* stopping drinking. He wouldn't let the woman – the women – he wouldn't let them, that was it. *He* was the master of his life and nobody else. This would *definitely* be the last swig, he thought, looking at the sticker with his name and the words "one spoon three times a day with meals".

# Friday, March 19, 1920

Sigurd spent most of the day sleeping, and Gunnar spent most of the day avoiding him. The darkness kept him company, casually hanging around, occasionally making a remark. *You're an alcoholic, you're worthless, and you're going to die. Have a good day.*

According to the calendar, it was nearly spring. According to the weather, it was a great day for frosty wind and a monotonous drumming of sleet that whipped the roof. What did the calendar know? The house felt suffocating, as Gunnar couldn't free himself from thoughts of unexpected visitors. His back emitted blunt, hot pain. Rest, said Doctor Brynjólf, so he would rest. *You're an alcoholic*, reminded the darkness, *he said that too.*

"Posture," said Gunnar drily, putting on his new sweater, the brown coat with celluloid buttons, new boots, old hat – it was still perfectly good, there was no point wasting money on another one. He held the door open for the dog to join him. Ragnar ran outside, wagging his tail encouragingly even though his own feelings were somewhat mixed, and not just because of the weather.

Gunnar briefly returned inside to fill his flask with moonshine, half as an act of defiance, half out of powerlessness. He saw no way out from his entrapment. Hunted by relentless "friends", haunted by an elf, and now unable to drink himself out of the thoughts, because the darkness found a way to use it against him. *Aye*, said the darkness, and Gunnar imagined a dark, human-like shape, nodding vigorously. *You're an alcoholic, and you're going to die. Two*, reminded the darkness, *just two days, and then we'll have a real good time together.*

If he died today, the moment would never come to pass.

*Suit yourself*, answered the darkness.

Gunnar dragged his feet to reach his usual spot, but he didn't make it. His limbs were getting heavier and heavier, until he surrendered, and sat down on the nearest patch of miserable grass. Ragnar tilted his head and barked questioningly. The blacksmith tried to open his mouth, say something, but he had no strength to explain that he had no strength. He tried to reach for the flask in his pocket, but his arms refused to cooperate. The darkness spread into his limbs, palms, fingers, eyelids. Gunnar's mouth moved for the last time in silent protest, and then he was drowning in the black soot, no longer hearing Ragnar's concerned barks and whines.

It was the sleet that broke through the dark armour, slapping Gunnar's face, pouring in cold streams under the collar, soaking his trousers. The blacksmith sat up with a groan, uncorked the flask, then emptied almost half of it before remembering it was supposed to last him all day. On Monday, Gunnar quickly decided, he'd cut down on Monday, since today was a bad day, and he's already had enough of it. No, on Tuesday, after the cleaning woman's visit. And if not on Tuesday, then very soon afterwards, once he helped Sigurd with his plan.

Thus reassured, Gunnar took a sip of moonshine, then spat it into the grass, because of the horrible taste and because he now remembered: Doctor Brynjólf was coming. At six. What time could it have been right now? Would there be other visitors? Visitors with Bibles, crosses, scones?

"I don't know what to do," Gunnar confessed to the dog, who didn't know either, but wagged his tail encouragingly. The blacksmith absent-mindedly scratched Ragnar's head, weighing the flask in his other hand.

When Brynjólf finally arrived, he found both of his patients half-asleep and barely able to put a coherent sentence together. He took Sigurd's temperature, sighed, shook his head, then attempted to converse with Gunnar.

"Gunnar. Wake up. Has he been eating or drinking? Anything at all?"

"Mmnay, he's jus' sleeping," answered Gunnar, raising his head from the table where it was resting. His face was red, eyes bloodshot and wild. He was holding on to a nearly empty bottle.

"He has to drink at the very least," worried Brynjólf. "Water or coffee with milk. If you could also make sure that he doesn't take too many of those pills, they're not sweets… Gunnar? Do you hear me?"

"Is nice," observed the blacksmith.

"What's nice?"

"When you don't jus' sigh a' me."

"Gunnar," said the doctor, softly. "I don't know what to say to you. You must drink less, it's absolutely essential that you drink less. You are killing yourself and that's not an exaggeration. I can help, we can help."

"Who's we?" muttered the blacksmith. He lifted the bottle to his lips and sucked out the last few drops, barely managing not to fall off the chair, then dropping his head to the table again.

"Oh. You know."

"Nay, I d'n't."

"Look at me. Gunnar, please look at me. Fine, then just listen. My wife and I, we've got a room upstairs. You could stay there for a while, until you recover."

Gunnar's head turned slowly, and his red eyes met the doctor's worried gaze. "Will I go to prison?"

Brynjólf's throat constricted at the sound of Gunnar's voice – resigned, flat. "No," he said, "of course not. Nobody will find out. We'll–I'll personally make sure. We'll get rid of everything in your shed, all your equipment…"

"My shed," muttered the blacksmith.

"No, no… I misspoke. I was just guessing that you probably don't make it at home, just a guess," babbled Brynjólf, angry with himself. Someone else should have conducted this conversation. "I must run. Other patients and so on. Promise to think about it, I mean about recovering, not about…"

Gunnar's head dropped to the table with a muffled thud.

"I'm going to send a girl over tomorrow to attend to your cousin," said the doctor. "Can you hear me? Gunnar? Warm him some milk at least. Make him coffee with a lot of milk." He stood up, took soap out of his bag, then started washing his hands. "Gunnar? Do you have a towel?"

No answer came. Brynjólf sighed again, wiped his hands on his own trousers, returned the soap to its box, then put it back in his bag. "I really have to go now. The girl will be here around twelve tomorrow and I'll visit sometime around six." He stopped for a moment. "I mean, sometime in the evening…"

Brynjólf's voice died out. He took in the sight, and his shoulders drooped under the crushing weight of guilt and shame. This couldn't go on any longer. He'd do his part first – Thóra and her friend whose name escaped him would have to wait. And then Brynhildur would take over. "It's going to be alright," the doctor said, more to himself than Gunnar.

"Doc'r," slurred the blacksmith, his face still flattened against the table. Brynjólf stopped, his hand already on the door handle. "You have some old clock at home? I'll pay."

# Saturday, March 20, 1920

As far as Gunnar could tell by what he could see through the window, he'd gotten up early. Sigurd's rhythmic snoring continued. Gunnar filled a thermos with coffee and milk, put it next to the bed, then retreated to the safety of his kitchen. The bread was dry, salted cod tasted mostly of salt, but coffee was coffee. An empty bottle stood on the table. He couldn't remember whether there was another one open. In fact, he couldn't remember anything that had happened after the doctor left.

The blacksmith was busy pondering whether he owed it to Sigurd to make a fire in the room, when he heard the snoring stop, and then a blood-curdling screech.

"I am blind! I can't see! I am blind! *I am blind!* I can't see!"

"Shut it," Gunnar called into the room, then he pulled away the blanket and stuck his head inside. "What's going on?"

"I am blind! I can't see! My plan," sobbed Sigurd. "My plan. I am blind. It's… it's so unfair! I waited so long!"

Gunnar cheered up. "Tell me," he encouraged as he entered the room. He switched the light on, then took a few reluctant steps, trying to stay as far away from Sigurd as possible.

"They will find out… I can't see! Help me!"

"I'll help you, with everything. Just tell me who *they* are…" started Gunnar, then the next step brought him close enough to see Sigurd's face. "Hell and all devils!"

"I can't see," sobbed Sigurd. "I am blind. They will find out. All those years… I can't see."

Gunnar couldn't escape quickly enough. He would sleep outside tonight. In the shed, with all his sheepskins… but they were inside, upstairs. The stable might be warmer. People in his condition were especially vulnerable! Forge, he thought. He'd build a fire on the floor…

A knock at the door interrupted his racing thoughts. Gunnar found himself past caring whether it was a Conservative Woman or a Brynhildur. He opened the door, then gawked at a face he didn't know.

"What?" he barked. If this was yet another candidate for a wife, she seemed way too young, definitely no older than thirteen, face covered in acne.

"I'm Kris. Doctor Brynjólf sent me," said the girl. "To take care of your cousin."

Gunnar instinctively looked around, then lowered his voice. "He's gone blind. His face is all swollen and awful."

"Ah," said the girl, unfazed. "That. Aye, it happens. Shouldn't last long."

The blacksmith let Kris enter the house, but didn't accompany her inside. No matter how unimpressed she seemed, she wasn't in his condition. Once she emerged again, he stared at Kris gloomily as she smiled and assured him that all was well. Gunnar's mind was set – he would not be returning to the plagued house, possibly ever. He sat on the stairs, hunched over, pondering whether it would be better to have a drink that would clean him internally or to not have one due to his condition. That was how Brynjólf found him hours later.

"You're putting yourself at risk of pneumonia," huffed the doctor. "That's not going to make anything better. Get up, and don't tell me your back isn't hurting now."

"It does," groaned Gunnar as he tried to straighten up, avoiding Brynjólf's disapproving stare. "I prefer this to being blind," the blacksmith murmured. "And you lied."

"I just didn't want to worry you. This happens sometimes, but I assure you… Oh, come inside," said the doctor. He hung his hat on the coat rack, then, along with his bag, disappeared behind the blanket. Gunnar had no intention of following. He made coffee, ate whatever was on hand, then waited, his fingers drumming a nervous rhythm on the table. The doctor emerged, pulled the soap out of the bag, and started vigorously washing his hands. "Please try to make him eat something," he said. "I gave him an injection. He's uncommunicative right now, but he must eat something, no matter what. Porridge at least. Give him lots of water. I'm so sorry, what was his name again?"

"Sigurd," reminded Gunnar. "He's from America. He has a mystery plan. I decided. I'm going to sleep in the forge. Is that safe?"

"Will you not freeze?"

"Nay. But I'm feeling sick. In my stomach. And I have a headache. I think I might be infected."

Brynjólf sighed, looking around. "You don't seem drunk."

"I'm not always drunk! I've got a very vulnerable condition."

The doctor looked crestfallen. "This is a terrible thing to say, Gunnar, but you *need* to have a drink. Not too much. But you should. I feel like a horrible human being saying this. You need real treatment, a friend to watch over you."

*Friend*, thought Gunnar darkly as he took the whisky out of the cupboard. "This much?" He poked at it with a dirty finger.

"Mmm. Let's say this much. Can you handle drinking just this much and no more?"

"Of course not," chuckled the kettle.

Gunnar turned his stare to the kettle and opened his mouth to admonish it, then noticed the doctor's gaze followed his. The blacksmith briskly returned to the subject at hand, downing the miserable amount of whisky immediately, under Brynjólf's worried stare. Ah good, Gunnar's body seemed to say. *Mooooore*. The blacksmith swallowed and gave the doctor a hurt look. "But it helps," he said meekly. "With my back, my head, with the dar... the..."

Doctor Brynjólf sighed heavily. "Have you been... vomiting? Incontinence?"

"A what?"

"Diarrhoea? Rapid heartbeat? Shivers?"

"I don't want to talk about it!"

"Gunnar, we have to talk about it."

"Nay. It's all good."

"You are killing yourself, Gunnar, bit by bit."

"Maybe that's what I want," said the blacksmith angrily. "Maybe then I would be happy."

"Are you unhappy?"

"Who cares."

"I do," said Brynjólf gently. "Please consider the offer. You could spend some time at our house. We'll put you in the spare room. I won't charge you much..." Guilt struck with such force he almost doubled over. "I won't charge you at all. I owe you a favour. My wife will cook for you, someone will take care of your animals. I know it seems hopeless now, but it's not over, as long as you allow us to help."

The thought of being stuck in a pretty room with pretty wallpapers, pretty curtains, and the doctor's pretty wife bringing him dinner terrified Gunnar more than death. "Nay, don't think... not yet, but soon I will." He paused, bewildered. "I didn't mean to say that! He's making me!" Gunnar was pointing accusingly at something and Brynjólf's worried stare followed. The blacksmith was pointing at a kettle.

"Gunnar, I have to say I'm becoming very concerned. I think of you as a friend and, as a friend, I must tell you–"

"Doctor Brynjólf," said Gunnar, "later. Sigurd needs to die in peace."

"Good Lord! He's not going to die!" Brynjólf looked away, crossing his fingers behind his back. "The coming days might be difficult. But then he'll get better very quickly. Hopefully you won't get sick either. Remember, you're at, uh, higher risk than… other people."

"Aye, because I am an *alcoholic.*"

"I am truly sorry, Gunnar, but you are indeed at higher risk for this infection. It's true. If you like, I can show you in a book."

"No books," shuddered the blacksmith. "It's bad enough without books. My belly is aching here, is that the infection?"

"No, Gunnar. That's a sign you must stop drinking. How is your memory? Do you find yourself forgetting things…? Oh! I almost forgot. This is your new clock. It's a present. You… you know how to read time, right?"

Gunnar recognised the paper – it wasn't an old clock, it came from the merchant. The thing was square with rounded corners, a case painted with fake gold, and it stood on four flimsy feet that looked far too thin to handle something that size. Two large, round bells sat on top. The hands of the clock pointed to 6:43. It looked cheap and ugly. "I'm not as dumb as everyone thinks," he answered, glaring at the thing. "I just don't *like* time. It's bad for you."

Brynjólf wondered whether poor Brynhildur and the Conservative Women of Iceland knew what they were taking on. "Why did you ask for it then?"

"Just so I know when you are coming. Will you be here tomorrow, too?"

"I'm afraid not. It's Sunday, and, well, I have a family… and other duties at home. I don't work on Sundays, unless there's an emergency. But he will be alright. I hope you sleep well. Try not to drink more than this bit, just try. Oh, and tomorrow…" Brynjólf tried to produce an encouraging smile, and the blacksmith cradled his medicinal whisky. "I just… hope it will be a nice occasion… I have to be going. Don't worry. Everything will be just fine in the end."

The doctor hastily departed, and the house was silent again, except for the ticking of the clock. Gunnar glared at it threateningly, but the clock didn't seem intimidated, so he redirected his attention to the bottle he was still holding. How odd. He didn't want to drink, but he… had to. It seemed like every cell in his body was sweaty with anticipation. The blacksmith still felt a mild burning taste in his throat, and he wanted more. True, Gunnar never managed to have just one drink, but there were always good reasons to have just one more. Perhaps he really needed help, although he'd die before he agreed to that…

"Oh," said the clock with slight disdain, "you will die if you don't agree, too."

Gunnar was so startled the whisky bottle almost slipped from his sweaty palms. It was 6:46. Three minutes closer to death than the last time he looked. Don't *you* start now, thought the blacksmith.

"Too late," chuckled the clock, then Grendel materialised. He was sitting in a chair, booted feet on the table, in a position that looked both flippant and uncomfortable.

"I didn't say that out loud," accused Gunnar. "Or did I? I didn't!"

"Oh, I can read your thoughts," said the elf. "That's the nature of hallucinations. We're in your head."

"So it's true. I'm crazy and you are a hallucination."

Grendel's stare was unusually kind. "See, that's the funny thing: you will not know whether I am a hallucination or not…"

Ragnar snarled at the elf, unsure whether to attack or hide.

"…except, of course, that the dog wouldn't notice me if I weren't real," continued Grendel, not missing a beat. "So, I suppose I am not a hallucination after all. Unless your dog is hallucinating too, which could be the case. Or maybe it's just accidental. Who knows?" he mused. "The important part is that I can read your thoughts. It's very useful."

"Can you read Sigurd's thoughts? Tell me about his plan."

Grendel shook his head. "Of course I can't read his thoughts. I am *your* hallucination. But I can tell you that you don't want to be helping him."

"Sure," huffed Gunnar. "Like I am going to believe you."

"Have I lied to you so far?"

The blacksmith pondered that. Mocked, laughed at, interrupted – yes. Lied – not that Gunnar noticed.

"Anyway," said Grendel, "I have to go."

"Why?"

"Because you had a drink." The elf's shape started blurring, and Ragnar whimpered. He, too, wasn't coping well with the number of visitors haunting the house in the recent weeks.

"It was a small one!" protested Gunnar, but no response arrived.

According to the clock, he had five hours and thirteen minutes left until tomorrow, with Ragnar as his only company until the inevitable arrival of the darkness. A drink, his body insisted, just a small one, just one more, a bit with coffee, to help with the pain, just one and no more afterwards…

# Sunday, March 21, 1920

Gunnar's eyes opened. He wished they hadn't.

For everybody else, today was the first day of spring. For the blacksmith, it was the day he was turning thirty-five. Gunnar celebrated it by locking himself at home and drinking by the fire all day, trying to silence the voice of the darkness which always accompanied him on that day. Now that he was going to stop drinking very soon, he had no idea what he would do the next time. But then, he didn't expect to see thirty-six anyway.

It was a Sunday. He didn't want to know that, but the darkness was there to remind him that other, normal people were doing family things. They went to the church, then celebrated the arrival of spring no matter how thick the snow outside was. The blacksmith felt lonely, lonely, lonely.

Sigurd was alive – the snoring could even be heard in the kitchen. Gunnar was still afraid of the infection, but right now he wanted to sit by the fire and listen to the story. His desire for fights and fires was gone. He wanted a happy ending, at least for Juana. The story made her seem almost like a real person. She deserved to find peace, see her dreams come true, at least some of them. Hopefully that's where the story was going. But in order to find out, he needed to ensure Sigurd would survive his infection. Dragging his feet, Gunnar filled a thermos with fresh coffee and not-so-fresh milk, then placed it next to the bed along with a bottle of water. He remembered vaguely he was supposed to keep an eye on the sleeping pills, but he had no idea where they were, and had no intention of touching anything that could have been infected. Once the good deed was done, Gunnar backed away, then proceeded to wash his hands in ice-cold water, wishing he had invested in soap after all, until they were red and raw.

At least today he didn't have to worry about visitors, he thought right before someone tapped on the door. Ragnar jumped to his feet and started barking, which meant it wasn't Thóra. With a stomach full of dread Gunnar opened the door just enough to see who stood in front of it, then nearly slammed it shut again.

"Hello," said Brynhildur pleasantly. "Just passing by on my way from church! Happy birthday, dearest Gunnar!"

"Hello," he muttered in response. Gunnar didn't know where exactly Brynhildur and Anna lived, but he was certain the shortest route from the Klettafjörður church to a house in Klettafjörður did not lead past his forge.

"Let's come inside and have some coffee, shall we? I brought you a nice present for your birthday."

"I don't want no presents. Go away."

"Gunnar! You don't even know what it is. And I am cold. Just give me a cup of nice, hot coffee and I will be on my way back very soon."

To her surprise, the blacksmith grinned. "Aye," he said, "come in, come in. I'm sure it's not infectious anymore."

Brynhildur's hand flew towards her mouth. "What's not infectious?"

"I've got my cousin here," answered Gunnar cheerfully. "He has ah, um, a *very syphilis* infection. No joke. Doctor Brynjólf said so. I might be infected, too. He's gone blind – my cousin, not Doctor Brynjólf. That's how bad it is." Then he put a hand on his stomach and groaned loudly.

Brynhildur's head jolted back as if he had flung a hammer at her. "Don't worry," she said, careful to keep what she hoped was a safe distance. "You will be just fine. You'll be taken care of. We will make you happy." She carefully placed a package next to his feet, then withdrew again, barely avoiding falling off the uneven steps. "Why don't you unwrap it?"

"Soon," he assured her. "Very soon. Now go home before you go blind, too." He put a hand on his forehead and groaned again. "*Very* infectious," he repeated, and Brynhildur became suspicious. "Ask Doctor Brynjólf."

"Oh, I will. We must see if it's safe for Halldóra to come here tomorrow. No need to thank me, it's my pleasure. If you don't mind, I will go now, I've got errands to do. Please promise me you will have a nice day, and don't get sick. I will check on you–"

"Don't…!"

"–on Tuesday. That's in two days. Thóra and Laufey might come too. I thought you could use a friendly warning."

The corners of Gunnar's mouth dropped in defeat.

"You know," Brynhildur continued with fake cheer, "I have a feeling that you would look so good if you shaved and got a haircut. Just a suggestion! It could be a nice present to give yourself for your birthday. I mean, once you're certain you won't go blind and die. There's a very good barber in Klettafjörður now. Ásta's husband goes to him *all* the time. In today's society, it is very important for men to take care of their–"

Something she saw in his eyes made her pause.

"–but I'll be going now. Goodbye, dear Gunnar. Spring is here! Enjoy your birthday!"

Gunnar watched her through the window until he was sure she was on her way. He weighed the present in his hand. It didn't feel like a book. He ripped the brown paper to reveal a shirt. White and blue stripes. He threw it on the table and wondered how Brynhildur expected a blacksmith to keep something like that clean.

"Gunnar," said a weak voice from the room. "I think I put my hand in the chamber pot."

The moment of joy at hearing the familiar voice was very brief. "The cleaning woman is coming tomorrow."

"Good God. I can't wait for Halldóra until tomorrow, not with my hand like this. Bring me some water and a towel at least."

The blacksmith hesitated.

"Gunnar! *Please!*"

"That must be extremely infectious," complained Gunnar. He did, nevertheless, bring over a bowl with water. "I forgot to buy towels."

"An old one will do fine."

"I forgot for a very long time," said Gunnar, as he took a few steps back, then watched Sigurd frowning and trying to clean his hands without seeing what he was doing.

"Can you make me something to eat? Porridge? Something like that?"

"I don't have no porridge. I can make you mashed potatoes. With butter. I have that."

"I'll take anything," said Sigurd. "But I still can't see, so you have to…"

"Hell no. I'm not feeding you. I'm in a very vulnerable condition. Don't touch me."

Generally, when Gunnar boiled potatoes it was to start on moonshine. He sat in front of the stove, waiting, rotating the same thoughts in his head: he could make a new batch – but he was going to emigrate – *no, you are going to die* – but maybe a new batch would make him feel better, maybe he just needed some more – but here and now water was hissing as it spilled on the hot stove. Gunnar stared at the boiling pot, trying to gather enough strength to finish Sigurd's meal. Sometimes splitting impossible tasks into smaller ones helped. Stand up. Pull the pot off the fire. Burn your fingers. Swear. Drain the potatoes. Mash them… no, too much too fast. Reach for the masher. Move it up and down. Make a plate. Walk towards the room, left foot, then right. Pass the food to Sigurd without touching him, watch the old man's hands moving around, uncertain, looking for the plate and fork. Retreat to the kitchen. Sit there motionlessly. Watch Ragnar's tilted head and worried stare. Wish it was possible to pet the dog. Try to explain. Fail to make a sound. Listen to the clock mercilessly bringing his death closer with each tick and tock. *Happy birthday, dear Gunnar,* said the darkness politely.

# Monday, March 22, 1920

Sigurd woke up and saw the light.

At first, it seemed like something was wrong. His eyelids seemed glued shut by some sort of crusty substance. The bedding he lay on was wet and he felt thirsty, hungry, exhausted. Sigurd rubbed the crust out and managed to open his eyes enough to see the faint light coming through the window. There was nothing wrong, in fact everything was right, right, right!

"Gun–" he tried, before a coughing fit interrupted him. His mouth was full of sand, or perhaps sawdust. "Gunnar," he wheezed. "I'm awake." When no response came, Sigurd turned to his side, and the sight was breathtaking, if somewhat blurry. Raw, cold walls! That rusty horseshoe! The cherry-red, maybe even plum coloured cracks of the good chair! The ashes in the fireplace! The dirt floor! Sigurd hadn't realised how many things he'd taken for granted. He had expected death, and felt ready for it, but blindness? Bacterial infections? Limping? Those were things that happened to other people…

Ignoring the rumbling in his stomach was becoming more difficult, but Sigurd wanted to examine his ankle first. From what he could tell, it had improved dramatically. Hope and joy filled his heart as he admired the sparse surroundings again, but a dry, painful cough brought him back to reality. His body needed water now. Sigurd prayed for another miracle and it briskly arrived in the form of a creaking forge door, then heavy footsteps. He tried to call Gunnar's name, but all he managed was another coughing fit, which was – luckily! – enough to attract Gunnar's attention.

"Here's water," said Gunnar, his voice muffled by a rag wrapped around his face, eyes bulging with fear. "Here's coffee. With milk. Doctor Brynjólf's orders. Have to go." He placed the items on the floor and began to withdraw.

"At least pass me the water," wheezed Sigurd. "I can't reach it from here."

"I am at risk. Not touching anything."

"The germs don't just jump through the air when you pass me water! I am starving, do you have some bread? Cheese? Fish? I'd love some fish."

"You really are much better. Doctor Brynjólf will be happy. Thought you would die. The cleaning woman will bring bread and fish. Just tell her to give you some."

Not even a mention of the cleaning woman could diminish Sigurd's happiness right now. "I can see you," he reported joyfully.

"Congratulations," said the blacksmith, then finally escaped into the relative safety of the kitchen. But he, too, felt happy. Thanks to his care, Sigurd survived. This time he didn't fail. Perhaps, thought Gunnar, he could even stay around during Halldóra's visit, seeing as he needed to practice for the Concerned… Conservative… *the Women* who were going to invade tomorrow. The thought itself made his stomach twist, and he quickly resolved to do something nice for himself instead. A long walk away from any people.

Ragnar was chasing his own tail, running in circles around Gunnar as they walked nowhere in particular. The blacksmith's back was still sore, although perhaps less than the day before. Work wouldn't be possible for a bit longer, but at least now he could stand up straight. *I saved a life*, he thought proudly. Of course, Doctor Brynjólf helped a lot, and Gunnar's appreciation for medicine had increased. Perhaps he could manage a month in Doctor Brynjólf's guest room. He'd get cured of his medicine problem, then take the money and emigrate before anybody noticed.

Halldóra arrived mere minutes after his departure. She barely noticed Gunnar's absence. She neither craved nor resented company. Other people were just *there*, same as chairs, dirty pans, empty bottles.

Her life was never supposed to be any different from that of her sisters or friends. All was going very well until she was sent away to work as a servant, like nearly every other girl she knew. But unlike the others, a few months later Halldóra was sent back home. Her shocked parents barely recognised their daughter. The energetic and imaginative girl was now unable to put together a coherent sentence. She couldn't hold a fork or spoon and had lost the ability to read and write. Within the next few weeks she stopped speaking altogether. Her right foot became a deadweight she dragged behind, and her right hand seemed to fold into itself, fingers becoming stiff and useless.

Nobody knew how she had fallen ill or what the illness was. There wasn't much sympathy for her. "Another mouth to feed," her normally calm father would yell, "even cows are of more use than you!" Halldóra cried every night. She couldn't speak, but she understood every word. As her father's outbursts continued, she began to hide in her mind, spin tales that became more and more elaborate, and found out she was able to tune the outside world out.

With her sister's help, Halldóra learned how to use her left hand to eat, cut vegetables and fish, peel potatoes, then eventually clean and cook. A couple living nearby took pity on the poor, stupid girl, and hired her as help. Halldóra was slow, not extremely meticulous, but her services came cheap, and soon she worked nearly every day. As time passed, her father calmed down again, ignoring her presence rather than yelling. But it didn't matter by then, because Halldóra had her own world, one where she was a princess, an elf, an angel, and nobody ever raised their voices. She ignored couples that openly fought in front of her, those who berated her for doing something incorrectly. Halldóra's hands did the work as her brain spun more and more tales until she could no longer tell what was real and what was borne in her imagination. It didn't matter anyway, since she had no way of sharing any of her thoughts, and they made her happy.

Halldóra hummed as her hands slowly did the work. The cooking was done. She took the pots and pans off the stove to cool down, covered the food from flies, then remembered the extra task she had to do – clean up after Gunnar's cousin. As her hands lifted the overflowing chamber pot, in her mind Halldóra was lifting a chalice filled with magical nectar. The elves around her played harp and harmonica, sang for her, and whenever her light feet touched the ground, the grass turned greener, flowers bloomed…

"Halldóra, dear," said Sigurd, when she returned to the living room with the broom, by now completely oblivious to his presence. "Halldóra," he said louder, and she ignored him again. "Halldóra!!!" he yelled, then started coughing, and finally broke through her happy trance. The music of the elves cracked, then stopped. The chalice was a chamber pot again and she put it down as fast as she could, then raised her eyes, frowning, hoping the interruption won't last long.

"Let me move a bit," said Sigurd, emerging from the shadow. "Can you see me now? I think I remember you, don't I? Although you've changed a lot, sweetie."

Halldóra dropped the broom. A gurgling sound came out of her throat. She took a step back.

"I see you remember," he smiled. "Thank you, that's a compliment. It's been so many years…what age were you when I last saw you? Ten, eleven? Look at you, you're a woman now. But hey, none of us is getting any younger."

Halldóra stared, frozen. She… sort of remembered. She had seen this man before. He was bad. He shouldn't be here. She began to withdraw towards the door and nearly tripped over the broom, flailing her left arm in the air, squeaking in fear. "Don't go yet," Sigurd said, and despite his gentle tone Halldóra bent as if punched in the gut, unable to take her eyes off the man's kind face.

"I'm sorry to see you like this. What happened to you, sweetheart? Did you hit your head or something? You were a nice kid…" He paused and stared at her thoughtfully. "Do you know, I can't remember whose you were… Guðrún's? You don't need to be afraid of me. Just don't let anybody know I'm here… and you won't get hurt."

As if jolted by electricity, Halldóra ran out of the room, or rather tried to, her useless foot like a trap, the sounds emerging from her mouth more like a crazed crow's shrieks than anything a human could produce. She fell off the steps, painfully scraping her elbow, but she couldn't feel the pain. Tears ran down her face as she crawled through the mud, crying, squealing, lifting herself to her knees, then falling again. All her visions were replaced by pure horror now, as if a raging blaze were right behind her. Never, she would never return here, not even if she had to starve or listen to her father's yells. This man was evil, he was one of *them*. It's just that Halldóra couldn't figure out which one.

Gunnar returned home cold and hungry, but in slightly better spirits. This didn't last long. Once he realised that the first thing he did upon returning home was look at the wretched clock, he decided he was having a bad day after all. His birthday had passed, true, but now *sixty-three* hung over his head. Sixty-three days until the anniversary of his mother's death. Once that date passed, the number would be replaced with *ninety-two*.

Sigurd jumped at the food, and Gunnar was slightly taken aback. "She didn't feed you?"

"She ran away, poor woman," Sigurd mumbled, his mouth full. "Mmph. Her mind is quite confused, I think. Can you make a fire?"

Gunnar shivered. He now felt brave enough to be in the same room as Sigurd, but not enough to actually touch him and transport him to the good chair. But, aye, they needed a fire… No sooner had he finished than the doctor arrived.

"He's better," reported Gunnar, opening the door and blocking it.

"That's good to hear," said the doctor. "May I come in?"

"Of course," answered the blacksmith, not moving, until Brynjólf demonstratively cleared his throat. "Aye… sorry. Come in. God bless," he added after quick consideration.

"How are you feeling, not feverish?"

"Not at all. And I'm not blind either."

"Well done," said Brynjólf. "Now if you excuse me…"

"And! He's eating, too."

"*Thank you*, Gunnar. Oh hello, um, um…"

"Sigurd," helped Gunnar, practically leaning on Brynjólf's back.

"Gunnar, please! Go play with your dog. Leave us alone for a minute."

It wasn't a bad idea, decided the blacksmith, spending a few minutes rolling over the floor with an ecstatically happy Ragnar, until the doctor returned and Gunnar discovered he couldn't get up. "So, he's not going to die?" he asked from his spot on the floor, gently pushing Ragnar away.

"Oh, Gunnar," sighed Brynjólf. "Of course he is not going to die. I told you he wouldn't." He took soap out of his bag and started washing his hands. "Brynhildur sends her greetings," he said. "I'll tell her you need a towel. You do look quite flushed. Are you sure you're not feverish?"

"No, just… too warm."

"Why are you on the floor?"

"Because… because…"

"Because your back hurts," sighed Brynjólf. "If you're going to lie on the floor, do me a favour. Let me lift you for a moment… here's your coat. Is it new? Lie on it. Yes, like that." He dragged a chair over. "Put your feet on this. Like that, yes."

"And now?"

"And now stay like that for a while."

"What's a while?"

"Oh," said the doctor, taking a quick look at the clock. "Half an hour. You can do it as many times a day as you feel like. It will speed up the healing, hopefully, and take some of the pain away."

"Thank you, Doctor Brynjólf," said Gunnar with a slightly choked voice. "Is it supposed to be so uncomfortable?"

"On your floor it must be, I suppose. Maybe try to fold that coat in half next time or use some sheepskins. Soon you'll be able to walk normally, but please don't start working yet. You can affo– I mean…"

"I know what you mean," muttered Gunnar.

Brynjólf quickly looked for a diversion. "Are you reading *The Picture of Dorian Gray*? That's interesting. Are you enjoying it?"

"Um. Aye."

There was doubt in Brynjólf's gaze. "That's good. What is it about?"

"It's, it's about, uh, love."

"Is it?"

"Between two people," said the blacksmith. He remembered Sigurd saying that. "Despite many obstacles. Thank you for coming, Doctor Brynjólf. Now why don't you go see other patients? We'll be good here."

### Then

In an unusual turn of events, despite the multitude of witnesses, the villagers couldn't figure out what exactly happened. There were as many theories as there were people interested enough to discuss them. Magnús's theory was that Arnar was simply a bastard who finally showed his true colours. Katrín knew for a fact that he'd wanted to kill her before she even started to reveal the secret, which she now refused to share despite her father's half-hearted threats. Bjarni felt secure enough to take the reins of his construction team again, announcing Arnar had finally gone completely insane. Nobody complained. Niels kept to himself, hoping to avoid questions about the source of the money he suddenly had, money that he had inherited from an envelope with the word "JUANA" written on it. Even less was known about why exactly Juana was now living under the pastor's roof, refusing to set a foot outside or talk to anybody at all, apparently wearing nothing but black.

"She must be really upset about Gullveig," said Guðrún to Fríða.

"Why would Katrín be upset about Gullveig?"

"Not Katrín! Juana. We were talking about Juana."

"No, we were talking about my silly daughter's secret. Which," said Fríða with a little wink, "she told to Jórunn, and Jórunn told me, and I could tell you, but only if you promise that nobody else will find out…" Fríða stuck out her hand, hoping for another coffee with brandy. Guðrún refilled the mug with coffee, but the only additive she offered was sugar. Fríða scowled.

"It's not Katrín's secret," said Guðrún. "It's Arnar's secret. If you had seen him that evening you'd have known why Katrín won't talk. He must have done terrible things to Juana. Anyway, I know it as well. From Bjarni. Of course I didn't tell anybody else…"

"But why wouldn't they be married?" wondered Fríða. "Or did I misunderstand something? I just don't know why somebody wouldn't want to be married."

Guðrún frowned, then looked away. "Sometimes," she muttered, "people don't really want to commit to just one other person."

"Oh yes," said Fríða. "That reminds me. How is your husband doing?"

Guðrún's frown deepened. "What does this have to do with Arnar's secret?"

"Oh, nothing! I just thought about it because we were talking about marriage and commitment. I don't see your husband much, that's all. My apologies, I don't even remember his name, could you remind me…?"

"My, my," said Guðrún after a pause, during which Fríða stared at her with an innocent gaze. "Look at the time. You must be going now. Take care of *your* husband and your children. God bless," she said firmly, opening the door and waiting for surprised Fríða to leave.

In the meantime, Katrín tried and failed to become Juana's confidante. The only time Katrín managed to elicit any reaction was when she started to muse about the differences between both brothers. The twins walked, talked, behaved differently – even the way they smiled was different. Arnar was a monster, said Katrín, looking at Juana in sympathy. Juana said nothing until the girl moved on to complimenting Ingvar, kind and loving, hard-working, true embodiment of everything that was good…

"Yes," said Juana flatly. "He's a very good man."

This was all. Katrín felt upset for a moment, then shrugged and went back to her duties. She was coordinating a fundraiser for a small library in town. It would kill two birds with one stone – save Ingvar's time, and give more people access to books. At least Juana took over the domestic chores, although she wasn't doing a very good job. But Katrín forgave her. Juana used to look like an exotic flower in bloom, she thought with pity. The flower was now wilted. Even Juana's hair seemed to have given up, resembling the dried grass of autumn rather than a flame.

Katrín knocked on Ingvar's door. He was staring at three pieces of paper at once, two in his hands, one on the desk, his brows furrowed. Since Juana's arrival he'd found it very difficult to focus on anything. Two out of those pages belonged together, the third didn't, but Ingvar was unable to figure out which was supposed to go with which, even though he had just finished writing. Jesus Christ, he prayed when he heard the knocking, not another funeral or christening, leave me alone…

"I'm sorry to interrupt," Katrín said, letting herself in without waiting. "The fundraiser ladies want to see you and one of them is downstairs. She's asking what a good time would be."

"Good God. What ladies, which fundraiser?"

"The ladies raising funds for the library. I'm so sorry, but they want to see you, I told them how busy you were, but–"

"Oh, Katrín," sighed Ingvar as he put the papers down. This fundraiser seemed to require an extraordinary amount of meetings. "You shouldn't overwork yourself. This is my job. Of course they are welcome here. Maybe on… What day is it today? Monday? Maybe Wednesday morning? As early as they can make it. Then I can go back to work. Please give them some coffee, something to eat, apologise in my name and thank them for coming. Make sure they don't leave angry."

"Wednesday morning. Thank you." Katrín hesitated. "I wouldn't dare to tell you what to do, Reverend…"

"Please call me Ingvar."

"…but you need to rest. I've been, um, watching you… I mean… I've noticed…"

"I don't have time for that," he mumbled. "I should be going around scaring the children enough so they study the Catechism." Katrín's face was worried. Good Lord, thought Ingvar. This sweet, innocent child worried about him – and he had no idea how he would function without her help. This wasn't how he envisioned his life would turn out.

Once she was gone, he sat back by the desk, hiding his face in his palms, trying to breathe long, slow breaths. By now, Ingvar expected to gain recognition, start receiving tempting offers which he would at first modestly refuse until a really good one came along as the wave of adoration carried him up. But if there was even a ripple of adoration, he had no time to notice it, too busy with all the menial tasks he had to perform.

Doubt appeared in his heart. Perhaps he should have soldiered on in Copenhagen for a few years longer, sent letters over here preparing for some sort of better position… But his bluff would have been called at some point. Yes, Ingvar was a part of a big political shift, but a much smaller part than his letters suggested between the lines. This, what he was doing, was the right way to go about things. Except for the fact it just wasn't working…

Someone entered the room, and without looking he knew it was Juana. She came to him and started to massage his shoulders.

"She's right, you know," she said. "You need rest. Is there no way you can take some time off? Even if it's just one day. Let's go to a hot spring."

"I've got to finish all this…"

"If you're too tired to even read, you won't finish it."

"I told you too much," said Ingvar, half-smiling in the tired way that broke Katrín's heart daily. "Would *you* want to go out if we went to the hot spring?"

To his dismay, Juana's surprisingly strong hands on his shoulders dropped. "I don't know. But you make me feel safe."

"Hmmm," said Ingvar. She was still his brother's wife, he reminded himself, but she smelled so nice, and he was wishing she'd go on with the massage. A hot spring, just the two of them… "I told Katrín to keep me informed if he shows up anywhere."

"I wish he would," said Juana. "I wish he would just find me and do whatever he wants, even if that means killing me…"

"Stop this nonsense! He will not kill you. We will keep you safe."

"Oh, Ingvar," she sighed. "I don't even dare to step past the door. I even fear going to Mass. If this is what safety feels like, I might be better off without it. I had… have a nice house. I should just go back there and…"

"And what? Wait for him? Unacceptable. Perhaps you should contact your family?"

Juana shook her head. "I've lived in sin with him for years. I stole my family's money. Never contacted them. I don't think I even have a family anymore. I feel so alone. I didn't know how much of my life revolved around him, not until he left. I thought getting married would change things, but…"

"I promise we will find a solution," murmured Ingvar. "And tomorrow we will take a day off, maybe an afternoon, and go to the hot spring together." He knew he was lying, but it felt so good to even just pretend to himself it might happen.

Ingvar closed his eyes when she departed. The thoughts he was having right that moment were decidedly ungodly. She was his brother's wife! He needed to step away, wash his face with very cold water, stop the alternating ruminations either on Juana's suffering and beauty or on the fact that his brother had never been found, dead or alive. It was the uncertainty that laid heaviest on his shoulders. If only Arnar would show up! Dangerous, wild, with an axe, a torch… If such situation arose, Ingvar would have to defend Juana, Katrín, himself…

His brother was a monster, there was no doubt about it. Ingvar knew from Juana that Arnar was capable of burning an innocent old woman alive, he had seen Magnús's face, his broken nose, a missing front tooth. But Magnús looked fine again, a missing tooth being nothing unusual.

Gullveig's old land was taken over. A new dwelling was being built. Nothing ever truly ended, nobody was irreplaceable.

Except Juana. And Ingvar would do absolutely anything necessary to keep her safe.

Anything.

# Tuesday, March 23, 1920

In his attempts to regain control over the situation, Gunnar found himself in a barber's chair. *This* would show the women he was already becoming an acceptable member of society, that there was no need to visit him and attempt to fix his wrongdoings. But the moment the barber reluctantly touched his hair for the first time, blood rushed from Gunnar's gut to his extremities, and he wished he had dared to use some medication first.

The barber withdrew his hand from the unruly mess he was about to work with, then discreetly sniffed and scowled. This man's hair looked like it had never been cut or combed, perhaps shortened every now and then by someone who barely knew how scissors worked. The beard would have served well as a nest for a family of small birds. The barber immediately doubled the price, praying for the man to leave, but Gunnar had no idea how much such a service was supposed to cost. He also didn't care. He kept his eyes closed the whole time, until the barber announced he was done, and encouraged the blacksmith to look in the mirror. The shiny surface reflected a complete stranger. The man was clean shaven, his hair short and glued with some sort of goopy substance. Without warning, the barber poured something into his hand and slapped Gunnar's face. The blacksmith flinched, even though he barely noticed the actual slap. But something stank and hurt his bare cheeks.

"What is this awful thing?" he asked.

"It's called *eau de cologne*," said the barber. "You might want to buy some. And pomade for your hair."

"O-the… Do modern people really do this?"

The barber rolled his eyes and mouthed a quick prayer. "Yes," he finally answered. "They do. Every day."

Gunnar, who had just about managed to relax a bit thinking it was over now, found himself sweating again. *Every day.* He didn't think about it, expecting that one visit would set him up for life. "Is it necessary?" he wailed.

"Oh yes," said the barber. "It might also help if you maybe washed more often…"

The blacksmith paid without saying another word. The barber counted the money and, despite the doubled price, frowned slightly at the lack of a tip. Muttering to himself, patting the flask in his pocket, Gunnar dragged his feet towards Anna's store, then stopped in front of the door. He tried to inconspicuously see whether Brynhildur was inside, but the window was almost completely covered with knick-knacks, including his own works. Yet again he tried to open the door slowly enough not to trigger the bell, and *almost* managed to stick his head inside before the sound startled both him and Anna. The shopkeeper gasped and grabbed at her chest convulsively.

"God Almighty, Jesus and Mary, forgive me for all my sins…"

"What is wrong with you?" snapped Gunnar, immediately forgetting about his own frail nerves.

"Gunnar…?"

"Who else?"

"Good God! I thought it was a ghost. I'm so glad it's just you. But Gunnar! You look *exactly* like Karl. I mean, your father. You look exactly, *exactly* like your father. Do come inside. Look, look!" Anna practically dragged him inside, shaking with excitement and impatience. "Look in the mirror!" Gunnar averted his eyes. "Look!" demanded Anna, then forcefully turned his head. "Don't slope your shoulders! Stand straight. Look at you! Exactly like your father! Gunnar, *do* look at yourself! Smile!"

"I am smiling," muttered Gunnar. "Can I go now? Oh. Hang on. I need a calendar. And a pomade. And… o-de-colon."

"You want to buy a *what*?!" shrieked Anna. "Has something possessed you? Or un-possessed you? Do you also want a comb? Shaving foam? A razor? Actually, don't answer that, we'll pack them all for you. Our best pomade for you! Do you know what to do with it? Brynhil–" She abruptly stopped. Her face turned purple, and she grabbed at her chest again.

"Not Brynhildur," muttered Gunnar, and to his surprise Anna nodded vigorously.

"The Conservative Women of Iceland," she continued, much quieter. "I will send them over to you. They will be so happy! There will be candles lit on the altar, let me tell you. Look at you! You look exactly like…"

"My father, aye, got it," said Gunnar. "Can I just take the things and go…?"

"I have to admit I didn't expect…" muttered Anna, her face slowly regaining its normal colour.

"What's all this shouting?" asked Brynhildur, emerging from the back room. "What's going on here? Oh sweet baby Jesus, is that Gunnar?"

"Go back there," snapped Anna. "You've got work to do."

"I don't. Mother, can you imagine what Thóra…"

"Just be quiet. And hurry up. Pack all the gentlemen accessories for Gunnar. Hair pomade, comb, razor, shaving foam, cologne. Shoe polish. And newspapers! A calendar, Gunnar wants a calendar!!!"

"I think I'll go," said Gunnar, and Anna grabbed his coat.

"Not before you get your shopping," she said. "You will now find a young lady in no time. I will introduce you to someone nice."

"Mother!"

"Don't you *dare* raise your voice at me. Look at yourself, Gunnar! You…"

"I look exactly like my father," muttered the blacksmith. "Please let me go." Never again, he promised himself. This would be his last visit here. If that meant he had to go to Reykjavík every week, he would. His naked face was itching, and the smell was so overpowering he sneezed and wiped his nose with the sleeve of his new coat.

"Handkerchiefs, Brynhildur," commanded Anna, scowling. "Ten." She no longer sounded friendly, but still held on to Gunnar's coat. "You need a scarf," she announced. "I will not take no for an answer. Something that would go well with your coat. Have I said it's a lovely coat? It must have cost a fortune!" She let go of him and rushed back into the storage at the back. Gunnar sighed in relief, readying for escape.

"You can't go now," exclaimed Brynhildur. "You look *wonderful*. Soap, Mother, we forgot soap!" With hands shaking in excitement she added soap to the cotton bag that was already so full it threatened to break. "What else? What else? Do you have socks? I can't wait to visit you and help you with everything!"

"Just let me pay," begged Gunnar.

Anna emerged from the back with a scarf just in time to hear Brynhildur's last words. "She will not visit you, Gunnar," she hissed, nearly strangling him with the scarf. "I'm sure you'll manage. It was lovely to see you. Now *go*."

The blacksmith bolted out before she had a chance to change her mind, losing the bar of soap in his hurry.

"I will… not?" repeated Brynhildur. "But why? I've been working so hard on him, and now that there are effects…"

"Stay away from Gunnar," snarled Anna. "As far away as you can. Don't you try to lie to me again, or you will be homeless the very same day. I know where you went for your 'walk'. People see things, people hear things, people *talk*, and you should be the one that knows it best!"

"Mother–"

"Don't you dare interrupt me! I will find you a suitable bachelor if necessary. But not Gunnar. You can see he's got all the genes of his father. Karl was not a good man. Gunnar is going to be exactly the same. At first he will be charming and sweet. He will treat you like a queen. At first. Then he will start disappearing. More and more often. There will be other women."

"How do you know that?"

Anna paused for a moment. "People talk," she finally repeated. "Now go back to work."

"I'll just–"

"No, you will not just. Go and fold everything. If it's folded, unfold it and do it again. Wipe the floors."

"He lost his soap, it won't take a moment…"

"You're not going anywhere. And that's the end of it. I will not hear about Gunnar from you again."

Brynhildur nodded obediently, already planning an inconspicuous little trip. Her future husband was waiting, and if Mother imagined the shy, introverted blacksmith would suddenly start "disappearing" to see "other women", she obviously knew nothing about people.


Gunnar returned home in record speed, or rather would have, had Karl listened to his pleas.

"If there is anything worse you could have done, I don't know what it is," huffed Sigurd. "Expect tons of visitors very soon."

"Nay," said Gunnar. "I did what they wanted. They will leave me alone now."

"You really know nothing about women. You just proved that you will change if they work on you a bit. The Constipated Hags of Iceland will be here the moment they hear what happened and, knowing people, I can tell you that will be very soon."

Gunnar didn't answer, eyeing the pomade jar suspiciously. His face kept itching. The blacksmith scratched his chin and withdrew his hand with a quiet groan. This wasn't his face. It was, apparently, his father's.

"You put this in your hair," said Sigurd. "It's called pomade."

"I know. The barber told me."

"You will have many friends now. Female ones. The Hags will come by with holy water, possibly dragging the pastor along. Hell, they might drag the altar here, too, and get you married to Brynhildur before you decide to stop shaving again."

"He's right, you know," said Grendel, sitting on the stove behind Sigurd, thoughtfully scratching his own beard, not even trying to hide the smirk.

"Please," answered the blacksmith resignedly, "just leave me alone."

"I don't think I can, not yet," said Sigurd. "My apologies if I am being too direct, but it's simply true…"

"Not you, eh… never mind. Show me how you stand up."

Sigurd put the good foot on the floor, grabbed the table top for balance, then lifted himself carefully from the chair before trying to rest on the other foot. "My ankle feels weird," he said. "I'm not sure about this."

"Let me help you."

"No, no," said Sigurd, still holding on to the table, his expression doubtful and worried. He tried again. "I don't understand. It doesn't hurt, but it feels like it's… crooked."

"Maybe it is."

Sigurd began to sweat. Not now. Not after all those weeks. Not again. "Maybe I just need to practice," he muttered. "It's possible to lose muscle tone when you don't…" His voice died out. "Boots. They might help."

"Take another day or two. It's probably still infected. And you haven't finished your story."

"Perhaps you're right…" Sigurd sat again, lifted his foot, and tried to forcefully bend the ankle into the correct angle. He hissed and left it alone. "I think you should put me in the forge," he sighed. "Trust me, I don't want to be there, but you *are* going to have visitors today."

"They always come in the evening–" started Gunnar, but banging on the door interrupted him. "Oh no," he cried. "Hide!"

"Put me in the forge! Now!"

"No time!"

"Stop talking and just do it!"

The person outside was so determined to come inside that the door shook. "Gunnar! I know you're there! Let me in!"

"It's Anna," said Gunnar, bewildered. "Get under the table," he commanded, then opened the door and stood in it, blocking the view. "What is it?"

"First of all," snapped Anna, "God bless. Second, you lost your soap. Third, you didn't pay."

"But you said–"

"Here are your ashtrays. Don't come to my store ever again. You are not welcome."

"But I went to the barber…!"

"I don't care where you went. Don't even try to speak to Brynhildur. Stay away from my daughter, I warn you."

"Oh," said Gunnar, perking up. "Thanks. That's good."

Anna's eyes widened in surprise. "Uh. Really? Well. Here are your things. Just keep the money."

"But where will I sell them now…?"

"Not my problem. Good-*bye*, Gunnar."

"That was interesting," remarked Sigurd from under the table when the door slammed. "Can you help me get out of here? What's wrong with you talking to Brynhildur?"

"Everything," said the blacksmith cheerfully. "First good news of the day. See? You were wrong. They will leave me alone now. And I don't need to sell anything anyway. I'm rich. All is good."

"A calendar," said Sigurd in disbelief, once he was back in his chair. "Are you sure you are Gunnar? The one who doesn't do time, but now has a calendar *and* a clock? Is there a ghost in this house adding things while I am not looking?"

Gunnar heard a quiet chuckle and jerked his head up. The elf might have disappeared again, but that didn't mean he was actually gone. "There is no ghost in this house," said Gunnar loudly. "Not at all. Not even one. But there is blood sausage and bread. You'll get some if you stop talking."

"I will," sighed Sigurd. "Please put me in the forge when we're done eating. I promise you this day is not over yet."

As they ate, Gunnar demonstratively topped off his coffee with medicine. Sigurd didn't even notice, busy worrying about the upcoming influx of uninvited guests. He swallowed the food without bothering to chew, and only breathed in relief once he was safely hidden inside the cold, windy forge. *The Women's Paper* offered a recipe for "Grandma's Cake". Sigurd had never even met his grandmother and he didn't remember seeing cake until he arrived in America. A pancake with powdered sugar was a luxury reserved for holidays. Maybe some raisins, he thought and smiled sadly to himself. Despite having just eaten he felt a pang in his stomach. After a steady diet of salted fish, stale bread, burnt soup, and porridge it was difficult to imagine cake even existed. Soon, very soon.

It wasn't until five thirty, as indicated by Gunnar's trusty new clock, that another visitor arrived.

"You look very handsome," said Brynhildur, who had now taken to letting herself in without waiting for Gunnar's permission. "Stop biting your fingernails. Let's make a plan. The Women will be here in half an hour. Are all the bottles hidden?"

"Aye. Your mother told me not to speak to you."

"That's nice. You could do with an extra sprinkle of cologne. Do you like the smell?"

Gunnar scratched his itchy chin, startled himself again, and said nothing. Brynhildur opened the bottle and stuck it under his nose. The blacksmith withdrew, appalled, and she shook her head. "Give me a plate," she commanded.

"Are you hungry?"

Brynhildur rolled her eyes, then pulled a blue and white metal can out of her huge bag. "I brought special biscuits. They're Dutch. Very expensive, but you are worth it. A gesture of good will. Pretend you're civilised and just put some on a plate. I brought candles, too. The nice ones, blue, to fit the shirt I got you. Perhaps put it on now. Do you have a candleholder?"

"I've made tons of them."

"Good! Give me the prettiest one."

"I sold them."

"Jesus, Gunnar. Don't you leave anything for yourself?"

"Money," muttered the blacksmith, and Brynhildur's eyes lit up. "Wait, I'll see." He unlocked the forge door, opened it as little as possible, squeezed himself in, then locked it from the inside. Brynhildur realised that the forge must have been one huge mess. Obviously not something he would like to show to his fiancée. She mindlessly stared at Ragnar, who lowered his eyelids until only the merest hint of a pupil was there, pretending not to observe her. "You'll be moving out soon," she whispered, smiling pleasantly, just before Gunnar squeezed himself back inside, balancing a massive candleholder. "That's wonderful! Is that copper?"

"Brass."

"It's delightful."

"You and Anna sold ten of them or so," Gunnar pointed out.

"True," she admitted hesitantly, "but it's still delightful. Make coffee. Do you have any mugs that are not broken? That reminds me, I completely forgot to ask. What have you done to poor Halldóra?"

"The cleaning woman? I haven't done anything. I haven't even seen her. Why?"

"She came home crying, apparently, went straight to bed and… well, she doesn't talk. Did you, uh, touch her? Her sister came to me to complain…" Her voice died out as she watched his expression – surprise, confusion, but not a bit of guilt. "I apologise. Of course you didn't do that. Did you offer her a drink–?"

An assertive knock sounded at the door. It was a person who did not take no for an answer, a person used to being listened to without protests. Gunnar enthusiastically opened the door. "Deary me!" he exclaimed. "The Constipated Women of Iceland! God bless!"

Brynhildur nearly choked on a biscuit. Laufey opened her mouth. Her eyes said all that needed to be said. Thóra let out a brief, piercing scream, then fainted. Gunnar, afraid to stain her coat, caught her at the very last moment.

"It was the heat," said Thóra meekly once she came back to, placed on Sigurd's bed. Brynhildur, who was about to throw a bucket of water on her, frowned in disappointment. Thóra's face was soft now. Her eyes were open wide, hurt, defenceless. She looked almost human, thought Brynhildur, amazed. "Or maybe it was the cold. Never mind… never… I would like a bit of brandy, I mean water, please."

"There's very good coffee and Gunnar bought biscuits," emphasised Brynhildur, "very good biscuits, if I may say so."

"You look lovely, Gunnar," said Laufey. "Truly a sight for sore eyes."

"Mother says he looks exactly like his father," said Brynhildur. "Bring the coffee, Gunnar. Now. And biscuits. Don't spill. Don't add *anything* to the coffee."

"I'd like some sugar," whispered Laufey.

"Of course," answered Brynhildur. "Gunnar!!! Sugar for Laufey!!! As you can see, Gunnar is putting a lot of work into…"

"Bringing God into this house, I hope," said Thóra weakly.

"I can't bring everything," complained Gunnar from the kitchen.

"I'll help," offered Brynhildur, already getting used to being the lady of the house.

Laufey watched her discreetly, then turned to Thóra. "Are you feeling better?"

"Yes, yes," said Thóra. "I'm *completely* fine, Laufey dear." Her voice sounded weak. She hardly resembled the disapproving regal figure she always presented. "He just looks so much like his father. It was as if I saw a ghost."

"His father must have been very good-looking, then," said Laufey. "They will make a lovely couple, those two. We mustn't stay long."

"Why don't you leave decisions to me, Laufey dear... I think we should go."

"Now?" asked Brynhildur, appearing with a plate of biscuits. Laufey swallowed.

"Yes," said Thóra. "We're going to leave you two alone. To your *Bible studies.*"

Brynhildur offered Laufey a biscuit nonetheless, then waited out the outburst of gratitude. "Thank you, thank you, those are delicious biscuits, excellent coffee too, and you look wonderful, Gunnar, we shall go now, yes, off we go." Laufey paused. "I'm so sorry," she added, just in case.

"Do you need help?" asked Brynhildur.

"Of *course* not," huffed Thóra, already storming towards the door. Brynhildur began to chew on yet another biscuit, watching Gunnar trying to avoid spilling coffee from two exceptionally non-chipped mugs. "God bless," he muttered uncertainly as they left. Before the door shut, he saw Laufey's bewildered expression. To his surprise, Thóra didn't even deign to give him the briefest disapproving glance.

"That was very interesting," said Brynhildur a second after the door closed. "I think I found a way to keep them away from you."

"Aye?"

"Put that coffee down already. Don't stand like that. We're going to do Bible studies together, help you find God," announced Brynhildur, clapping her hands joyfully. "Thóra will make sure my mother has nothing to say on the matter. Then I will tell them we are very busy preparing you for confirmation, and I'll keep them away from you. It will just be the two of us. Isn't that lovely?"

"The two of us?"

"Of course! You and me. We *will* study the Bible. And," she said, winking seductively, "we might study some other things, too."

"Nay. I don't want you here."

"But why?"

"Anna told me not to talk to you. And I won't. Go home."

"But Gunnar... I just want to help!"

"You're not helping. Go away." He opened a cupboard, pulled out a bottle and drank a good half without breaking for breath.

"Good God," said Brynhildur in awe. "That's impressive. I mean, it will have to stop, but it's really impressive."

Gunnar didn't respond, his face carefully expressionless. *Just go*, he prayed.

Brynhildur stretched herself on the chair, looking comfortable and relaxed. "Cards on the table," she said, flashing her foxy smile. "You have friends in town, more than you'd think. We know things about your parents and about you, things that you do not know, but you're not going to find out until we are married." Gunnar seemed to wobble a bit, and Brynhildur became concerned. "Sit down and have some coffee. Would you like a biscuit?"

"Talk."

"More for me," said Brynhildur, continuing with her mouth full. Those biscuits were worth the price, especially if Mother wouldn't notice she stole a can. "It's very simple. A group of friends – Brynjólf, my mother, me, and some others, all of whom you will meet soon – gathered and decided." She swallowed the biscuit with some coffee. "I spoke to Brynjólf and he is going to cure your alcoholism. I mean, your condition. We will tell the Constipated Women that you have gone to visit your family to beg their forgiveness and their permission to marry me. You will spend that month with Brynjólf, I will come and visit you every day, and we will work on preparing you to be confirmed. You will not go with all the kids, of course, as that would be ridiculous. It might take more than a month, since you've never read the Bible…"

"I have read the Bible," interrupted Gunnar angrily. "Many times. You don't know as much as you imagine you do."

"That's excellent! It will save us so much time!"

"How dare you just decide to live my life for me!" He banged his fists on the table so hard the plate jumped, Brynhildur dropped her mug, and coffee spilled all over the table and her clothes. "It's my house! I did not invite you over here, I don't want those women to come here either, I just want to live my life in peace! I don't want to marry nobody, I don't want to be confirmed, I don't want to go to Doctor Brynjólf for a month!"

Anna's words rang unsettlingly in Brynhildur's head. *His father was not a good man. Gunnar is going to be exactly the same.* "Leave and never come back," continued the blacksmith, before instinctively straightening one of the candles dripping wax on the table.

"Gunnar, my dear," said Brynhildur through clenched teeth, examining the damage to her thick skirt. "You don't have a choice. Unless you would like the authorities to be notified about the fact you've been producing moonshine and selling it to many people."

"I have never sold anything!"

"It's been noticed that you've been spending money." A victorious grin emerged on her face. "We wondered – Mother and me, and maaaaybe some others – where that money could be coming from. It's probably because you've been working so hard and the market has been thriving, even though we're in a recession again. Well done, I would say! Unless, which I am sure is not the case, it's because you've been illegally producing alcohol and providing it to other people? Maybe if the Sheriff and his men came to search your farm they would find some sort of equipment and lots of bottles? Perhaps money?"

"I… I will tell them…" The moonshine was coming back, the bile in his throat was disgusting, he…

"Yes, dear, what will you tell them?"

Brynhildur watched as Gunnar stormed outside, then cast an uncertain glance at the clock. She really should be going. The biscuits attracted her attention again. Clearly they wouldn't be necessary anymore, she decided, replacing them in the decorative can. She winced when Gunnar returned, slamming the door so hard the horseshoe over the door fell right next to his head. He didn't seem to notice.

"I don't believe you," he burst out. "You said you and your friends know things about my mother and father. Tell me what things."

"They are *your* friends," said Brynhildur, standing up. "Sit there, next to the stove, behind the table."

"Why?"

"So you can get warm." Both of them stared at each other as Gunnar took his seat. Brynhildur positioned herself tactically next to the door.

"You're blackmailing me," said Gunnar. "Is that how Christians and their God act?"

"*Our* God, my love. Our God. You better get used to it." Brynhildur paused, realising she was enjoying herself. Of course, she was only saying all those things for Gunnar's own good, but she still decided to say an extra Hail Mary before sleep.

"To hell with both Gods, yours and mine. Tell me about my mother and father."

"I will tell you just one thing to begin with. There's more, but you must promise that you will not hit me, hurt me, or anything else. And that you will stay with Brynjólf and stop being an alcoholic."

"Tell me."

"Promise me first that you will start curing your alcoholism next week."

Gunnar snorted. "I've got things to do. I can't just leave everything…"

"Oh yes," said Brynhildur, "you can. What is it that you have to do? Drink? Come on, dear Gunnar. It will be good for you and for us. The faster, the better."

Not for Sigurd, thought Gunnar. The one secret he still had left. "First of May."

"First of May is weeks away."

"What does it matter? We'll spend the rest of our lives…" The blacksmith convulsively grabbed the nearest of four coffee mugs and emptied it. "Together," he continued in a strangled voice. "So. Tell me the one thing."

"I will," said Brynhildur, putting her hand on the door handle. Stjarna was waiting outside, she reminded herself, and Gunnar was stuck behind the table. Nevertheless, she could feel the little hairs on her skin standing up. "Please remember this is not my fault. In fact, it has nothing to do with me at all. It's just information."

"Tell." His face was red, eyes bloodshot. A vein pulsated on his forehead, teeth bared again, his hands folded into fists so tight that the knuckles became white, and Brynhildur felt something unusual: fear. She quickly considered her options, but there weren't any. She'd already said too much.

"The woman who died…" she began reluctantly. "The one you remember… She wasn't your mother. Your real mother is still alive. Once we're married, I will tell you who she is." Her body tensed, ready to escape, but Gunnar didn't move. The fury on his face turned into confusion.

"I have no idea what you just said."

A bit of guilt and sympathy emerged, but Brynhildur quickly pushed them aside. She'd feel sorry for Gunnar when she was safe, far away from here. "Your father met a lady when he was already married. They… had relations together. Then she became pregnant and gave birth – to you." She cleared her throat, as her mouth felt strangely dry, then opened the door, letting the cold in, making sure Stjarna was close enough. "She is still alive. Your real mother was not the woman your father married."

# Wednesday, March 24, 1920

Gunnar descended down the ladder and found Sigurd snoring. Clearly the sleeping pills were working very well. It also meant he'd brought the lodger back to bed, even though he couldn't remember doing so. The blacksmith scratched his chin, which was now becoming stubbly and rough like sandpaper. He dragged his feet to the kitchen, ready to begin his morning as usual, then froze in horror. Someone had destroyed everything. Mugs, plates, even two of the chairs. His big butcher's knife stuck out of the wall, and Gunnar felt a chill run down his spine. Who in their right mind would do something like that?! A blurry thought emerged: it was him. He had caused all this mayhem. But why?

The blacksmith started cleaning up, muttering under his breath, trying to figure out what had happened. The Conservative Women came over. He remembered that. There were biscuits. Candleholder… Worriedly he jerked his head. The candleholder stood in its spot on the table, safe, untouched, although the candles were completely burnt. Gunnar never left an open fire unattended. What happened?

"Ragnar," he said, then turned and barely contained a shocked cry. The dog was gone, his blanket strewn with pieces of glass and porcelain. A wave of blood rushed into Gunnar's head, and he groaned in pain and fear, touching his forehead. It didn't feel hot, it was cold and sweaty. The infection! He would have to get to Doctor Brynjólf – something in his memory stirred – but Ragnar was more important. Gunnar opened the forge door with shaky hands and looked inside. "Ragnar?" There was no answer.

With a sinking feeling the blacksmith returned to the room, where Sigurd continued to snore. "Ragnar," Gunnar whispered before noticing movement out of the corner of his eye. The dog whimpered quietly, withdrawing from his master, and Gunnar stumbled as if slapped. He dropped to his knees. "Ragnar, good boy," he whispered. "Come to me. I'm sorry. I'm going to clean it all up. I don't even know what happened. Do you remember?"

The dog didn't move, whimpering quietly, his eyes filled with fear. He remembered.

Gunnar's lip began to tremble. "I didn't hurt you," he whispered, "right?" Ragnar didn't answer, but another thought made it through the haze of Gunnar's mind. Something about his mother… Ragnar growled when the blacksmith slowly extended his hand, and Gunnar nearly cried. "I'm sorry," he whispered. Ragnar watched him, his gaze wary. The blacksmith withdrew, defeated. There was nothing for him to do but clean the kitchen.

The guilt felt like an anvil had been placed on Gunnar's chest. Broken plates and mugs didn't matter, and neither did spilled coffee. The stains wouldn't come out. Who cared? Gunnar intended to disappear very soon, perhaps even tomorrow. Sigurd would have to fend for himself somehow. *He* could stay with Doctor Brynjólf. Once Gunnar managed to convince Ragnar to trust him again, they would go… somewhere. To America, maybe? Or Denmark. Reykjavík wouldn't be far enough. Did they take kronur in America? Sigurd would know that…

Emigrating.

Women.

Brynhildur.

His mother.

Gunnar's hand stopped mid-movement as he was about to pull the knife out of the wall. All of a sudden the little energy he had disappeared, sucked out by the darkness. "Lies," he whispered, and a vague memory resurfaced of himself yelling "Lies! Lies!" while throwing things at the wall.

*You are completely alone now,* said the darkness. *Even Ragnar hates you.*

The blacksmith dropped to his knees, unable to breathe.

*Only Brynhildur is going to keep you company. Forever. Unless… unless… think about it…*

Gunnar fell to his side, not even feeling the pain when his head hit the floor. The darkness would swallow him whole this time, he was certain. It would be over soon, he thought, and felt grateful. There was nothing left, only lies.

*What about me?* asked the darkness. *I am the only one to tell you the truth. Think about "your friends". Then about me. Who's always been by your side?*

Gunnar couldn't find any fault in those words.

*You have no choice,* the darkness reminded him.

Sigurd limped into the kitchen. "Gunnar? What's going on?"

No answer.

Sigurd slowly and carefully lowered himself to the floor and sat next to the blacksmith. Unsure what to do, he clumsily patted Gunnar's shoulder. "Are you unwell? Can I help?" Gunnar's eyes were open, unblinking, fixed on the wall. If he weren't shivering, Sigurd would have been worried the blacksmith was dead.

"Listen," he said. "It's going to get better. I promise. Let's have some coffee. I'll see if I can make breakfast. But you need to light the fire. You're the best with fire. I've never seen anybody build a fire faster than you. Please? Ragnar needs to eat, and Karl, and you too. And me. We need you."

A single tear rolled down, then Gunnar's lips moved silently.

"I can't hear you…"

"I don't know what's happening," mumbled the blacksmith, and then a sob that came straight from the deepest, darkest corners of his soul shook his entire body. Sigurd sat next to him, muttering platitudes, patting his head clumsily. Ragnar emerged from the room, still wary, eyeing his master carefully before forcing himself between the wall and Gunnar in a way that allowed him to lick the scruffy face. Gunnar blinked, wrinkled his nose, then lifted himself to all fours. Ragnar's tail wagged so fast it was practically a blur. As the blacksmith crawled towards the stove, Sigurd began to worry about the potential infection. Gunnar had to survive a bit longer. A few more days, he begged quietly.

It turned out that preparing breakfast was easier than serving it. Wooden planks had to serve as plates, a little saucepan as Gunnar's mug. Sigurd was the lucky recipient of the only actual mug that survived the massacre. It was cracked and leaked, but it had to suffice. He knew better than to complain.

"I have to buy some new, uh, everything," said Gunnar. "I'm going to Reykjavík. I'll be gone all day."

Sigurd looked alarmed. "What if someone comes?"

Gunnar looked up from his plank. "Nobody is going to come here anymore."

"I see… Say… what time do you think it is? I think your clock stopped working."

The blacksmith looked bewildered. He had destroyed everything he could find, including the huge cross, yet the clock stood untouched, just silent. "Eleven," he said.

"Are you sure?"

"How would I know? Just set it to some hour and wind it, then you'll know how long I've been away. Doesn't matter anymore."

Ragnar approached Gunnar again, staring at him with sympathy. Gunnar dropped to his knees and hugged the mutt. Sigurd observed the two of them, marvelling at how human the hug was. The dog was just large enough to place his paws on Gunnar's shoulders, and all seemed forgiven.

Soon both of them departed, and Sigurd realised this was a different sort of being alone. He could now do anything he wanted without fear of being caught. He remembered the last night, unlike Gunnar, and agreed with the blacksmith. There would be no visitors for a while.

Sigurd limped towards the forge door, resting against the table, afraid to fall. This was a good time to look for the money, but unless it was somewhere he could easily reach, he might have to threaten the ursine blacksmith first. Sigurd chuckled at the very thought, absent-mindedly scratching his itchy armpits. Then something occurred to him. He was now alone, and there was a sink. With a bar of soap on it.

Pulling off his sweaty, dirty clothes proved to be quite a challenge. Trousers were the most difficult, as he had to free himself from them while sitting. Casting worried looks at the curtain-less window located right over the sink, Sigurd splashed some water on his face, then stifled a surprised cry at how awfully cold the water was. He ground his teeth and, with all the determination he could muster, started to rub his skin with a rag dripping with soapy water. With every rub he felt better, even though he now stood in a cold puddle, and his teeth began to chatter. As Sigurd looked around for something he could dry himself with he noticed movement outside. The person waved, and a moment later Brynjólf let himself in without knocking.

"I can explain," blurted out Sigurd, trying to protect his modesty as well as it was possible using a small, wet rag.

"Absolutely no need! I'm sorry, didn't mean to interrupt. Can I help you get dressed? I have a clean towel with me."

"Please!"

"I just came to check on Gunnar," confided the doctor. "I must say your ankle doesn't look very good… You should have visited me immediately when it happened. Another day or two should wipe out all of the infection, but at this point the ankle is not going to get better."

"But I can't walk," complained Sigurd bitterly. "Is there really nothing you can do? I will pay as much as necessary."

"I could send you to the hospital in Reykjavík, I suppose. They would break the ankle again, and hope for the best…" Brynjólf noticed the colour of Sigurd's face. "Otherwise, you will have to get used to it. I suggest you get a cane." The doctor sighed. "What are your further plans?"

"I, ahem, decided to return to my family, I mean to our family home. I'd rather not talk about it, if it's alright." The speed at which gossip spread here was unbelievable and Sigurd didn't trust anybody, including the doctor. "Being at Gunnar's is difficult. I am sure you understand."

"You could have stayed in town."

"True, but Gunnar is family after all, and my ankle… Also, I'd never actually met him before."

Brynjólf's eyebrows moved up his forehead. "How come? Is it because you're just back from America?"

"Yes! That's exactly it. I am his… uncle's… wife's brother. I don't have a family of my own, because… because they died, and Theodór told me about Gunnar being all alone here. We were very worried. I ended up staying here longer than I expected with the ankle and all. But I realise now that, in your hands… I mean, I am aware of the plan you and Gunnar's friends have made and I fully agree with it."

"Oh," said Brynjólf. "This was supposed to be a secret."

"Not with Brynhildur around," smiled Sigurd. "Speaking of which, Gunnar was very distressed yesterday after Brynhildur and the… Icelandic Ladies…"

"Conservative Women of Iceland."

"Yes, those. Thank you. I would suggest giving him a bit of a break. I'll try to talk some sense into him. As good as the plan is, I can tell you he's so upset he might do something silly. In fact, he demolished most of the kitchen yesterday. He is very determined not to speak to anybody in Klettafjörður again. But I know him enough by now, in a few days it will pass. I'll talk some sense into him."

The doctor nodded but said nothing.

"Poor Gunnar," sighed Sigurd, "don't you think? He needs all the help he can get. He doesn't realise how worried his uncle is – he thinks all Theodór wants is the farm. It is important that he… this sounds horrible, but it's important that he feels that he has no other choice than to follow your plans. Just not too fast, or he'll run away. He's been talking about running away quite a lot. Make him feel more at peace. One step at a time."

"I think this makes sense. I'll tell them Gunnar's family–"

"No," said Sigurd quickly, "please don't tell them about me. You and me both know the moment they find out I am here Gunnar will not catch a break."

"Where is he now?"

"I believe he's either in Reykjavík or on his way there."

"I'll see what I can do. To be completely honest, it's not like they listen to me," confided Brynjólf. "So, I will try my best, but…"

"Thank you, doctor. Nobody can help him better than you. I heard that you intend to take him in and help him get over his drinking. That's very generous. Theodór will be *most* pleased. So will Gunnar, eventually. Could I please make a request? Could you set the clock in the kitchen to the correct time when you go? It would be good if you didn't stay here long, he might be back any time and he shouldn't know that the two of us spoke about him."

The doctor nodded again. "How are the sleeping pills?" he asked.

"They're working great. I have a few left. No more than one a night, of course."

"Have you been dizzy in the morning? How long do you sleep?"

Sigurd looked up thoughtfully. "I sleep very long and deep. I don't remember any dreams. It takes me a long time to wake up, but once I have a cup of coffee all is good and well."

"Excellent," said the doctor. "I shall leave you to it. Do you need me to help you with something else?"

"No, I believe that's it. Thank you for all you are doing for me. And for Gunnar."

"It is my pleasure," said Brynjólf, but his face darkened. No explanation came, and Sigurd was soon left alone with another question without an answer.

He spent a while with a bitter feeling in his mouth, his head in his hands. So, the ankle wouldn't get any better… The only silver lining was the realisation that there was no point in waiting any longer. One to two days for the infection, said the doctor. Sigurd now wished he'd known that beforehand, as now he would need to send the blacksmith to Reykjavík again. Other than that, Sigurd intended to finish the first part of the story, having found the one listener who would never be able to share it with anybody else. And then he would write the few remaining chapters.

There were four sleeping pills left, and at least two nights, possibly three. This constituted a problem, unless he would be able to fall asleep without them, despite the excitement he felt, despite his nerves… The pills were dangerous when mixed with alcohol. The latter part would be easy. But Sigurd was worried. One pill probably wouldn't be enough. Two? Two and a half? Maybe he could skip sleep tonight, tell Gunnar more of the story? Sigurd was furious with himself for having missed the opportunity to ask the good doctor for another pill or two. He had to sleep before his departure, no matter what. He needed to be rested, clear-headed and *walk*, for Christ's sake…

Sigurd ate some stale bread, drank cold coffee, then tried to walk without crutches again, his mind plagued by the image of Halldóra and the "sshhh... *tap*" that accompanied every step she took. After a while he fell back onto the chair, covered in sweat, gasping for air. The ankle was now pulsating with pain again. The crutches would have been a great help had it not been for the fact Sigurd needed his hands free. Outdoors there would be no walls to lean on...

The door opened, and Gunnar nearly flew inside along with a particularly brutal gust of wind. Ragnar followed, more than ready to hide under his blanket, nearly sending the blacksmith to the floor. "I'm back," panted Gunnar. "Any visitors?"

Sigurd's eyes widened, his mouth agape.

"Just kidding," said the blacksmith. "This wind! Not a good day to go out." Sigurd paled further. To call Iceland's weather capricious would be a major understatement. The elements were yet another thing his plan didn't include. "Going to bring everything inside," sighed Gunnar. "What a day."

He had never grown to like Reykjavík. First of all, it felt enormous — ten, perhaps twenty times the size of Klettafjörður. Street sellers shouted, peddling their stuff, as did boys with newspapers. Every now and then Gunnar saw a car and invariably shuddered. It was unnatural for a carriage to move on its own without a horse, donkey, or even a bloody dog to pull it. Gunnar patted the pocket that hid his flask, but didn't dare to get it out, not with all the people around. What a nightmare, he thought, deciding that wherever he would be moving it wouldn't be Reykjavík.

Once he was done with the shopping, Gunnar found himself passing by an inn. His stomach grumbled in hope, and the blacksmith stuck his head through the door. There were people inside, but he found a table that was unoccupied, stuck in a corner where nobody liked to sit. Worried about attracting unwanted attention Gunnar started casting suspicious looks around him, examining every other patron, which caused each of them to stare back. What they saw was a good-looking, neatly dressed man with big, dirty hands and a face that betrayed that he was very, very uncomfortable. A woman bent towards a man, covering her mouth with her hand, whispering something without once taking her eyes off Gunnar and, had it not been for a smiling girl who came to take his order, the blacksmith would have bolted out.

The waitress seemed nice, her smile genuine, and Gunnar went with her recommendation: soup of the day and some bread.

"I'd like some whisky," he said.

"We don't sell alcohol, sir," she answered. "It's illegal." Nevertheless, she didn't seem surprised.

"That's right, aye, that's right," said the blacksmith and scratched his itching chin. "I've been away for a while. Just bring me a pot of coffee." He tried his best to smile, and the girl blushed slightly before smiling back. He seemed strange, but very handsome, even though he clearly had no time to shave.

When the coffee arrived, Gunnar poured himself a nice, steaming mug, added sugar, and took a big swig. He coughed and grinned. Some nice person had added a generous bit of brandy to his coffee. That nice person would be getting a big tip. Gunnar closed his eyes, enjoying the warmth. The other patrons had lost interest in him by now, and his wide shoulders relaxed. The waitress smiled when she brought the soup, and he smiled back. It was becoming easier. She didn't talk much, and clearly understood that a man had needs. At the end Gunnar stayed for an hour and a half, finished the nice coffee, and realised he didn't feel like leaving. Had it not been for poor Ragnar, who stayed with Karl on the outskirts of town… oh, and Sigurd, of course…

As Karl trotted home faster than usual – she, too, disliked the wind – Gunnar began making plans. Perhaps Reykjavík wasn't so bad after all? It felt good to be a stranger, surrounded by other strangers, none of whom inquired about his religious views, tried to marry him, or asked questions about his money. Such a big city must have had thousands of inhabitants. Maybe he could get used to shaving and having his hair cut, and then nobody would notice him, except perhaps the nice girl at the inn. A new name, he thought, new identity, new life. The outskirts of town were much quieter, and Gunnar could imagine himself living there. Maybe he could even start a little forge. Surely in a town this size it was possible to buy alcohol as well…

Proud of his willpower, he resisted the temptation to reach for his flask, still feeling warm from the special coffee. But if he were to be completely honest, there was another reason. Gunnar's supply was down to two bottles, unless there was one hidden somewhere he'd forgotten about. There would be no more visits to see Doctor Brynjólf. So, his "friends" wanted his life to change? Aye, it would. On Gunnar's terms.

The blacksmith whistled joyfully as he made a fire, helped Sigurd hobble to the good chair, made fresh coffee, and served dinner on new plates.

"You're very happy," observed Sigurd. "Are you alright?"

"Is it bad when I'm happy? It was a nice trip. Almost no rain."

"Ah," said Sigurd, listening to the roof creaking in protest as the wind tried to tear it off. The blacksmith seemed unconcerned. "So – why?"

"Just making some plans. What do you think I should do?"

"I assume you don't mean the option with Brynhildur in it."

Gunnar snorted.

Sigurd looked at the ceiling thoughtfully. "You can move pretty much anywhere you want. The money will last you longer or shorter, depending on where you go. You can sell this place and you'll be even richer. Do you want to stay in Iceland?"

"Don't know."

"Did you like Reykjavík?"

"Sort of."

"Reykjavík is close," pointed out Sigurd. "You know news travels fast, and people from Klettafjörður visit Reykjavík often enough. You could go to Akureyri, if you want. It's smaller and far away from here. I suggest you avoid small villages like Klettafjörður. Everybody thinks nobody's paying them any attention and everybody is wrong. The more people, the better. I know you don't like people, but you don't have to befriend them. Just be one of the crowd."

"Crowd," muttered Gunnar. "Aye. So, I did shopping," he said, perking up.

"Yes?"

"I bought you the papers. And some books." The blacksmith chuckled. Sigurd glanced at him. "What's so funny?"

"Nothing. Just thinking that it's nice when I can go shopping and nobody in the village knows about it. It's funny. There were more people, but I felt better."

"Good," said Sigurd. "Because I will have to ask you to go to Reykjavík again, I'm afraid."

"Why?"

"I will be leaving soon."

Gunnar found himself at a loss for words. Despite having spent so much time telling himself and Ragnar they would be alone again very soon, he had become used to his companion, his... friend, the storyteller.

Of course, Brynhildur would have lots of stories as well. About Ásta, Ásta's husband, her kids and dresses, about Thóra and Laufey, the poor dead Helga with her cats, about Halldóra and her family, about their families' families, but worst of all… "We have to leave together," he muttered. "Or they won't leave me alone. That dumb Brynhildur was telling lies about my mother. If I never see her again it will be too soon. So. When do we leave?"

"In about a week," lied Sigurd. "My apologies, I haven't thought about it earlier. I will need some clothes, boots, shaving utensils, that sort of stuff. I assume you don't want to go to Klettafjörður for all that. Do you think you could go tomorrow?"

"I only just came back. You've got a week. Why the hurry?"

"Just growing impatient, I guess. Excited."

"You've got a story to finish," reminded the blacksmith. "Let's eat. I'll bring a bottle. Hey, I'll have whisky – nay, I won't, because I'm not visiting Doctor Brynjólf tomorrow." He scratched his chin, scowling. "I decided I don't like Arnar at all. Get rid of him."

### Then

One evening, when Katrín went home, Juana knocked on Ingvar's door.

"Don't you want to go to bed?" he asked, surprised, before noticing tears rolling down her face. His heart trembled. Before he knew, he wrapped his arms tightly around Juana, who sobbed and cried on his chest. Ingvar clumsily caressed her hair, making soothing noises. Her hair was so soft, her body, covered only with a nightgown – warm and pleasant to touch… Ingvar felt a pierce of something that took him a moment to identify. Lust.

Stop it, he told himself, mortified. No matter what, Juana was his brother's wife, and he should know, having officiated the wedding. Even though Katrín admitted that the wedding certificate didn't exist anymore, and no copies had been made either… Ingvar shifted uncomfortably, his body betraying his iron will. Those were bad thoughts, sinful ones. It's just that he hadn't held a woman like this, not once. His clumsy advances towards Danish girls never got him as far as smelling their hair.

"I'm scared," she sobbed.

*I want her*, he thought. *No, I want to* save *her*, he quickly corrected himself. He just wanted her to be happy, to smile, to see her out of those godawful black dresses she was wearing… no, no, that was wrong, no…

No.

"You should go to bed, Juana," he said, gently. "I'll tuck you in. Come. You are safe under this roof." He led her by the hand to the guest bedroom, where she slept every night. It cost him all his strength not to kiss the tears from her cheeks. When he closed the door, he stood outside for a while. Now he feared more than just Arnar.

Katrín liberated him from almost all of the paperwork by now. This gave him time to finally get some writing done and catch up with everything, but for some reason he discovered he couldn't do it. For the first time in his life, words didn't come to him, and Ingvar sat in front of his Remington, staring at an empty page, wishing the words would appear. They would have to be God's words, since he had none of his own.

Every time Juana appeared at his desk, smiling apologetically, bringing food or cleaning up empty cups he couldn't resist noticing something new. The soft curves of her body. The way she unconsciously pushed an unruly lock of hair behind her ear. The gentleness of her neck. Ingvar happened to know the origin of the name Juana – it meant "gift of God". What could be a better sign…? But no, no…

The unwanted thoughts kept tormenting him and Ingvar was now even more tired than before. At night he lay on the church floor, praying to be freed from temptation, only to be thrown back into its arms when the dawn came. Juana never massaged his shoulders again, and it cost him all his willpower not to beg her to do it just one more time. But even though she kept a polite distance, something always seemed to distract the pastor. Sometimes it was a soft, accidental brush of Juana's breast over his shoulder as she brought him coffee. Sometimes it was a whiff of the smell of her skin that threw him off. The impure thoughts were always mixed with the fear of the unknown. Arnar was still out there somewhere and could show up any day. Every time Ingvar had to leave he worried what he would find upon his return. He kept reminding Katrín and Juana to lock the doors, to be careful. There was nothing he wouldn't do to protect the women, he told himself and God, and a wave of shame immediately washed over him. There was nothing heroic or pure about his intentions.

An article he sent to the newspaper was returned. The editor pointed out that the two pages seemed to be parts of two different texts, which meant the other newspaper would be in touch very soon with the same problem. Ingvar confused the places he was supposed to visit, surprising both the villagers and himself. He found himself dictating letters of apologies to Katrín, who kept suggesting he needed rest. As if he had time for rest, he answered, and as if by a miracle time freed itself when editors of both newspapers informed curtly that they were terminating their arrangements. Ingvar cried that night, begging for redemption, for one more chance. He knew God was punishing him for his arrogance, lust, greed. Ingvar understood the right thing to do would be to send Juana away, but there were so many reasons not to. She was so helpful. She'd be in danger – someone like Juana couldn't remain unnoticed for long. She'd be… not here. He kept postponing the decision, begging God for strength if forgiveness couldn't be had.

According to Katrín nobody knew anything about Arnar's whereabouts. The girl was the only person who dared to visit the house, as everyone else avoided it. As far as she could tell, nothing was missing. Katrín brought Juana her American Holy Bible, the family photograph, and some clothes, and reported that from what she could tell all Arnar's things were still there.

"He probably went into the countryside," said Katrín. "He's working somewhere far away. Perhaps he left for America again. There's no need to be afraid. It was long ago. He's not coming back." Nevertheless, Juana couldn't shake off the dread. That night, when Katrín went home, Juana waited a few minutes to make sure the girl wouldn't return, then knocked gently on Ingvar's door. Neither of them had the courage to talk about their shared fears, and after some empty chit-chat both of them fell silent.

"Can I ask you a question?" whispered Ingvar, and she nodded. "Why did the two of you get married after all that time? What happened?"

The dam broke. Juana forgot all the good times, the love, the warmth, the joy. She could only speak of pain, broken promises, words she believed to be lies. She blamed Arnar for everything, and Ingvar believed her – he *wanted* to believe everything was his brother's fault. Feelings overcame him, sinful, evil feelings: hatred, anger, spite. If he could, he'd have killed Arnar right then and there. Of course, his brother was a strong man and an experienced brawler, while Ingvar's fights were at best verbal, and ideally conducted in writing. But if his brother could be somehow… disposed of… Everyone would benefit, he told himself, as Juana sobbed. The whole village would breathe more peacefully. It would be for the greater good… When Juana impulsively threw her arms around him, still crying, his lips found her neck and remained there for a second too long.

Both of them stiffened. Juana withdrew just far enough to look into his eyes. Their gazes locked in silent understanding. It wasn't Ingvar who raised his hand to caress her cheek, his hand seemed to move of its own accord. Juana shyly touched his leg, then withdrew her hand. Her lips were half-open, and Ingvar couldn't resist anymore. He kissed her clumsily, then again, shivering with excitement and fear, and it was her turn to envelop him in her arms. They lay down on his bed, their lips never parting. Ingvar allowed her to take initiative, fully aware of the fact he didn't really know what to do. *Sin. Shame.* The thoughts were surprisingly easy to push away. He was doing the right thing, providing Juana with love, tenderness, and care. His brother was never the right man for her, self-obsessed, angry, rough around the edges. Juana was a gem that deserved to be treated like the precious object that she had always been. A princess. They fell asleep in each other's arms, safe and satiated.

In the morning Katrín let herself inside. One glance was enough to notice Juana hadn't bothered to make breakfast. She was probably still in bed. Katrín sighed heavily, but didn't mind too much, as it meant she would have the pastor to herself. She prepared a tray with coffee and a special treat – sweet buns her mother had baked especially for the pastor. She was just about to take the tray into Ingvar's room, when she got interrupted. Poor Ingvar, thought Katrín, informing the guests he would be with them in a minute, then unsuccessfully attempting to smuggle the tray with coffee and sweet buns away before they noticed.

The tray was large, and Katrín stuck out her tongue in concentration, attempting to open the door without dropping anything. She barely stopped herself from cursing out loud, but finally made it inside. "I'm sorry to wake you, pastor, but the fundraiser ladies are here *again*, yes, the same ones, I *know*, I–" Her gaze reached the bed and the tray fell to the floor.

Ingvar sat up, rubbing his eyes. Next to him, Juana raised herself on her elbow. Both needed a moment to realise what was happening, but once they did, their faces slowly morphed into identical horrified expressions. So did Katrín's before she ran out of the room, slamming the door shut. The fundraiser ladies, who had travelled in the rain from another village, were unceremoniously sent home. They huffed at each other about how rude the pastor's servant was. Perhaps they visited the pastor a bit more often than they really had to, but they knew how kind and pious Ingvar was, and couldn't believe he would employ someone so unpleasant.

With shaking hands, Ingvar clumsily pulled on his nightgown, cursing nastily. Juana sat in bed, her eyes open wide, face pale, blanket wrapped around her body as tightly as possible. The pastor ran downstairs, tripping over the nightgown. "Katrín!" he shouted. "Wait!" But Katrín was nowhere to be found. Ingvar went outside, covering his eyes from the rain that whipped him mercilessly. "Katrín!" he yelled once more, then briskly returned inside and shut the door, unaware the girl was standing right around the corner, hugging herself, raindrops and tears dripping down her face.

Katrín had done so much for the pastor. She'd sacrificed time and energy, all to help him, to take the burden off his shoulders. Ingvar was such a good, pure man, and he was *her* future husband, this much Katrín knew for sure. Juana seduced a man of God even though she was married herself! That witch! So that was what she has learned from Gullveig! Tonight everyone would find out, Katrín promised herself, biting her lip to stop the tears from flowing. Then anger towards Ingvar struck her as well. Out of all people he should have been the one to resist her poisonous embraces! Well, from now on Ingvar could open his own post, write his own apologies, beg for forgiveness as much as he wanted. Katrín would never again speak to either of those two. Never ever. She had learned a lot from Reverend Ingvar about preparing carefully before delivering an important message and was already planning what she would say later that evening at the inn.

"She will tell people," said Juana weakly.

"We could say she's jealous," burst out Ingvar, "and–"

"Lie?" she asked quietly, and his words died. They didn't speak about it again, not even after days passed and it became clear that Katrín was not coming back. Ingvar and Juana were too isolated without Katrín around to know what was being said and done about their sin. But once they had already broken the sacred vows and been caught in the act, there was no point in pretending further. The guest bedroom was free again.

The pastor found himself a new man, once more rejuvenated and inspired. Instead of writing another round of apologies to the editors he sent them finished articles, sparkling with inventive metaphors, clarity, possibly the finest writing he had produced in his entire life. One of the editors never responded, but the other one was delighted, and all was forgiven. After some consideration Ingvar sent the other article to the same editor, and his name began to regularly appear in the paper again. He was no longer afraid of his brother, but new bitter feelings consumed him.

217

Every time he stood behind the pulpit he failed not to notice the attendance at Mass seemed to drop. The constant stream of visits slowed down to a trickle. Even the fundraiser ladies never returned. Was he just imagining the disdain in people's eyes? Were they whispering? Until now it hadn't occurred to Ingvar that this was a tight community and that he was not a part of it, as if the church was surrounded by an invisible fence that could only be opened from the outside.

One evening, when Juana and Ingvar sat in the kitchen worrying about the future, a visitor arrived. They exchanged pleasantries, but Bjarni took a step back when Ingvar tried to hug him. The pastor's smile abruptly disappeared.

"So," Bjarni said casually, "word goes around that you're sleeping with your brother's wife."

Juana raised her hand to her mouth, eyes open wide. "Go upstairs," Bjarni commanded, and she retreated hastily, her hand still covering her mouth. Bjarni paid her no attention, glaring at Ingvar. "This is where you are supposed to say those are filthy lies."

Ingvar didn't answer.

"You care about her a lot, don't you?"

"Arnar has tortured her for years…"

"How do you know? Have you spoken to him about it? Every story has two sides, sometimes more."

"May I remind you," the pastor said quietly, "that he burned an old woman alive in her own house? I was thinking that it should really be reported to the authorities after all. It was a murder in cold blood."

"You have no proof," snapped Bjarni. "It's all Juana's words. She was not there."

"How do you know she was not there?"

"I– of course she wasn't, she would have done something, she would have told you…"

"She *did* tell me," pointed out Ingvar. "She wouldn't lie. She is too pure for…"

A satisfied smirk appeared on Bjarni's face. "Oh, brother," he said. "We know every little detail of what happened. We know it's been happening for months, behind Arnar's back. Katrín tried to defend you, but even she had to admit that you didn't stop your illicit affair even when you married them…!"

"No!" exclaimed Ingvar, jumping to his feet. "Those *are* filthy lies…!"

"Which ones? Oh, Reverend, I wish I could believe you. But we have no reason to doubt Katrín, she has nothing to gain or lose by telling the truth. You, on the other hand? It's clear to everyone you've got *feelings* towards Juana. Otherwise, why would she even still be here? Arnar is a bad man, I can't disagree with that, but it looks like you are, too, just in your own special way." Bjarni paused to give Ingvar a chance to defend himself, but the pastor just dropped back onto his chair in defeat, head hung in shame. "You think that somehow the entire village doesn't notice you until you go out to teach and preach. But they – we – all know. You, on the other hand, know nothing. We hardly ever saw Reverend Kristófer, you know? He never had time for us. We thought you'd be different. But you just sit here in your ivory tower, with your important papers. What do you really know about us all, what do you even know about me? I know you never forgave me for the delay–"

"I have," blurted out Ingvar, "absolutely…"

"Why did you come here? You could have had such a career. We all knew how busy and important you were. We felt privileged to have you here. And now? What is it that you're doing?"

"I wanted to touch lives," said Ingvar. "I wanted to change the country, to make things better, starting here, then moving further. And now… Bjarni, I live in constant fear…"

"So, you *do* remember my name. Fear of Arnar?"

"Of everything! Of the words you are saying now. Why did you come to tell me all this?"

Bjarni barely suppressed a smile. "Oh, brother. We need someone to be good. We're all human; we make mistakes, we sin without even knowing we sin. You were supposed to be the one to tell us, show us how to live with God in our hearts. But the only thing you've done is show us that nobody is truly pure."

"I am just helping her," burst out Ingvar. "She needs love, compassion, tenderness, she's been hurt so badly…"

"You're lying to yourself, pastor. It says in the Bible 'do not commit adultery', and there are no exceptions that I can remember. Am I wrong? You should know best. Is adultery allowed when the pastor decides his brother's wife needs love or compassion?"

"Please," said Ingvar softly. "Do not raise your voice. I understand your point. But I am human, too. You can't put me on a pedestal and expect me not to slip." This was a good sentence, he thought, momentarily distracted. He'd need to write it down later… Pride. Lust. Greed. Anger. He only had three left to complete the set, and if he were completely honest, there was envy as well. Arnar was the legal owner of this treasure. "Where do you think Arnar is?"

"He could be anywhere, in Iceland, in America, Denmark, Spain, you name it. Do you really want to find him? Let's face it, none of us wants to see him again, and neither do you. What you should do is send her away, *my good man*. Get rid of her. Confess your sins to the bishop and to us here. Take penance for what you have done, and maybe – maybe you will be forgiven, *my good man*."

"I'm living in fear," repeated Ingvar. "All I wanted was for everything to be well. Now every single day I worry that Arnar will return here to finish what he started. I wish he'd be found, so that… so…"

"Aye," interrupted Bjarni. "You wish he'd be found dead, huh?"

"I don't wish death on any being, human or animal," muttered Ingvar.

"I'd better go," said Bjarni. "I don't like being under this roof."

"No," pleaded Ingvar, "listen, this went completely wrong, it's all a misunderstanding, I can explain…"

"No," snarled his brother. "You really can't. No need to show me the door, I installed it myself."

The next morning Katrín arrived to formally give her notice. "Too busy with other work," she said, avoiding Ingvar's pleading eyes. "Also, Juana helps you with everything, so much better than I ever could."

"Katrín, she can't write or read half as well as you can. I greatly value your help. Why… why did you invent all those things and tell them to people? What is it that you want? Money? Revenge for something I have or haven't done?" The corners of his mouth dropped, and… were those tears? He looked pale, emaciated, clasping his hands to hide the trembling.

Katrín's firm resolve melted. Of course he didn't understand. He never had. There was never any love for her in his heart apart from what she made up in her head and convinced herself was true. "My mother… doesn't want me to work here anymore. She's got other things for me to do. I need to go into the country, work for other people, learn more about life. My hands are getting soft…" Her voice was choked by tears now. "Thank you for everything, pastor, but I– I just…"

"Yes," said Ingvar. "I understand." He reached out his hand to pat her head absent-mindedly, as he was prone to do. Katrín winced, and Ingvar quickly withdrew his hand. The innocent gesture she used to enjoy so much hurt both of them.

"It's her fault," Katrín whispered. "She made Arnar become so angry and evil. And now she corrupted you. I'm sick of her. We all are. Get rid of her."

Ingvar didn't tell Juana about the visit, a forced smile plastered upon his face. "Be careful," he warned her like he always had. "Today I have to start visiting the children and make sure they're preparing for their exams. I might be gone for a few days."

Juana nodded, saying nothing.

"Be careful," repeated Ingvar, kissing her stiffly. He mounted the horse with guilt and shame bouncing endlessly inside his head. He found Katrín's list and hoped it was complete. The first one was Hannes. Ingvar remembered Hannes, a smart boy who one day might become his protégée. Ingvar quite fancied the idea of helping a poor boy gain education, like the old pastor had helped him. It would be a nice gesture, and it wouldn't go unnoticed.

Elín, the boy's mother was home, and Hannes sat next to her. "God bless," said Ingvar.

"God bless," whispered Elín, looking down at her lap. She pulled a handkerchief out from her pocket, then began to fiddle with it nervously.

"Hello, Hannes," said Ingvar encouragingly. "What is it, boy? Have you forgotten all the words?"

"My father says you are a bad man," mumbled Hannes, staring away from the pastor.

Ingvar flinched, as if slapped in the face. Elín let out a quiet gasp. "Go out," she barked at the boy. "Play outside." Ingvar sat quietly, watching Elín's hands clutch the handkerchief. It was a habit she picked up many years ago as a girl and had never managed to get rid of. Every time she was nervous she fiddled with the nearest object she could find. Handkerchiefs or pieces of fabric were best, because they didn't break.

"Why am I a bad man, Elín?"

"I don't really think you are," she finally whispered, "but others…"

"Which others?"

She didn't answer.

"Tell me, Elín. There's no right or wrong answer. It's about Juana, isn't it?"

"She bewitched you, pastor," exclaimed Elín, raising her eyes for a moment, then dropping her gaze again. "We all know it's her fault, we know it's not you. She just doesn't belong here. You need to get rid of her. She is his wife. She is his to treat however he wishes."

"He is not a sane man. He hurt her many times."

Elín shrugged. "We don't care."

"We?"

If the handkerchief were a twig, it would have snapped. "I don't really have time right now, pastor. I've got to get back to work. I'm sorry for what Hannes did– said– please go," she pleaded in a whisper. "I don't know what to say. Please, get rid of her."

Ingvar stood up and let himself out without another word. Hannes was nowhere to be seen. The pastor suddenly bent over and threw up, unable to imagine going further, talking to other families, receiving the same treatment. Nothing could possibly be worse, he thought. If only he had an idea what the future held in store for him…

# Thursday, March 25, 1920

It was Sigurd's turn to suffer from a headache. After rolling in bed for a few hours he broke down and took half a pill, but he kept drifting in and out of consciousness. It seemed that every time he was on the brink of falling asleep his nose would begin to itch or his arm would tingle. The ankle was hurting as well. He counted sheep, recited psalms, but the harder he tried the more agitated he became. All he achieved by taking half a pill was an unpleasant feeling of dizziness.

"You look tired," observed Gunnar over breakfast.

"That's because I am tired. What an observant person you are."

"Are you out of your pills?"

"I'm running out. Isn't it Thursday today? When you see the doctor…"

"Hell no. Never going to go there again."

Sigurd poured himself another coffee, then yawned again, nearly dislocating his jaw. "What if I promise to finish the story today?"

Gunnar scowled. "I can get you to the outskirts of Klettafjörður, then wait there until you return."

"You know I can't walk that far."

"And you know I'm not going there ever again."

"But… you will go to Reykjavík tomorrow?"

"Aye, I will. I'll buy more food, too. I don't think the cleaning woman is coming back. What the hell happened to her?"

"I don't know. Possibly nothing. Your fiancée just wants to take over." Sigurd smiled pleasantly, watching the horror on Gunnar's face. "I'm just joking. Soon you will never have to worry about those women again. Pour yourself a drink, and I'll finish the story."

"This is my last bottle," said Gunnar, and he began to sweat. "I'm not making any more," he said in a strangled voice. "No point. I'm emigrating anyway. So I have to save it for when I need it."

"The… very last one?" It was Sigurd's turn to feel the cold tentacles of fear.

"Aye." The blacksmith sighed heavily, staring at the bottle. Maybe he could have just a tiny bit with coffee…

## *Then*

As weeks passed, things seemed to calm down. Another scandal broke, diverting people's attention. Apparently the bishop, the same one who was so kind towards Ingvar, couldn't keep his hands off little boys and, despite his threats of eternal damnation, one of them finally complained to his parents. Our pastor wasn't so bad after all, muttered the villagers. Elín, holding on to Hannes protectively, demanded that her husband apologise to Ingvar. The trickle of visitors started again, and most of them brought something nice, smiling apologetically. The fundraiser ladies hadn't returned, but Ingvar wasn't too troubled by that. Juana became a fact of life. She was there, nobody was harmed by her presence, and it wasn't like the other inhabitants of the village were examples of moral purity. After a heated discussion at the inn it was decided that everything was Arnar's fault.

Even Katrín found herself on the brink of apologising to Ingvar, maybe even Juana, as long as the pastor would agree to take her back. Now that she no longer worked for him it felt like the only things surrounding her were sisters that needed to be kept in check – and fish, so much fish. Gutting fish, beheading fish, drying fish, cooking fish, preserving fish in salt. She longed for the days when her day started with opening the pastor's post. Juana was frail and old, she thought. Twenty-something, perhaps even thirty? She might die soon and then Katrín would be around to soothe Ingvar's nerves. She was still too young to marry anyway and who knew what would happen in a few years... Magnús gave her his permission to ask the pastor for her old job back. Katrín immediately boasted about it to her younger sister, Jórunn, who was only getting on her nerves more as time had passed.

Jórunn's job was collecting driftwood from the shore. That was real work. She was being productive, muttered Jórunn to herself, pretending she wasn't envious. Who would have wanted to return to work for the sinful pastor? She was staying true to God, helping the household... She cursed when a splinter embedded itself in her finger. She dropped the wood and tried to pick the splinter out with her bitten fingernails, then with her teeth. Of course Katrín never had to deal with anything like that... From the corner of her eye Jórunn noticed a particularly thick piece of wood. It was as thick as a man's arm. It *was* a man's arm.

Splinter forgotten, Jórunn took a step closer, wondering who could have been drunk enough to fall asleep on the beach. Tsk-tsking in disapproval, she bent to take a closer look at the man's face. Driftwood scattered as she ran back home, screaming, barely taking breaks to breathe.

Katrín sat outside, half-covered in fish guts, murmuring to herself under her breath. Tomorrow couldn't come soon enough. Her pride took second place to her hatred of fish. As she decided to take a long bath in a hot spring before visiting Ingvar, hoping to get rid of the smell, she heard some sort of terrible racket and raised her eyes, only to see her own sister.

"He's there," cried Jórunn. "He's there!"

"Who?" asked Katrín to no avail. Jórunn sobbed hysterically, pointing toward the shore, repeating "he's there". Katrín clucked her tongue, pretending to be irritated, quietly grateful for a break. "Come with me," she said, "show me what it is." But Jórunn just cried louder, ran inside and slammed the door.

Katrín considered herself an adult, but still felt a pang of fear. She'd never seen Jórunn behave like that before. What in the name of God could it have been? She strode towards the shore. A few minutes later she was running towards the inn, holding on to her stomach, trying not to throw up.

"If it's really Arnar," grumbled Guðrún, "he can wait. He probably fell from the cliff and broke his neck. Drunk as a skunk..."

"No," gasped green-faced Katrín. "He really didn't." She wanted her father to hold her, assure her that everything was going to be well, that she wouldn't spend the rest of her life with that image embedded under her eyelids haunting her every night. Because Arnar didn't just fall from the cliff.

"Good for nothing," muttered Guðrún, walking briskly towards the shore, Katrín a few steps behind. "If it's really him, I can't say I'm–" She sucked her breath in sharply between her teeth. "Oh, Ingvar... what have you done? Katrín," she commanded, "go get every adult you can find. Except Ingvar and Juana. Everyone needs to see this."

There was nothing left of the face. Someone must have sat on Arnar's chest, repeatedly hitting him with the bloodied rock that laid next to the body. Guðrún looked around, but any traces had been washed away by the ocean's ebbs and flows. It was an exceptionally beautiful day. Birds sang, the breeze whispered, the waves peacefully washed the shore... and Arnar's booted feet. Guðrún forced herself to look down again, avoiding looking at the gaping hole that used to be his face. Something on his hand caught her attention. Guðrún knelt next to the body and tried to remove the ring from the corpse's finger. She had seen this ring many times before. It was made of two sorts of gold, and the large jewel shone in the pale sunshine. The jewel was the same colour as blood.

"Jesus Christ," said Niels behind her, and Guðrún jumped up with a shriek, the sudden pull leaving the ring in her hand. "That is the worst way to die I've ever seen. Someone must have really hated him."

"You think?" asked Guðrún sarcastically. "Who else is in the village?"

"Me," said Niels proudly. "Bjarni should be back in the evening, I think. Magnús, too. Fríða and Sigurveig are away. I don't know, Ásgeir? Haven't seen him for a while."

"He's gone with Bjarni," said Guðrún. "If Bjarni comes back, so will Ásgeir. Trust me on that." She took one last quick look at Arnar's body. "I can't believe this. Of course Ingvar wanted him dead, but this…? Looks like his neck is broken. I'd say he was pushed off the cliff first, before… before *this*."

"Coward's way," said Niels dismissively as they were walking back. "A real man would have had a proper fight."

"Can you imagine Ingvar in a fight with Arnar?"

"It's not about imagining, it's about honour!"

"I don't think Ingvar has much honour left," said Guðrún. "This has gone way too far. Ah, there you are, Katrín. Come with me. We need to talk about this."

"What about me?"

"You go home and nurse whichever body part is making it impossible for you to work this time," barked the innkeeper. "Meet us at Bjarni's when it gets dark. His brothers, his responsibility."

"I refuse to have anything to do with this," huffed Bjarni a few hours later. "I don't know anything, and I don't want to know anything."

"Why don't we light some torches," said Guðrún, "and walk to the shore so you can see it yourself? You might change your mind."

"I've made up my mind."

"I'm not going there," said Magnús. "And neither will any of my girls." He awkwardly patted Katrín's head the same way Ingvar used to do, and she winced.

"You mean you're not going to the shore or to the church?"

"Anywhere. Bjarni, it is your responsibility. They are your brothers."

"We told him to send her away," whined Katrín. "It's her fault. She forced herself upon him. She seduced him. Then she made him kill his own brother."

"Nonsense," said Guðrún. "She's just a—"

"Remember the witch?" interrupted Niels. "When the accident happened? We could…"

226

Bjarni's face reddened. "We will not set fire to the church. Are you insane? It's a *church*, no matter who the pastor is! If anybody cursed it, it must have been Ingvar. We all were wrong about him. I should have told you what he said to me when he first saw me."

"What was it?" asked Guðrún, missing the fact that the problems with the church started when Ingvar was still living in Copenhagen.

"Eh," muttered Bjarni. "He called me his good– never mind. We have no proof. All we know is that Arnar is dead. Anybody could have killed him."

"Who?" huffed Magnús. "Name one person that benefits from his death. One person other than Juana and Ingvar."

"Katrín," said Ásgeir.

"Sit down, Magnús," barked Guðrún. "Katrín, go home. It's too late for you anyway."

"But I have to know!"

"No, you don't. You've got your sisters to take care of."

"She's my daughter," snapped Magnús, and slammed his fist on the table. "You don't have the right to tell her what to do!"

"Haven't we had enough fights?" asked Bjarni, and silence returned to the room.

"Good," said Katrín, offended. "Let me just remind you that we have the proof. Guðrún found that ring. Goodnight."

Guðrún reluctantly placed the ring on the table, and everyone stared at it. There was only one like it in the world.

"That's still no proof," muttered Bjarni.

"It's clear," said Niels. "He showed up at the church. Then Ingvar threatened him and chased him to the shore…"

Magnús chortled.

"What? It could have happened!"

"Niels, why don't you go home as well? Your arm, ankle, or whatever it is this time surely needs rest," said Guðrún. "Leave us grown-ups to talk."

"Good," said Niels, offended. "Let me just remind you that Juana inherits everything, and Ingvar can marry her any time now. Goodnight."

The remaining four stared at each other until Guðrún interrupted the silence. "Go talk to Ingvar, Bjarni. Give him one last chance to explain himself. And if the explanation isn't really good, we're going to report him as fast as possible, before someone else dies."

"She has to leave," muttered Magnús. "They both do."

"I don't believe Juana had anything to do with this," said Guðrún. "I don't think she could even lift this rock."

"Maybe she held him at gunpoint..."

"Even you can't believe that," huffed Bjarni. "Arnar would kill her before she figured out which end of a shotgun is which."

"What I think," said Magnús, patting his pockets in search of his pipe, "is that this church needs to be consecrated again. We'll get the bishop–no, not the bishop. Reverend Kristófer, if need be." He frowned. "But Ingvar needs to leave first. And so does she. Nobody else is going to die, and I am not helping to build yet another church."

"Maybe I will go tomorrow," said Bjarni.

"You will go now. The body is still... fresh. Drag him there if need be."

"I'll come with you," said Magnús.

"No," said Bjarni. "If I must go, I will go alone. Guðrún is right. It's up to me. You go and check on Nilli, I don't trust him not to get overenthusiastic with a torch."

"To think," said Guðrún amused, "that there were *two* evil twins, not one, and we never knew that. Bjarni?"

"Aye?"

"Take the ring," she said. *Juana inherits everything*, she thought as she watched Bjarni departing. Not that it proved anything, as convenient as it seemed to be...

"We know everything," muttered Bjarni to himself, dragging his feet. The church was beautifully lit by the moon, and the closer Bjarni got the slower he walked. "We have proof," he mumbled. "We know everything..." He stood in front of the door, his hand raised, but couldn't convince himself to knock. "We know everything," he said to himself, louder, closing his eyes and slamming his fist on the door until it opened.

"We know everything," he said sharply.

"Bjarni," said Ingvar, already in his nightgown, holding a candle. "Is everything well? Can I help? Come in, I'll make coffee. What is it that you know?"

Bjarni didn't move. "Why did you do this?" he finally asked.

"You mean... coffee?"

"We know everything, and we have proof!"

"Sshh, sshh. No need to raise your voice. Come in and tell me what's going on."

Loud voices from the kitchen woke Juana, who quietly descended down the stairs. She stood in a dark corner, unnoticed, observing the fight.

"No!" yelled Bjarni. "It was not a drunken accident! At least stop smearing his name now that he is dead! It's clear, just admit it. It will be easier for both of us, for all of us."

"I did no such thing! I would never–"

"Ingvar, the proof is right here on the table!"

"That's my ring," said Juana in disbelief, and both men winced, surprised. "I left it behind when I left. Arnar must have taken it."

"He was wearing it as he died," said Bjarni. "Arnar still loved you, Juana. He came here to beg for forgiveness, and he was rewarded with death."

"Arnar… is dead?" Her voice rang with sincere surprise. "What happened? How?"

"The good pastor here murdered him. Arnar came here, Ingvar forced Arnar to go to the cliff, pushed him off, then finished the job with a rock."

"What rock?"

"It's better for you not to see that," said Bjarni. "Tell me, Juana, and speak truthfully. I will know if you are lying. Did you know anything about it?"

Juana slowly shook her head.

"Do you know when Arnar came here?"

"I don't–"

"She doesn't know anything and neither do I," interrupted Ingvar, "because it never happened! How can I make you believe me? What can I do to prove it to you? Tell me!"

"You've done enough. My suggestion is that you pack and depart before the dawn, brother, or you will burn along with the church."

"Isn't it enough that Arnar…?"

"Arnar is dead," repeated Bjarni. "As dead as can be. You wouldn't believe how cruel your beloved pastor was." His voice broke. "We've had enough, Ingvar. Do as you want. Leave, or die. It will be a mysterious fire, like before, probably a candle that fell when you were asleep. We don't want you here anymore. For your own good," Bjarni accented, "it is better if you are gone by dawn. Remind me, who is responsible for this? Ah, that's right, you are. Goodbye, *my good man.*"

He dragged his feet on his way home. He imagined revenge would have tasted sweet, but all he could think of were the two pale, horrified faces staring at him. "Bjarni!" he heard, turning to see Juana running after him. She tripped, and Bjarni grabbed her just in time.

"Juana."

"I had no idea," she whispered. "I… had no idea. You believe me, don't you?"

Bjarni exhaled slowly. "I do," he finally said. "Come with me. You can stay the night, or longer if need be. I will keep you safe from Ingvar." The irony was not lost on either of them.

Magnús waited in front of Bjarni's house. He cast a look at Juana but said nothing. Bjarni nodded stiffly, let Juana inside, then shut the door. "What?" he whispered.

"Did it go well?"

"What's 'well'? He'll be gone by dawn, and if not, we'll report him."

"Did he admit?"

"He did," said Bjarni, averting his gaze. "Even he couldn't deny it."

"What about her?"

"She's innocent. He admitted that much as well. She's in shock. Why are you here?"

"We've got one more job to do. Come."

Guðrún was waiting at the shore, holding a lit torch. Reflections of the flames flickered in the water. "Fill the pockets with rocks," she commanded. "Take his boots off. Get him up to the cliff, as far as you can go."

"We're destroying evidence," muttered Bjarni.

"No," said Guðrún. "We're cleaning up. Nothing ever happened here. We have never seen Arnar return. This village is a peaceful place."

She watched as the body landed in water with a splash, quickly disappearing under the surface. "Nothing wrong ever happened here," she reiterated, talking to herself. "And nothing ever will."

### Now

"And then?" urged Gunnar.

"Then nothing," said Sigurd. "That's it."

"Really?"

"Here's where the story ends."

"But I want to know what happened next," complained the blacksmith. "Where did Juana go? Did Ingvar leave? Why did Bjarni lie to him?"

Sigurd looked at Gunnar dismissively. "Every story has an end, and this is it. You have to make up the rest yourself." He half-smiled. "They all lived happily ever after," he said. "*Þetta reddast*. Mostly. As I said."

Gunnar stood up and stretched his arms, then cracked his knuckles and grinned. "I might find out what happened later, anyway."

"Oh? How so?"

"You see, I bought myself a book, too."

All blood left Sigurd's face as Gunnar presented his purchase. "Þetta Reddast: All Ends Well," he read. "Memoirs of Ingvar Jónsson. Apparently it sells very well. Does it have more chapters than your story? Are there photographs inside?" Gunnar quickly browsed through the book. "Nay," he announced. "Shame. You wrote all this and got an award in America, it says."

Sigurd's lips formed a thin, white line.

"Does it talk about America? I'd like to find out more about America. Might still move there."

"Yes," snapped Sigurd. "It does talk about America."

"And Juana?"

"No," said Sigurd through clenched teeth. "Every story can be told in many ways. Everyone has their own version of the truth, sometimes more than one. Sometimes people lie without even knowing, and sometimes they tell the truth when they should have stayed quiet." He extended his hand, and Gunnar automatically handed him the book. Sigurd clutched it to his chest. "I only want to ask you two more things. Go to Reykjavík and bring me what I need. And don't open this book until I am gone."

"Why not?"

"Because I asked you to. I wouldn't feel good having you here reading it, asking questions. I made a lot of things up when I told you the story. This book… I assure you that whatever answers you're looking for, you won't find them here." Sigurd's headache was drilling into his skull, nausea so strong he felt he could vomit any moment, anger more and more difficult to contain. Of course Gunnar had to find The Book sooner or later when Sigurd kept on sending him to a bookstore.

"Tell you what," said the blacksmith cheerfully. "I'm going to go to Reykjavík now. It's not late. I thought there was more story left. If anybody comes over, I'm not in. I emigrated. Make me a list of all you want, just hurry up. I don't know what time it is."

"Quarter past eleven."

"How do you know that? Thought the clock stopped."

"I… I just watched the sun until noon, and then set it to the correct time. Give me a piece of paper and a pencil. And some coffee." Sigurd lifted himself from the chair and began to stumble towards the room, trying to grind his teeth quietly.

"Hey," called Gunnar. "Don't be upset. I won't touch it until you go. Promise. I can wait a few days. And you're walking better and better each day, aye? I'll make you a nice big fire."

Sigurd rapidly jerked his head, and the hatred in his eyes made Gunnar flinch. He was holding on to the book so hard his knuckles became white. The blacksmith had to remind himself that, without a weapon, Ingvar was more or less harmless, barely able to walk, weak, thin. He found himself oddly afraid to follow Sigurd, who placed himself in the good chair, his face now expressionless, the book in his lap.

The blacksmith handed him a piece of paper and a pencil, then busied himself with the fire. "You can tell me about America," he said when the first flames appeared. "What is it like?"

"There's a lot of America," muttered Sigurd. "I'll tell you when you're back from Reykjavík, or tomorrow."

"What if I promise to read your book quietly and not ask any questions?"

"It would feel too weird. Imagine people coming to your forge, walking around while you're there and commenting on everything, as if they couldn't see you."

"Aye! They do that. All the time. And they ask me the same questions. 'Why is this so expensive' and 'why is it taking so long'. And it's not children that are the worst. It's their fathers. They say, 'I could make this in my sleep', and then I tell them—"

"Here's the list," interrupted Sigurd. "I'm going to have a nap while you're gone. I didn't sleep well last night."

"Pills not working?"

"Just… go already."

"They couldn't even make a nail," muttered Gunnar as he was getting dressed. Ragnar looked at him with sympathy. "They don't know the difference between hardened steel and wrought iron. That's the sort of people I have to deal with, you know?"

The dog didn't respond, but his gaze expressed deepest sympathy.

"Wish me luck," said the blacksmith. He ensured Ragnar had enough water, then left, smiling at the thought of drinking the nice coffee served by the nice waitress. After the door shut, Sigurd waited for a while to make sure Gunnar hadn't forgotten anything. Then he began to tear pages out of the book, crumple them, and throw them into the fire.

Once the stress wore off, tiredness returned, and his eyes began to close involuntarily. Sigurd forced himself to get off the chair, where he was a bit too comfortable by the warm fire, then hobble towards the bed. He fished a little paper bag out from under his pillow, but no matter how many times he checked, there were three and a half pills, and not a tiny bit more. He'd need one to sleep. That left him with two and a half. Sigurd cursed again, wishing he'd remembered to ask the doctor for more. But they were dangerous when mixed with alcohol, and Gunnar only had one bottle left... Sigurd limped towards the kitchen and froze momentarily as he looked at the table. The bottle was no longer full. The blacksmith failed to resist the temptation to refill his flask before leaving. After a moment of stunned silence Sigurd laughed out loud. He no longer had to worry whether Gunnar would be able to drink enough for the poison to work.

Sigurd put one of the pills aside, then ground the rest into powder, which he carefully poured into the bottle. He shook the bottle until the powder completely dissolved. He stared at the last pill, wondering what to do. Gunnar had to die, but Sigurd had to sleep, and this would not be an easy night for him. Unless Gunnar decided to finish off the moonshine tonight, in which case... Sigurd hesitated again. There was no way he could predict the exact timing.

He opened the door and looked doubtfully at the three steps in front of Gunnar's door. The air seemed stale and warm, but random gusts of wind chilled Sigurd to the bone. He was barefoot and stared at his feet as he took uncertain steps. There was no way around it – he couldn't place one of his feet flat on the ground. The ankle was stiff and unwilling to bend as far as he needed it to. Sigurd's only remaining hope was that boots would make it easier. He stood on top of the stairs, wishing there was something he could rest on or hold on to. They were practically two steps, he told himself, if you didn't count the ground... But Sigurd's feet became so cold he retreated back inside, relieved and worried at the same time. Boots would help, he was certain of that. Until then there was no point in abusing his poor ankle without a need.

Eighteen days he'd spent here, eighteen long days. Sigurd no longer felt tired or sleepy. Energy and excitement filled his veins. He was ready.

# Friday, March 26, 1920

"I'm done with drinking," announced Gunnar over breakfast, and Sigurd froze. But the blacksmith's eyes kept returning to the bottle until he finally put it away in a cupboard. "There," he announced. "Out of sight, out of mind." But now his gaze kept escaping towards the cupboard. Sigurd's stiff shoulders relaxed a bit. Had Gunnar poured his medicine into the sink, the plan would have been ruined.

According to the clock in the kitchen it was a few minutes past four, which meant it hadn't been wound. Sigurd rolled his eyes, then washed himself as well as he could under Gunnar's curious stare. With great relief he started to shave off his awful beard. "Don't you want to shave as well?" he asked. "Your beard is growing back."

"Nay. I had enough people tell me I look just like my father. You're bleeding."

Sigurd turned, half of his face still covered in soap. "It's just a cut. You don't know how to shave, do you?"

"I don't need to know."

"You should shave before you leave. You're going to attract attention if you don't. Try to blend a bit."

"I'll go to the barber in Reykjavík," muttered Gunnar. "The nice girl wasn't at the inn yesterday."

"Ah," said Sigurd politely. "Wasn't she now." *Why don't you have a drink? You could, you should have a drink…* "You know," he said as an idea appeared in his head, "why don't I shave you now? Just sit here on the chair…" A sharp blade, an exposed throat…

"Nay. You're leaving in a few days. Maybe then. I'd like to hear more about America."

"Sure," said Sigurd, returning to shaving. "Pour yourself a drink and I'll tell you all you need to know."

"I don't want to drink," said Gunnar. He put his hands in his lap, trying and failing to stop them from trembling.

"It's easier if you finish it all," encouraged Sigurd. "I'll tell you what, I know how it is. Just finish it, throw the bottle away, then you're done and you can't go back to it. You didn't make a new batch, is that right? So no more for you ever again?"

"N-nay. I might… maybe I should have, but, but I am… leaving soon."

"Up to you. You get to decide everything now. Unless of course the Conservative Women of Iceland come over," said Sigurd mercilessly. "Or Brynhildur. Or the doctor, just to check how you're doing. Or even the pastor. You know they have great hopes for you, and they haven't been around for a few days. They're planning something, don't you think?" He washed his face, dried it with a real towel, then used Gunnar's cologne. It stung in a pleasantly familiar way, and Sigurd sighed in pleasure. It was the first time in weeks he felt truly human.

"First you don't like me drinking," muttered Gunnar, "now you want me to. But… you're right." He took out the bottle and looked at it doubtfully. "It's not much, even," he said as if to himself. "Just half. I think this bottle is smaller than the others, too. Hell and all devils! It's bloody bitter!"

"Add it to coffee," said Sigurd. Now he was trying and failing to stop his own voice and hands from trembling. "Add sugar. Just drink it, so it's gone. It might help with your back as well. How is your back today?"

"Quite good," muttered Gunnar. Sigurd stared at his hands as Gunnar added a generous portion of moonshine to his coffee. "Think I should be able to work again soon. Just not lift the anvil."

Sigurd was too busy watching the mug travelling towards Gunnar's mouth to notice the last sentence. "No need to worry about work. You will be free from all this very soon." He paused. Gunnar only sipped a tiny bit. "You know, you can still decide to go on with Brynhildur's plan. It *might* work out fine in the end. She talks a lot, true, but you will be the man of the house." Gunnar took a gulp from the mug. "She'll put you back on track, give you beautiful children. She will be just like your mother…" Gunnar emptied the mug and reached for the bottle, his face blank. "Of course she won't be, my apologies. Your mother was special. So was your father. But imagine how much love you're going to give and receive," Sigurd blabbed. Gunnar's shoulders were slightly shaking. "God will take you into His arms. You will be a respectable member of society. Everyone will want to spend time with you. You'll go to the theatre, visit people every week, Brynhildur will introduce you…"

"Stop," wheezed Gunnar. "Stop." The blacksmith's hands were shaking so badly now that some of the liquid splashed on the table, and Sigurd let out an involuntary nervous gasp. Gunnar remedied the problem by emptying the mug in one go. The bottle was almost empty.

The blacksmith greedily sucked out every last drop, no longer complaining about the bitter taste, then returned the bottle to the table. It fell, and Gunnar's brows furrowed.

"You can be happy if you decide to be," continued Sigurd, so tense his entire body was rigid, voice throttled. *Die. Please. How long does this take?!* "If you let Brynhildur and the hags do what they want to do, you'll be able to stay here. No need to go anywhere, no need to continue forging, since you're rich now. Brynhildur will renovate the whole house, make sure everything looks good…"

"I don't need any rev– renove– I don't feel so well–" Gunnar tried to reach for the coffee pot, but his hand missed. "Do you th-think moonshine can spoil?"

A wave of relief washed over Sigurd. *It was working!*

Ragnar's eyes opened.

"Just going to brush my teeth," said Sigurd, turning away from Gunnar.

"I need to… care of… Karl," said the blacksmith. His voice sounded gruff and raspy, and he cleared his throat, then tried to spit on the floor, almost falling together with the chair. He leaned heavily against the table. "I think I'm– I've got your infection… but no drink anom– any– I will recov… my cond'tion…"

"Of course," Sigurd said, buttoning his shirt, noticing with satisfaction that his hands were no longer shaking, as if Gunnar's medicinal alcohol had calmed him down instead. He heard a loud thud and turned to see what had happened. Gunnar lay on his side, rubbing his eyes, trying to sit. Ragnar approached his master carefully, tilting his head. "C-m-here… boy," said Gunnar, looking around in confusion, blinking. "Rg– where are you? Can't see… Grendel," he spat out, "Grendel!"

Sigurd was too mesmerised with the shotgun on the wall to wonder why on Earth Gunnar would be quoting *Beowulf*. "Lie down," he said absent-mindedly. He was so used to the sight of the shotgun he had stopped noticing it. A grin slowly appeared on his face.

Gunnar gave up his attempts to sit up and fell to his side. Ragnar started to bark, poking his master's face with his muzzle. "M'st…" muttered the blacksmith. "Hell… devils… call… doct'r…"

"You don't have a telephone," Sigurd pointed out politely. "But I will greet him if I bump into him. Any last words?"

Gunnar's mouth opened, but no sound came out, and then he finally stopped moving. Ragnar became hysterical, whining, barking, pushing his muzzle into Gunnar's face, licking his cheeks, whimpering. Holding on to the chair, Sigurd carefully knelt next to the blacksmith, pulling at his shoulder until the body faced the ceiling. The open eyes didn't move or blink. "Gunnar?" he called, pushing Ragnar away. He slapped the blacksmith as hard as he could. "Gunnar! Wake up!"

Ragnar sat down and howled loudly, then moved a pleading gaze to Sigurd and barked questioningly.

"Shut up," answered Sigurd, pulling on his boots. The dog returned to licking Gunnar's face, barking, howling, crying. The boots were tight and seemed to help Sigurd's ankle a bit, but not enough. Ragnar continued making noise. "I'd kick you if I could," barked Sigurd, looking around for something that could serve as a cane. His gaze landed on the shotgun.

Excitement buzzed in his veins as he examined the shotgun curiously. Sigurd had never used a shotgun in his life, but he had experience with revolvers. The thing was double-barrelled, which meant he'd have two shots – just enough, especially as he also had Gunnar's butcher's knife. Sigurd laughed to himself, a slightly hysterical, high-pitched laugh, then aimed at the dog, carefully setting a finger on one of the two triggers. It was difficult to keep the shotgun still, as it was heavy and he was weak after spending so much time in bed. It would be a good idea to eat breakfast, but Sigurd couldn't imagine sitting by the table and eating in the company of a dead blacksmith and a howling dog. There would certainly be something in the pantry that he could help himself to.

Ragnar's laments were working his last nerve, and Sigurd was no longer able to take things slowly. He tried to place the shotgun in the backpack, but the damned thing was too long for that, and half of it stuck out. He limped outside, briefly worried that the dog would attempt to attack him, but Ragnar was busy and didn't even notice when the door closed behind Sigurd.

It was time to finally brave the treacherous steps. What kind of blacksmith neglects forging a rail for himself? After consideration, he sat down, removed the shotgun from his backpack, and carefully descended the steps using it as a cane. It worked surprisingly well. "Thank you, God," said Sigurd, raising his head to the sky, ignoring the howls and cries he could still hear through the door. He began to hobble further. It was time to get acquainted with Karl.

The stable, like the rest of Gunnar's house, was clean, neat, and sparse. The horse barely looked at him, uninterested, chewing on some fodder. "Hello," said Sigurd. "Good girl." He reached to pull at the harness, then realised it wasn't on. He looked around and with a sinking feeling realised there was no saddle either. Apparently Gunnar rode bareback. But Sigurd knew that Karl was capable of getting to Klettafjörður without any steering. He just had to get her out of the stable, then mount her. The rest should be easy.

Unfortunately, the mare was not interested in leaving the stable, still waiting for her breakfast and ablutions. Sigurd's heart was beating so fast he could feel the blood pumping through his veins. The stable wasn't tall enough for him to get on the horse. She had to come out. After some patting, pulling, pushing, and attempts to sound pleasant whilst simultaneously grinding his teeth, Sigurd managed to get Karl out of the stable. He was already tired, his foot already hurt, and the hard part was still in front of him.

The first attempt to mount the horse using the shotgun as a cane resulted in Sigurd falling into the mud. He placed the shotgun in the backpack again. When he almost managed to get on horseback, cursing the lack of a saddle, the shotgun fell out of the backpack. It took five attempts, after which Sigurd felt almost as weak, sore, and hot as on his first day here. Karl remained placid, used to drunken Gunnar doing pretty much the same thing.

"We're going to Klettafjörður," announced Sigurd. He didn't know how to steer her without the reins. He gave Karl a very gentle slap on the backside. "You know where that is. To the left. We're going to visit old friends." To his enormous relief, the horse started moving slowly. Sigurd didn't turn to take one last look at the place that had been his prison for almost three weeks. In his head, he was already rehearsing the next part.

Inside the house a somewhat desperate elf kept attempting to get a hysterical dog to cooperate. "Ragnar! Listen to me!"

The dog whimpered and took a step back, staring at the bearded creature.

"You have to make your dad throw up," explained the elf.

Ragnar tilted his head questioningly.

"Hit him in the belly. Or stick something down his throat?"

Ragnar tilted his head further, eager to do the right thing once he figured out what it was.

"Like this," said the elf, then tried to push Gunnar's body. His hands went through and emerged from Gunnar's chest, which immediately threw the dog into terrified hysterics. "Not me!" shouted Grendel. "I'm bloody incorporeal! You have to do it!" He withdrew his hands, and Ragnar switched to a deep growl complete with focused, distrustful glare.

"Damn you, dog! Listen to me! Come here…" Grendel scratched his beard, then beamed up. He disappeared, only to immediately appear behind Ragnar, screaming "AAAHH!!!" With a terrified yelp, Ragnar jumped over his master's body and continued to growl, now from the other side of Gunnar's body.

"Idiot," snapped the elf. "Look! I am going to kick him! Really hard! It will hurt!" He raised his booted foot menacingly and the dog lost it. His furious attack resulted in nothing, because Grendel was already elsewhere.

"We don't have time to dance! Lick him, I don't care, make him throw up! Or… I will kick him in the kidneys! Do you know how bad that hurts? Go on! Attack me!" He assessed Ragnar's position. The dog was clearly prepared to leap, which wouldn't help. "Dumb creature," barked the elf, then squatted. "*Now* I am going to kick him," he announced. "It will be difficult, but I am very, very angry! Do you understand? Bite me!"

As Ragnar leapt over Gunnar's body again, tightening his jaws over thin air, Grendel reappeared on the other side.

"You," he said accusingly, pointing his finger, "are the most useless dog that ever lived. Go get the doctor!" But the door was closed, Grendel couldn't open it, and neither could the dog. With a deep sigh, the elf sat on the floor, cross-legged, staring at Ragnar. Neither of them blinked. Both startled when a gurgle came from somewhere deep inside Gunnar's stomach.

"Too late," groaned the elf, but a split second later the blacksmith's body straightened, then bent in a spasm, as though touched by an electric wire. As Gunnar's body curled on the floor, a loud burp was followed by a retch, then a small amount of vomit spilled from his mouth, followed by more and more.

"Well done," said Grendel to the dog with a hefty dose of sarcasm, then disappeared, leaving Ragnar on the brink of a nervous breakdown. Another cramp struck, and Gunnar retched again, his hands convulsively grabbing his stomach and twisting in an attempt to push out its poisonous contents, adding more and more to the disgusting puddle.

"Si–" the blacksmith managed before another retch filled his mouth with bitter bile. His body didn't listen to commands, jerking around on its own. Disgusting, acidic bile poured out of Gunnar's mouth as he coughed and coughed, trying to turn onto his back. His eyes opened, bulging out, and everything around him was dancing, making him sick again.

Gunnar begged God to spare him, promising he would never even look at alcohol again, he would marry Brynhildur, get confirmed, baptised, crucified if need be, if only God saw it fit to keep him alive. Another shiver, less brutal than before, went through his body, but nothing more came out, only a loud burp. His stomach felt as if someone had put him under a power hammer. Gunnar was cold, sweaty, some of the vomit was glued to his face, and nausea-inducing snowflakes danced ruthlessly in his vision, even with his eyes closed.

"I'm dying," he mumbled through half-glued lips. The darkness finally got its wish. But... the darkness was not here. Doctor Brynjólf's words came back to him, in short, disconnected phrases: liver failure, alcoholic, keep your posture, straight back, incontinence, memory problems... vomiting. Gunnar groaned when another spasm bent him, sending his head back into the disgusting puddle. *Sigurd*, he thought. Sigurd would bring the doctor over, he had to...

The darkness often came up with various suggestions regarding his death. An accident at the forge. Being crushed by a large piece he was working on. Breaking a leg somewhere far away where nobody would find him. Falling off the treacherous cliff that Sigurd somehow managed to scale. Sometimes Gunnar found himself nodding in agreement, only wishing for his death to be immediate, unlike this torture that seemed to last forever. "Sigurd," he whispered, his tongue stiff, mouth sticky. "Help." He was drifting into sleep, warm, inviting sleep, but somehow he knew that if he were to fall asleep, he would never wake up. *Doctor Brynjólf was right*, he thought. *Drinking is going to kill me. It's killing me* right now... Another violent cramp followed by a hammer striking his skull wiped out his thoughts. The blanket in the corner was shivering and whining.

Gunnar had thrown up from drinking many more times than he would have liked to admit. However, this taste was different, metallic, bitter, even worse than the breath mints – like poison, he thought. Yet after all the times when the darkness told him death was the only way out, after all the times he obediently agreed, right now every part of Gunnar wanted nothing more than to stay alive. To breathe, to drink – not the medi– the *alcohol*, never again! Water, coffee, anything that could flush this taste from his mouth. He wanted to stand up, but couldn't even move, crushed by the invisible weight, heavier than anything the darkness had ever subjected him to. It took superhuman effort for him to move his fingers, and something about wiggling toes wandered through his mind. "Si–" Gunnar tried again, then coughed and bit his own tongue. "Sigurd," he mumbled. His lips felt strange, both numb and sore as if they had been used as a pin cushion. "Where are you?"

At this particular moment Sigurd was busy trying to contain the horse. Karl was content to walk at pretty much the same speed Sigurd would have achieved if his ankle wasn't hurt. Every now and then the mare, who didn't get her breakfast, stopped to graze on whatever she could find. Then she found a puddle of water and stopped so abruptly Sigurd almost fell off. "Curse you," he yelled. Karl ignored him until she felt suitably refreshed, then resumed her lazy stroll. Sigurd simultaneously wanted the horse to hurry up and felt terrified of falling off Karl's back if she decided to trot more energetically. He tried to kick the mare's sides, and a white flash of pain exploded in his ankle. Karl didn't seem to notice.

It was too cloudy for Sigurd to assess the time. His thoughts were at fever pitch. The shotgun in the backpack kept pulling him to one side, and Sigurd couldn't stop worrying that it would fall out. "Move," he shouted, powerless, "hurry up!" In response Karl slowed down even more before wandering towards another patch of grass. Sigurd cursed furiously. With a normal, saddled horse he would have reached Klettafjörður within fifteen minutes. All he could hope for with Karl was that the mare would remember where they were heading. At this pace it could take hours until they got to town, and when, or rather if they got there at all, Sigurd would have to find a solution for another problem. He had the addresses, but no clue how to find them. Back in his time Klettafjörður didn't have street names, because there were no streets. "Hurry up!" he yelled, tightening his knees. "Leave that grass alone! Klettafjörður! Go!" He looked up and froze, his hands convulsively grabbing Karl's mane. Someone was approaching from the opposite direction. The rider could only have been heading towards the forge.

Not so far away, Gunnar lifted himself up using a table leg as a prop. He was now standing, breathing heavily, leaning on his fists, but the movement cost him all the energy he had, and everything began to spin again. The sink was close, yet too far for him to reach. The blacksmith was now discovering whole new sorts of physical pain he'd never been subjected to before. A drink would help, he thought momentarily, and his stomach reacted with another spasm, nearly sending him back to the floor. Goddamn Sigurd must have picked this exact time to go for a walk, he realised.

The sink was just a few steps away, but first the room had to stop spinning. Ragnar alternated between joyfully dancing around Gunnar and furiously barking at the door, contributing to Gunnar's headache. The blacksmith looked around, trying to focus his gaze. Something was missing, but he couldn't tell what. Sigurd's coat was gone – understandable, since he went for a walk. What else? The blacksmith blinked a few more times, wondering if he was seeing things, or rather not seeing them… The shotgun. The shotgun was missing.

"Find Sigurd," Gunnar said to the dog. "Get that bastard over here…" His raspy voice died. Sigurd had taken the shotgun and left. Gunnar had already drunk from this bottle before and there had been nothing wrong with the taste… The pills were very dangerous when mixed with alcohol…

White-hot fury helped him get to the sink, wash his face, greedily drink water, hobble a bit, rest his hand inadvertently on top of the stove that – mercifully – was barely warm by now, then stumble towards the room. He grabbed the new curtain for balance, and tore it off the doorframe, dropping to his knees. Even from here he could see the backpack was gone as well as Sigurd. Or, rather, Ingvar.

Gunnar needed to get to town and warn… someone. Doctor Brynjólf! It shouldn't be too difficult. He just needed to get to the stable, get on the horse and let Karl carry him as she always had. Everyone around Gunnar lied to him, used and abused him, tried to force him to do things he didn't want to do, attempted to kill or marry him. But Ragnar and Karl never failed him, not even once, loving him exactly the way he was, the same as he loved them.

The blacksmith tried to lift himself back to his feet, but instead fell to the ground with a groan, hitting his elbow painfully. His face landed on the soft fabric of the curtain. He was so exhausted now. He would only rest a minute, definitely not longer than that…

Gunnar's breath slowed. A little bubble appeared on his lips. A few minutes later someone began to shout outside, joined by Ragnar's furious yapping. But Gunnar's eyes remained shut, and the bubble in the corner of his mouth stayed exactly as it was.

"Let me… no," muttered Brynhildur to herself as she neared the forge. "My dear Gunnar," she said in a different tone, then took a cursory glance at a man approaching from the opposite direction. Too old, she decided. She sent him a sour smile, then returned to the task at hand without paying any attention to the man's pale face or the vaguely familiar horse. She pulled the reins and Stjarna slowed down. Brynhildur needed a bit more time. "Sweet Gunnar," she muttered, staring into space, thinking. "Why don't we…"

Anna might have thought her daughter would give up, too afraid of being thrown out of the house, but Brynhildur wasn't going to spend the rest of her life serving her mother and watching new wrinkles appear in the mirror. She *was* going to get married, move out, have a house and family of her own, and if Mother thought she could do anything about it, she clearly didn't know her own daughter very well.

Brynhildur's plan was simple and foolproof. All she needed to do was seduce the blacksmith, then explain to him that now she was pregnant with his child and he had no choice other than to become a respectable Christian and marry her. But Brynhildur had never actually seduced anyone before, and she was nervous. Should she seduce him first and then explain his situation, or the other way round? "Let us… warm ourselves," she purred to herself, "my dear Gunnar. Why don't I – we – do something nice… no, no! Why don't we go, and I'll show you… no, good God!" *The Women's Paper* had absolutely nothing to say on the subject. Brynhildur ground her teeth in frustration, then decided to cease rehearsing and improvise instead.

She could already see Gunnar's dwelling, and couldn't stop her displeased grimace. In the full light of day it couldn't be denied that this place needed a lot of work. Gunnar had to tell her how much money she– *they* had at their disposal. Ah! Gunnar would soon be locked in Brynjólf's guest room for a month! That would give Brynhildur more than enough time to start redecorating, as long as she got her hands on the money first. Gunnar would have no choice but to accept the changes. And things were going well, Brynhildur cheered herself up, he was already starting to look acceptable, even handsome – exactly like his father, but without the bad bits, once Brynjólf would cure his alcoholism.

Before she began envisioning the new dwelling, she had to remind herself that the conception had to come first. All she had to do was sleep with him one time, despite the smell and the dirt under his fingernails. Once she told Anna that she was pregnant and the wedding had to take place as quickly as possible, everything would be settled. Brynhildur's foxy smile brightened her face. Blackmail, tenderness, accidental nudity, even tears if necessary. Gunnar was hers whether he wanted to be or not.

Brynhildur led Stjarna to the stable and noticed something unsettling. Karl was gone. *Now* was when Gunnar chose to go on a trek…? Where the hell did he go? Definitely not to Klettafjörður, as they would have met on the way. She had only seen some old man. Brynhildur pulled Stjarna out of the stable again, then briskly walked towards Gunnar's door.

"Gunnar!" she shouted, frustrated, but all she heard in return was the stupid dog's barking. Her hand, already on the handle, withdrew. The blacksmith clearly wasn't home, but his dirty mutt was, and right now sounded like a whole horde of hungry rabid dogs. "Shut up!" she yelled. "You go first! He is mine, this place is mine, get used to it!" The dog's relentless racket continued, and Brynhildur lost the remains of her composure. "You have no choice!!!" she screamed as loudly as she could, then gave the door a kick and yelped in pain – her tall boots were soft, warm, and completely unsuitable for kicking things. But the door opened a bit, and Brynhildur almost managed to stick her head in before massive jaws filled with what looked like hundreds of sharp teeth flew towards her face. She gasped and pulled the door closed again just in time to hear the thud of Ragnar's body hitting it.

Brynhildur was breathing heavily, her knees were so soft she could barely stand, and her toes hurt. That beast wouldn't just get thrown out. It would get shot. By her.

Gunnar's eyes opened rapidly just in time to hear a furious "I'll be back!" loud enough to drown out Ragnar's hysteria.

Karl and Sigurd were definitely not headed towards Klettafjörður anymore. The mare seemed to be going towards the mountains, further and further away from the shore, grazing on patches of grey grass. Sigurd, stressed beyond imagination, lost any patience he still had. "Go back!" he shouted and slapped the horse's backside as hard as he could.

A second later Sigurd's body hit the ground. The shock was greater than the pain, and instead of screaming he only let out a little surprised yelp. Karl didn't even bother to give him a scornful look. She just continued her stroll, now free from the deadweight that dared to raise its hand at her.

"Karl!" yelled Sigurd. "Come back! I'm sorry! Good girl!" As he helplessly watched the horse slowly departing, something inside him snapped. Sigurd started screaming – at Karl, at the sky, at God who was playing with him so mercilessly, at everything around him. He only stopped when his throat grew sore and he realised that he was so thrilled to finally leave the suffocating walls of Gunnar's dwelling that he'd forgotten about provisions. Sigurd was now lost in the middle of nowhere, hungry, thirsty, equipped with a backpack containing only a butcher's knife, a shotgun, and The Book. He started to weep in frustration, wishing the infection had killed him.

There was a puddle near him and Sigurd crawled towards it on all fours, then drank a few sips of dirty water. He spat out some sand and mud. That bloody rat of a horse! It was the horse's fault, and Gunnar's, and...

And then the unthinkable happened.

"You were very lucky," said the doctor, as Sigurd carefully placed himself in the passenger seat of the car. "I've made the silliest mistake. I had the address, I had the name, but either the name or the address was wrong. That's what happens when I make the notes myself... Please, don't tell my wife, let this be our little secret. Good God, I should go to the other address, but I don't have it, where was my note... Erm, do you mind reminding me what your name was...?"

"Sigurd. Thank you so much for the rescue. Gunnar disappointed me so much. He found out that you and I have been talking, I don't know how he figured it out. He threw me out of the house, then left. I barely had time to grab my backpack, he didn't give me any food or—"

"And the shotgun?"

"I, er, didn't know where my crutches were, so I grabbed it from the wall at the very last moment. It's broken anyway, he told me. I'm just using it as a cane."

"How very unfortunate," said the doctor, sighing. "I can't believe he'd treat his own family member like that. I've always thought..."

"He's done this before, when Theodór came to help him after his father died. He wouldn't have any of that. He set the dogs on Theodór."

"Theodór..." muttered the doctor. "Theodór..."

"His uncle," helped Sigurd.

"Ah! Of course. I remembered that. And you are Theodór's..."

Sigurd paled. He didn't bother remembering the lie he told the doctor earlier. Was he a brother, or a son-in-law... How old could Theodór even be...? "I'm..." he started, and suddenly remembered whom he was talking to. "I'm his brother, of course," he said with a big grin, barely stopping himself from adding "twin".

"Ah," said the doctor. "Of course! I remember. Do you have any idea where Gunnar could have gone? Did he take the dog along?"

"No," improvised Sigurd wildly, "I mean, yes, he did, I suppose! You know Karl, the horse – she's very slow." His hands curled into fists for a moment, but his voice remained calm. "The dog probably just followed. Gunnar would never leave Ragnar behind. His own blood relative, sure. But the dog? Not a chance."

"Oh yes. That reminds me again. I've been wondering... You said you just came from America, and Sigurd is such an unusual name. So why would Theodór send his brother, of all people..."

Sigurd cleared his throat aloud. "This is a very nice car."

"Oh, thank you! Most people have no appreciation for them. Have you ever been in a car?"

"Yes, but I've never driven one. It seems very complicated to me. Is it safe?"

"That depends on the weather. The moment it gets slippery, especially when it's black ice, it becomes dangerous. So, I'm mostly driving very slowly, unless there is an emergency..." The doctor's voice died. "Oh no, I remember. I was supposed to see Katrín. Or maybe Halldóra. They're sisters and live together, so it's not a problem, I swear I had the address somewhere..."

"Halldóra is Gunnar's cleaning woman, is that right? Whatever happened to her?"

The doctor half-smiled. "Oh, poor girl. She's practically brain-dead, but harmless, as far as I can tell. I'm writing a paper on her, she's a very interesting subject. That reminds me... you didn't, by any chance, take too many sleeping pills?"

"Of course not," Sigurd assured him. "But I noticed that I can't sleep without one."

"Hmmm... I hope you will be able to regain your regular sleep again."

"You *hope*?"

Brynjólf frowned. "I must admit – please don't take this the wrong way – I haven't prescribed them to anyone before. I was worried that, ah, if someone here at Klettafjörður..."

"I understand," said Sigurd cheerfully. "It was easier to start with an outsider. You said they were dangerous, especially with alcohol, so I was very careful to only take one every night."

"Oh, I'm... almost certain they wouldn't have killed you. It's just that mixed with alcohol they can cause vomiting, and since they put you into such a deep sleep, you might suffocate on your own vomit. That would be a horrible way to die, right?"

Sigurd's heart was beating very fast and had somehow elevated itself to block his throat. "Right, and, say, um, if someone took two or three, just by accident…?"

"I am sure," said Brynjólf carefully, "that nothing really bad would happen. The person would probably simply sleep for forty-eight hours or longer."

Sigurd exhaled slowly, counting to ten forwards and backwards in his head. Forty-eight hours would be more than enough. "Good to know," he said, then began to worry again. They were now driving through what was probably the outskirts of Klettafjörður. Nothing seemed like he remembered it.

"Is the inn still somewhere here?" he asked. "Guðrún's old inn?"

"Oh no, she sold it right before prohibition started. You can say many things about my mother-in-law," Brynjólf said, missing his passenger's sharp intake of breath, "but she definitely isn't stupid. Here we are. Let me help you get out. Er, would you mind if I carry the shotgun?"

Sigurd wordlessly handed the shotgun to the doctor, then held on to Brynjólf's arm to spare his ankle as they approached the entrance. They made it just in time, as it was starting to rain.

The doctor excused himself and tended to the patients who were waiting for him to return. His wife led Sigurd upstairs to the guest room, brought him some food and coffee, then left him alone. Sigurd tried to figure out which out of Guðrún's children she could have been. As far as he could tell, she was somewhere in her mid-thirties. She would have been little, if she had even been born, when he left the village. Now she was a very pretty, if slightly nondescript, woman. Sigurd couldn't see any similarity between her and Guðrún. To begin with, the doctor's wife seemed very quiet.

Dinner was served early, and Sigurd was grateful for a chance to inquire a bit more about Klettafjörður. Where fifty people used to live, now it was more than three hundred. There were two actual stores, Brynjólf said, and Sigurd politely oohed and aahed. When the conversation started to take a turn towards Gunnar, Theodór, and the rest of the family, Sigurd decided to excuse himself, explaining he was very tired and had a raging headache. He couldn't resist sneaking a look at the shotgun resting against the wall.

"Yes," said Brynjólf, noticing. "I'm going to give you an actual cane."

"No need to bother, not at all. I am good. It's surprisingly comfortable, really."

"It's no problem at all," the doctor assured him. "Is there anything else you need? Do you need help going upstairs?"

"Hmm… no, thank you. I already managed to get upstairs with the sh– with this thing. Since you've said my ankle is unlikely to improve, I have to get some exercise anyway. So maybe I'll just take it for now–"

"Oh no, I'll give you a cane right away. I'm going to put the shotgun in a closet in the hallway, it will be safe there. I must admit I'm a bit scared of weapons."

"Thank you," said Sigurd calmly. There couldn't be many closets in the hallway. "That's very kind. Say, what time do you usually go to sleep?"

"Oh, we go to sleep before nine – in about an hour, maybe an hour and a half," answered the doctor's wife. "My husband rarely gets a full night of sleep, it seems like all emergencies happen in the middle of the night. I forgot to ask, love, how did things go with Katrín?"

"Erm…"

"Just one more thing," interrupted Sigurd, earning a grateful look from Brynjólf. "Doctor, would you mind giving me one more of those sleeping pills? I've had so much excitement today, I'd like to make sure I can sleep all night."

"Of course. We'll wake you up in time for breakfast. Then we'll decide what to do next." Brynjólf sighed. "Poor Gunnar. He should have been taken care of a long time ago. I hope it's not too late for him."

As the doctor uttered those words, Gunnar was hoping for exactly the same thing. Within the hours that had passed he had managed to regain some of his mobility, brush his teeth twice, drink some coffee, promptly throw up, then ingest some porridge, which mercifully had stayed down so far. But Gunnar's stomach continued to contract randomly, and every now and then he found himself getting dizzy or losing all sense of direction. He knew he had to get to Klettafjörður, to stop the insane pastor, and this thought was sufficient to force him to go outside. The drizzle woke him up a bit and Gunnar dragged his feet towards the stable, followed by an ecstatic Ragnar. When the blacksmith discovered Karl was missing, his body suddenly stopped demanding that he curl up on the ground and fall asleep. *Now* it was personal.

Gunnar couldn't tell how long he had been walking. The drizzle stopped, the skies cleared, but as time passed it grew darker and darker. It was then that the blacksmith found himself developing a sudden appreciation for nature's wonders. The new moon was nearly invisible. Had it not been for the murky glow of the Northern Lights, their green, blue, sometimes purple flames licking the sky, he could as well lie down and fall asleep. But nature gave with one hand and took with the other. Sometimes the rapid movements of the lights seemed to obscure the way rather than reveal it. The mountains in the distance should be familiar, but they weren't, not in this light. The blacksmith was no longer sure where the shore was. Every now and then it grew completely dark again, and all Gunnar could determine was that he was on a mostly flat surface. Ragnar, excited by the fact that his master was alive and well, ran circles around him. The dog didn't care where they were going, as long as they were together. Ragnar was a great friend and a lousy guide.

It had been years since the blacksmith actually walked to Kletta-fjörður. He usually instructed Karl where to go, then dozed off until she arrived. It was like having a carriage with your own coachman. Fog began to creep around him, taking away more and more of the ghostly landscape. Gradually the land and air were turning into a sickly, bilious swamp, ominously coloured by the aurora. The thicker the fog became, the slower Gunnar walked, until he realised he couldn't even see the mountains anymore. Uncertain, he turned back, only to see exactly the same alien-coloured mist.

Unexpectedly, Gunnar roared in laughter. "I'm alive," he said to Ragnar, proudly. "The bastard failed." They were nowhere, but they were somewhere; Gunnar was freezing, but he was also breathing. He looked where the dog had been just a second ago, but Ragnar was gone, and Gunnar's triumphant laughter died on his lips. "Ragnar?" he shouted, shivering in his new coat, feeling tired, sleepy, and cold again. To his relief, Ragnar, clearly overjoyed, ran back to him, yipping excitedly, then disappeared into the fog again, returning a moment later to give his master a stern look.

"Okay," growled the blacksmith. "I'll go with–" Before he took his first reluctant step into nothingness, he heard a whinny and happiness exploded in his heart.

Gunnar kissed the horse excitedly, then hugged her neck. Karl lay her head on his shoulder, nearly crushing him with the weight. "I knew you wouldn't leave me. I love you," professed Gunnar. "Let's go to town. Let's find Brynjólf. If you could try and go fast…" The mare politely allowed him to mount her and began to walk at her usual relaxed pace.

Gunnar started to doze off, then shook his head and automatically patted the pocket where his flask used to be. Never mind. He would no longer be the alcoholic heathen, he would be a saviour. Half of Gunnar's mind sang hymns of life and joy. The other half really wanted dinner, followed by a good night's sleep.

# Friday night

Gunnar shyly knocked on Brynjólf's door and listened for a response. None arrived. After a while, he banged on the door with his bare fists. Then he noticed the doorbell, and his first thought was that all those years he'd been doing it wrong, possibly offending the posh couple. The blacksmith forced the thought away, then relentlessly pressed the button until the doctor finally opened the door, candle in hand, nightgown on. "Which is it, labour or deathbed," he wearily asked, then yawned loudly.

"Doctor Brynjólf!" exclaimed Gunnar. "Thank God you're awake!"

Brynjólf raised the candle to look at the visitor. "Gunnar? What in the name of God are you doing here? Are you drunk?"

"No," answered Gunnar. "I was poisoned. Why do you think I'm drunk?"

"Because, uh, you're quite often drunk. And – kicking your cousin out of the house? He said you'd left, but I guess not…" Another yawn. "Food poisoning, then? Couldn't you have waited until sometime later?"

"Eh?"

Brynjólf's forehead wrinkled in confusion. "What, eh?"

"I didn't kick nobody out of my house. He's not my cousin either. He's a pastor and he's here to kill people." Having explained matters so thoroughly, Gunnar straightened his back proudly, felt a sting of pain, then returned to his previous crooked position.

"Why don't you come inside," sighed the doctor, now almost completely awake. "Your cousin is staying in the extra room, he took a sleeping pill. He won't be up until sunrise, perhaps later." The dog pushed past the doctor's legs, and Brynjólf almost set himself on fire trying not to lose his footing. "Try to be quiet, my wife is asleep."

"Doesn't she mind the doorbell?"

Brynjólf shrugged, spilling some wax on the floor. "She's used to it. But if she hears me talking to someone, and we will talk, because you have to explain all this to me, she'll wake up."

"Could I get something to eat?" asked the blacksmith. "I threw up everything I ate in the last week or so. And everything I drank. So I am no longer an alcoholic."

"That is not how it works, I'm afraid." A loud sigh. "Coffee and some bread?"

"I'd like to see him first," said Gunnar. "To make sure he's asleep. I don't trust him a single bit. He tried to poison me."

"Yes," said Brynjólf, "I got it. Please be quiet. He's upstairs, to the right, where the door is open... Oh my goodness!"

"Where's my shotgun?!"

"Lower your voice," hissed the doctor, but his wife had already emerged from an adjacent bedroom. "What's going on?" she asked, holding her belly as though it would fall off without support. "Do I need to help?"

"No," said the doctor. At the same moment Gunnar said "aye". Then they both paused for a moment as she watched them with certain confusion. "Nay," assured Gunnar, just as Brynjólf said "yes".

"I think you two need coffee," she said, resigned, already heading downstairs.

"And something to eat," said Brynjólf. "Gunnar had a poisoning. Apparently." He checked the spare bedroom again, but Sigurd was still missing. "There's something very strange going on."

"But after I eat, we need to leave immediately..."

"We're not going anywhere immediately. First you're going to explain all this to me, and I hope your story will make some sense. Otherwise you'll be meeting the Sheriff in the morning."

Gunnar was surprised to notice that, in the middle of the night, the doctor's wife didn't look as pretty as he was used to. Her hair was messy, her make-up-free face made her look less like a porcelain doll and more like... an actual person. Her dressing gown, decidedly rounded around her waist, looked quite old, including a rip on the bottom. The blacksmith continued to gawk until the doctor cleared his throat very loudly.

Once coffee was served, Gunnar began to talk, taking quick breaks to swallow the saliva gathering in his mouth – the pancakes smelled divine, and he couldn't wait to sample them. His efforts to condense the story as much as possible initially resulted in Brynjólf thinking that Arnar and Ingvar were one person with some strange personality disorder and that Juana had married herself in order to become a witch, but eventually he understood enough – Sigurd was in fact someone else and needed to be stopped.

"Hang on," interrupted Brynjólf just as Gunnar was getting to the bit where Ingvar was chased out of the village. "I have to check something." The doctor disappeared for a moment, then returned, looking deflated. "You're right," he sighed. "The shotgun's gone, and so is his backpack."

"He's a pastor gone bad," said Gunnar. "Very, very bad. He said he didn't kill his brother. I don't believe him. He tried to kill *me*, and now he's on the loose. With my shotgun. How could you have trusted him?"

"Uhm, you kept him under your roof for weeks, did I understand that correctly?"

"That was before he tried to kill me!" Ragnar's ears moved rapidly. He'd already found a cosy spot by the stove, got some water, but he still felt guilty about letting his master down. "We have to find that pastor," continued Gunnar, licking his fingers. "Thank you. They were delicious."

The doctor's wife smiled, saying nothing.

"But where do we find him?" asked Brynjólf, sighed, then turned towards his wife. "Love, do you know any of those people?"

"You've seen someone called Bjarni once or twice, but it's a popular name. Also, from what I understood, all this happened a long time ago. You see," she explained to Gunnar, "I've got files on everyone who ever came here. But older people don't trust modern medicine. If all this took place a few decades ago, most of those people will be either my mother's age, or dead. My mother would probably remember more, she used to own an inn back then."

"What's her name?" whispered Gunnar.

"Guðrún."

A few minutes later a small fight started in the hallway.

"There's no need for you to go," huffed Brynjólf. "Go to sleep, love. I know where your mother lives."

"My mother has heart problems. I'm not letting two strange men go alone."

"I'm not a strange man!"

"He might be after her," warned Gunnar. "He didn't seem to like her much."

"Oh no, then I must go with you!"

"You're in delicate state," started the doctor, then looked at Gunnar, who was petting Ragnar's head, and looking at the doctor with pleading eyes. "Oh no, Gunnar, the dog is not coming. Not in my car."

"But…"

"He's got water, he's got food," said Brynjólf, then sighed. "The dog stays, we go." Ragnar curled up by the warm stove, fast asleep and the blacksmith stopped protesting. At the sight of the car he momentarily froze in fear, then decided it could be an exciting experience, even if he did not expect to survive the trip.

"How does it know the way?"

"It doesn't," said Brynjólf. "I turn this wheel and it goes where I want it to."

"Well," answered the blacksmith proudly, "Karl knows exactly where I want to go, and I don't have to turn anything. But this is a very nice thing to be in if it's raining. With a roof and everything. Does it have to be so loud? Ingvar might hear us."

"He won't expect a car. He thinks we're sleeping."

"You thought he was sleeping too," Gunnar pointed out. "Maybe we should drive around. He's a limping man. He might be lost somewhere."

"We're going to check if my mother is safe first," snapped the doctor's wife. "Are we almost there, love? I can't see anything."

The car shook without a warning, and all present gasped.

"What was that?" asked Gunnar. "Does it do that all the time?"

"No," barked Brynjólf. "The wind is too strong. We shouldn't be in a car at all."

"Surely it can't be that dangerous," said his wife. "Not in comparison with a—"

"If you were not with us, we'd just walk. Please be quiet, both of you."

At glacial pace the car rolled next to Guðrún's house, every now and then shaking violently, causing Gunnar to feel nauseous again. When the car finally stopped, Gunnar crawled out and looked at the building. The windows were dark. There was nothing unusual about the absence of lights in the middle of the night, but chills ran down his spine nevertheless. "There might be a murderer in there," he whispered, and the doctor's wife squeaked in fear.

"Do you know, Gunnar," said Brynjólf, "I would be most grateful if you didn't make any more comments." Then he tapped on the door gently. "I hate that we have to wake her up in the middle of the night," he confessed in a whisper.

"Oh, Brynjólf," snapped his wife, as she pushed him aside and started to ring the bell mercilessly until they heard shuffling feet.

"Who is that?"

"It's me, Mother! Please open, it's an emergency."

The door opened and an old woman looked at them uncertainly, raising a candle, blinking. "What is this emergency you speak of? What are you doing here, Karl?" She rubbed her eyes with her free hand.

"I am not Karl! I am his son. No matter how many times people ask."

"Are you sure? Ah, I understand," said Guðrún. "I must be having a nightmare." She made a move as if to close the door, and Brynjólf quickly placed his foot inside.

"Mother! We're really here, it's not a dream. We need your help. Just maybe sit down first…"

"Ingvar is out there to kill!" said Gunnar. "He's chasing after you, or someone else, we don't even know! You know? Arnar and Ingvar? Bjarni? Juana?"

Brynjólf opened his mouth to protest, but Guðrún silenced him with one glance before fixing her gaze on Gunnar's face. "Well, well," she finally said. "I would have preferred a nightmare. Come inside if you must."

"No! Ingvar's out there with my shotgun and poison, murdering people! We must go!"

"Ingvar is dead," said Guðrún wearily. "I need coffee. Follow me."

"He can't be, he stayed with me for weeks," insisted the blacksmith. With a groan he sat down and was just about to start drumming on the table when he noticed the white, embroidered tablecloth. Gunnar quickly clasped his hands in his lap to avoid temptation.

"Suicide," said Guðrún shortly, kneeling by the stove. "Half a year ago or so, soon after his memoir was published. He hung himself."

Gunnar opened his mouth, but no sound came out.

"Are you sure you didn't make all this up?" snapped Brynjólf. "Is this why we're all awake in the middle of the night?"

"He didn't make anything up," said Guðrún. "I just don't know who this man is. Ingvar is dead, so is Arnar. Bjarni married Juana soon after–"

"Bjarni did *what*?!" erupted Gunnar.

"I don't know why this stove won't light," Guðrún said, slamming the metal door shut. "I can't host you like this. Would you like to drink something else? I've got a special herbal drink here that my son-in-law prescribes, it's very healthy."

"I would like some herbal drink," said Gunnar quickly, as Doctor Brynjólf hid his face in his hands, groaning quietly. "So, she married Bjarni? Are you sure?"

"Of course I am sure. Poor woman. She never had much luck. All she wanted were children, and Arnar made sure it would never happen… But you know all that."

"I don't understand. I thought he wanted to have children. What did he do then?"

"He was a violent man," muttered Guðrún. "I'd rather not get into details in front of Ísabella…"

"Ísabella!" exploded the blacksmith. "I remember you!" It never occurred to Gunnar that the doctor's wife actually had a name. He certainly had never heard it before, apart from the story. "You were a baby," he explained, which made Ísabella's expression even more confused. "Never mind. That is a very nice herbal drink…"

"Mother," Brynjólf started, then sighed. Guðrún was already refilling Gunnar's glass.

"Why don't you make yourself useful, Brynjólf," she said, "and light that stove."

"So Bjarni lives here?" repeated Gunnar. "With Juana? Then it can't be him. Sigurd, Ingvar, whatever his name is, came from America. Are you sure he's dead?"

Wrinkles on Guðrún's forehead deepened. "After he ran away, he was gone for a while, then apparently moved to America and became a famous poet there. I read his memoir, and I can tell you that man had no shame. He barely mentions Klettafjörður at all! A small village where he started from the bottom before moving on to bigger things. Then he talks about his career abroad. He got a prize from our government for this book! Posthumously, but still…"

"So you don't think he was a good man?"

She pshawed. "I'd have a hard time deciding which one was worse. You know, Arnar was violent, drunk, unpredictable. He could be your best friend, then suddenly erupt in your face. He threatened me with a knife more than once. We knew he was tormenting Juana and when she moved under Ingvar's care it looked like things would get better, but then of course she was pregnant…" She frowned. "Arnar kicked it out of her, and that was the end of it."

Ísabella gasped, automatically wrapping her hands around her protruding belly.

"Gosh," said Guðrún. "Maybe I should have phrased that differently."

"But that's, that's impossible! That was not in the story!"

"The story?"

"Aye," answered the blacksmith, trying not to watch Brynjólf's attempts to light a fire. "He said it was called 'Þetta reddast', and then I found the book. In a store. So then I knew it was all true. But I didn't read it. He said he had a plan. Are you really sure Ingvar is dead?"

"I think your stove is broken," announced Brynjólf, wiping his hands in a towel. Without a word, Gunnar took his place and removed the pile of ashes, fuel, paper, and wood scrapings.

"Obviously I haven't seen his body," said Guðrún slowly. "I've seen Arnar's alright, and sometimes I still see it in my nightmares. Ingvar didn't just kill him, he massacred him. So much hatred. Don't get me wrong. We were relieved. But for a pastor…"

"There," said Gunnar, wiping his hands on his trousers. "It will be hot in no time. But if it's none of the brothers, then who is it?"

"What does he look like?"

The blacksmith shrugged. "Very nice coat, let me tell you that. Fur-lined boots. He's kinda old, and he had a lot of mo–"

"In his sixties," interrupted Ísabella. "I'd guess sixty-five, perhaps a bit younger. Grey hair, looks like it was dark blonde before. Shorter than Gunnar, maybe half the weight. Pale blue eyes, quite intense. Scar on his lower lip. Possible broken nose. He was shaven, but not very well. Obviously that's not helpful. Dressed in brown and blue. Smaller shoe size than Gunnar's or Brynjólf's." Both her husband and the blacksmith stared at Ísabella with admiration.

Guðrún shook her head. "I can't remember people's eyes after more than thirty years. We all age. I don't see or hear like I used to. My memory isn't what it used to be either."

"Niels," said Gunnar. "It could be Niels."

"Absolutely not! Niels wouldn't know his right foot from the left one. Not to mention making plans or going to America."

"But he always broke his wrists and other legs, aye? Sigurd had a broken ankle."

"Not possible," said Guðrún. "Trust me on that. I'd sooner believe that Arnar got out of the grave. Also, what would Niels want? The longer I think, the clearer it is. Ingvar, the planner. Ingvar didn't believe in forgiveness. He faked his own death to come here for something or someone… Who do you think he's looking for?"

"Uhm," said the blacksmith. "He wasn't very fond of you."

"The feeling is mutual," said Guðrún dismissively. "And I've got a knife."

"He's got a shotgun," said the doctor. "But now we're here, so you are safe. Any other ideas?"

"Juana? But I wouldn't know why. Oh my," said Gunnar. "Bjarni. He called him 'a good man'."

"How is this a reason?" asked Ísabella.

"I know!" exclaimed the blacksmith. "Guðrún, it's your husband!"

"I've never had a husband," said Guðrún absent-mindedly. "Brynjólf, how is that coffee…?"

"What?" said Ísabella in a weird, strangled voice.

"The best thing to do…" started Brynjólf, but one look from his wife silenced him.

"Mother, you never had a husband? What about my father?"

"Why don't we talk about it later, over a piece of cake? We should really be going," said Guðrún. "There are lives at stake."

"Oh no," barked Ísabella, and, surprised, Gunnar instinctively moved his chair a bit further from the table. The pretty, doll-like woman sounded like Thóra all of a sudden. "*Your* life is at stake if you don't answer me right now. You told me my father's name was Máni, and that he died right before I was born. Did he even exist?"

"Goodness me," said Guðrún. "By golly. What can I say. Circumstances… I didn't feel the need to… I mean, men, who needs them? A man can't survive without a woman, but a woman…"

"So, it's not your husband," interrupted the blacksmith, swallowing the remaining liquor. "Must be Bjarni. Let's go."

"None of us is going anywhere until you answer me," said Ísabella, her gaze fixed on her mother's face.

Guðrún grabbed her chest theatrically. "My heart is aching right now," she gasped. "I can't have such difficult discussions, I am too old for that."

Brynjólf, without a word, reached for her wrist and held it. "She's fine," he mercilessly announced. "Also, Mother, your heart is on your left."

Guðrún looked at him angrily, then emptied the bottle into Gunnar's glass, to the blacksmith's content and the doctor's chagrin.

"Ingvar didn't know who your husband was," said the blacksmith. "Only that he was never around. And came by to get you pregnant every now and then. So, you didn't get married?"

"Well, deary me," said Guðrún. "Sugar, anyone?"

"Mother," warned Ísabella.

"Very well. You asked for it. There was… more than one. I'm not sure which one was your father. But I can definitely tell you he was very nice and good-looking, they all were."

"Ooh," said Gunnar excitedly. "So, they just visited?"

"I can't believe it," said Ísabella, ignoring his remark. "My own mother. You've been lying to me for so many years. Have you no shame? At your age?"

"There was a time when I wasn't my age yet, you know," said Guðrún. "Brynjólf, what's wrong with you?"

"Do you have standards, Ísabella?" asked the doctor quietly. His Adam's apple was convulsively moving up and down, face redder than Gunnar's despite the lack of herbal drink.

"What do you mean, my love?"

"Don't call me that. You're the last one to talk about shame."

"Let's go and find Juana," said Guðrún. "You can have a fight later."

"I can't drive right now," barked the doctor. "This wind can blow a car off the road, and that's assuming there even is a road. It would be suicide to drive a car in this weather, even if I had working lights."

Gunnar muttered something about Karl never having had any problems with wind or darkness.

"Yes, love, I tried to remind you," said Ísabella quickly, "the lights are very important–"

"I know it's not mine. Who?"

"I have never..." muttered Ísabella. "You are mistaken, my love, I swear..."

"For the last time, don't call me that. Who?"

"Do you have some more herbal medication?" Gunnar whispered to Guðrún. She pointed at a closet without saying a word. Gunnar briefly marvelled at the selection, then poured himself a generous serving. Despite minor bouts of dizziness, he felt better than at any time in the last days, which could only be attributed to modern medicine. Guðrún pointedly tapped her glass with a fingernail, and he filled it up as well.

"It only happened once," whispered Ísabella. "It was a mistake. I never planned..."

"*Who?*"

"Thorsteinn, Ásta's husband. He came by in the evening, when you were out to see a patient. We got... carried away. But I swear it only happened once. And..."

"I'm infertile," said Brynjólf. His usual concerned expression was gone, replaced with something between sadness and anger. "I never told you, because I thought you wouldn't have married me if you had known. When you got pregnant, I knew it wasn't mine. I would have known even if we were still trying. But I lied to you as well. So I told myself I had to forgive you, raise it as my own."

"I forgive you," said Ísabella quickly, "if you can only find it in you to–"

"*You* forgive me?! You think you have the right to talk to your mother about shame? You–"

"Get out of here if you want to have a fight," snapped Guðrún. "Go upstairs, or outside. None of us wants to listen to that!"

"I don't mind," said Gunnar quickly.

Brynjólf reached for Gunnar's glass and emptied it, then stormed outside. After a brief moment of hesitation, Ísabella followed him, but didn't close the door.

"…I was just feeling so lonely…"

"…you disgust me…"

"…always out, treating me like your secretary…"

"Mothers, fathers," said Guðrún loudly. "What difference does it make?"

"Mothers," said Gunnar, suddenly losing interest in the voices coming from behind the door. "Fathers. Tell me about mine. You know, don't you? Aye, I can tell you do. Everyone knows everything, except those who should."

"It was a very long time ago," tried Guðrún.

"…it wasn't like that, I swear…"

"…like you didn't even want to touch me!"

Gunnar stood up, closed the door, then returned to his seat. "Don't lie to me, I will know. Tell me about my parents."

"Oh, Gunnar. Nobody is ever a villain in their own story. But this one is an exception. Your father confessed it to Brynjólf on his deathbed. It's going to hurt. You can still decide you don't want to know." She refilled his glass again, and the blacksmith realised he was quite drunk. But it wasn't his fault. He'd stop being an alcoholic tomorrow.

"Aye, I decided. Goddamn Brynhildur knows more about my parents than I do. Tell me."

Another muffled yell sounded behind the door and Guðrún sighed. "Karl was very popular with the ladies," she said loudly. "Like some women were with men. Or so I hear. Your father spent a lot of time socialising, helping at the church, organising things like fundraisers. He wasn't much help at home. Him and your mother… Sóley fought a lot, because they couldn't have children, and each blamed the other. But then one of the women he was seeing got pregnant, and she swore many times Karl was the only one she had ever… He paid her some hush money every month, and she agreed to keep things under cover. But then he got another one pregnant, and she was the daughter of the pastor."

"Ingvar?!"

"Of course not! The one who followed, Reverend Guðmundur."

Gunnar swallowed, then refilled both his glass and Guðrún's. He remembered Reverend Guðmundur vividly. Grandfather Guðmundur, which meant his mother was…

"Poor Þóra was such a pretty, sweet girl," continued Guðrún, staring into space. "Very innocent. She was sent to her aunt somewhere deep in the countryside, then returned with a lovely baby that was apparently found at the church steps, and in her good heart she couldn't resist helping it. We all knew the truth, of course. Reverend Guðmundur didn't want that baby under his roof, and more or less demanded that Karl take it. Which he did. Karl convinced his wife that this would be their baby. Things went very well for a while, until you started growing up…" Guðrún paused. "Gunnar, it's not too late to stop."

"Go on," said Gunnar, pushing away his glass. He was dizzy and had to close his eyes again to stop things from doubling in front of his face.

Guðrún slowly exhaled. "You really do look like your father, you know. You took nothing from Þóra. As you grew older, Sóley started asking questions, a lot of them. They started fighting, really fighting. Karl would slam the door and leave. But he'd come back home, because by then nobody wanted to be around him anymore. You see, people talked…"

"I've noticed."

"He was no longer liked. He was happy to have his fun, but not so happy to face the consequences. Everyone's always first to blame the woman," said Guðrún loudly, briefly moving her gaze towards the door, "it's always the woman's fault! Gunnar… Karl simply wasn't a good person. I know he was a great father for you. But nobody wanted him near their daughters, wives, even mothers. He was expelled from the church. Reverend Guðmundur refused to even go near your dwelling."

She stopped as the door opened and the indignant couple returned to the kitchen, ignoring each other. "I hope you're done. You tell him about Karl's confession, Brynjólf, and about the promises you've made."

The doctor sighed. "When I saw him, it was too late for any medical help. I asked if he'd like to see the pastor. Karl said he had sins to confess, but the pastor wouldn't come near him. So, instead, he told me everything.

Then he made me… I promised him I would take care of you as if you were my son." He swallowed. "I've done a lousy job at that."

"Tell him, or I will," said Guðrún.

"Your mother, his wife…"

"Sóley," said Ísabella, automatically.

Brynjólf glared at her before continuing. "She became crazy, Karl told me. She grabbed a knife and threatened him. He laughed in her face. But then she threatened *you*. She said she didn't want to spend the rest of her life… looking at proof of her husband's… infidelity… No. I'm sorry, I just can't." He stormed out of the room, and Ísabella promptly followed, remembering to slam the door this time. The mask had dropped and nothing about her seemed delicate anymore.

"The hell," muttered Gunnar.

"Sóley didn't want to spend the rest of her life looking at the proof of her husband's infidelity," continued Guðrún as if nothing had happened. "He was scared for your life, or so he said to Brynjólf. Nothing personal, Gunnar, but when I saw you outside my door I really thought he had returned. You don't realise it, but Karl ruined your life. And Thóra's. She grew up to be this terrified woman."

"Terrifying?"

"No. Terrified. In her head, she had sinned, and then sinned again by giving you away. Don't forget whose daughter she was. She blamed herself for everything that went wrong, Karl's death, Sóley's death, you becoming… you. So, she devoted her entire life to making sure others would follow God's word in the way she hadn't. She may seem a bit uptight, but she's got a heart of gold once you get to know her, trust me on that. Back to Karl, Sóley's death wasn't an accident, nor was it an illness. I beg you, don't ask for details."

Gunnar sat stiffly, eyes closed, holding on to the table, no longer caring about the tablecloth, wishing Sigurd's poison had killed him. Guðrún put her hand on his. "I am sorry. But there are good sides to it. Your mother is alive, and all she cares for is your well-being, in her own way. Also, you are safe from Brynhildur. If necessary, we will all ensure she stays away from you."

"Why?" Gunnar's voice was croaky, and the word seemed to emerge from great depths.

Guðrún pursed her lips, then clucked her tongue. "Because Karl is her father too. Anna from the store was that other girl. Brynhildur didn't take after him, not as much as you. But now that your beard is gone people are going to notice at some point. Same nose, same lips, chin…"

"That's why Anna doesn't want anything to do with me," said Gunnar flatly. "Does Brynhildur know?"

"Of course not! Not even *she* is desperate enough to try and hook her half-brother just to finally marry someone!" Guðrún pushed her chair away and stood up with a groan. "You must excuse me," she said before walking out. Gunnar didn't register her departure, staring into space with unseeing eyes. His mind was completely blank, free from the darkness and feelings that would come later.

"Times change," said Guðrún so suddenly Gunnar winced, returning to reality. Brynjólf was now sitting in front of him, staring away from Ísabella, who moved her chair away from him. "Names change, so do the clothes, years pass by. But inside we all stay the same."

"So, Juana and Bjarni are married," said the blacksmith, rubbing his eyes. He was so tired now, and his body wanted sleep again, a very long sleep. "What happened to Ásgeir?"

"He died in an accident," answered Guðrún.

"Aye, an *accident*."

"It really was an accident. I know what you mean, but Arnar was long dead by then. Ásgeir was fixing the roof of the church, because Bjarni refused to have anything to do with it. It was a rainy day. Ásgeir slipped, fell off, broke his neck, and that was it. Poor Bjarni… There is not a single word in Ingvar's wretched memoir about his own brothers, either of them. Now I find out he faked his own death only to return after all these years to settle scores, and we don't even know which scores."

"He might still come here," muttered Brynjólf.

"I'm ready," shrugged Guðrún. "I've lived long enough. To be honest with you, Brynjólf, I don't see much point in going on. I just want to see my grandchild."

"Then we have to make sure you don't get shot," Gunnar pointed out. "It's getting lighter. Let's go."

"In your head, perhaps," muttered Brynjólf, then looked at his watch. "We can leave in an hour. How fast do you think someone with his limp can walk, without a horse or a car? He probably doesn't even know where they live."

"No more waiting," said Guðrún. "If necessary, I will walk in front of the car with a torch."

"Don't be ridiculous! We'll go, as long as Ísabella stays here."

"You can't leave me here when a maniac with a shotgun…"

"Do you know what? Right at this moment—" started Brynjólf.

"You have the rest of your lives to settle this," snapped Guðrún. "Just give me a moment." She opened a dark wooden box, one that looked so ordinary that even Ísabella never noticed it before. "I'm sorry, Gunnar. Maybe this cheers you up. I've held on to it for too long. You could probably sell it," she said, then handed something to Gunnar, who put it in the pocket without looking. The item was small, about the size of a ring.

# Saturday, March 27, 1920

The atmosphere in the car was, to put it mildly, tense.

"I can't see that well," Guðrún repeated for the tenth time. "But I think it's further there. Turn left!" she suddenly screamed, and everybody jumped in their seats. "Deary me… the other left. Can you go back?"

"I need space to turn," said Brynjólf.

Gunnar muttered something about Karl not needing any space to turn.

"I forgot exactly where she lives," confessed Guðrún. "We don't see eye to eye very often. Don't get me wrong, she's got a kind heart, keep going straight, Brynjólf, back then all of us adored her, and felt for her when Arnar was doing all those horrible things to her."

"Just not enough to actually do anything," observed Ísabella dryly. The car shook violently. "Don't fall off the road!"

"There's no road, it's dark, and it's snowing. If you're so smart, you can drive yourself. There better be no emergencies today…"

"We are out on an emergency," said Guðrún. "Is this the church?"

"It's your old inn," said Ísabella. "Mother, are you sure you know where we're going?"

"Oh," said Guðrún, "if it's the inn, then we're very close…"

"My father is Karl, too," said Ísabella. "Isn't that right, Mother?"

"Don't be ridiculous! No. I would never have touched him with a pole." Next to her, Gunnar took a breath in sharply between his teeth. "There were more men in this country than just one, even back then. Do you know, I am sure it's here… Oh yes, it must be here, unless they moved. Tell this thing to stop, Brynjólf. What time is it now? I don't want to wake up poor Bjarni. He's been unwell…"

"They might be dead," said Gunnar. "I'd prefer to lose sleep than be dead. I checked."

"Hush now," hissed Brynjólf.

When the indignant four found themselves in front of the door, Brynjólf gently knocked on the door, or rather tried to. The door opened by itself. The lock was broken.

"He's here!" boomed Gunnar, pushing past the doctor and running inside, only to be greeted by a small hallway with four doors. One of them was half-open.

"I'm here indeed," shouted Sigurd. "Come in."

Gunnar got there first, stopping abruptly in the doorway. The others were not able to stop in time to avoid crashing into him, and the small group practically fell forward into the room. Sigurd had made himself comfortable in bed and was now casually aiming the shotgun at them. Someone lay next to him. A dark stain was quickly spreading on the pillow. Ísabella squealed, and her hand flew towards her mouth.

"Oh," said Sigurd. "That's… unexpected. Where is my beloved? Why are you all here?" He squinted, trying to see in the faint light of a small lamp. "Who did you bring here? Good God, can it be Guðrún?"

"Yes," said Guðrún. "Still a genius. What are you doing, Ingvar? What was important enough to fake your own death?"

"Ingvar is dead," said Sigurd. "He committed suicide. I watched him as he did it."

"Then who are you?" demanded Gunnar.

"You," Sigurd said aiming the shotgun at the blacksmith, "should be dead." The shotgun moved again. "I wasted perfectly good sleeping pills, doctor, just because you said they were dangerous with alcohol. I *paid* for those pills."

"I said they were dangerous, not murderous. Who are you then?"

"My name is Arnar," said Sigurd. "Gunnar might have heard about me. Guðrún's probably demented by now, but even she might remember me."

"No," whispered Guðrún. "You cannot be. I saw his– your body! You hardly had a head, for God's sake."

Arnar chuckled. "You saw *a* body. I found some poor bloke – can't even remember where. Took a while to find someone who looked a lot like me, the unlucky bastard. Got him drunk, broke his neck, brought him to the beach, then made sure nobody would recognise him anymore. Left the ring in case all of you were too stupid to figure out it was me. It worked, didn't it?"

"It did," muttered Guðrún. "That's a horrible way to die. He must have suffered so much!"

"Not at all. He was dead before I even transported him to the beach. Now explain – why are you all here and where the hell is my wife?"

"That I can tell you," said Guðrún. "Juana has a key to the chapel. Every morning she goes there, and spends an hour lying in front of the cross, begging to be forgiven for her sins. For *your* sins."

"It will take a lot of begging, she's slept with all three of us. Even with Bjarni!" He spat at the bloodstained sheets and the motionless body that lay underneath. "What kind of desperation, what kind of evil drives a woman to do something like that? What did she think she would achieve, other than hurting me as badly as possible?" Arnar paused, then looked down at his shotgun. "It's unfortunate that there are four of you. That's too many."

"Let my wife go," demanded Brynjólf. "And my mother-in-law."

"Of course, valiant knight. So they can run and get help. You're all staying here until I decide what to do with you." Arnar grinned. "I was going to pay you a visit anyway, Guðrún. Thank you for saving me the time, I appreciate that."

"Stop looking so pleased with yourself," muttered Guðrún. "You killed both your brothers. Why?"

"I didn't touch Ingvar! We just had a conversation. He had his pretty words, and I had a very sharp knife. I love knives. They're very persuasive. The funniest thing is that he was so afraid of getting the smallest cut that he wrote a goodbye letter and put a noose around his neck instead."

"No," gasped Gunnar. "Really?"

"Really. He thought he was so smart, yet until the last moment he thought I'd let him live. If he'd had a day or two to write himself out of it, he might have managed, but unfortunately I was in a hurry. You see, while Ingvar wrote his poems and books filled with lies, I was doing things. I'm still doing things, and he's dead, both of them are. Who wins?"

"Wins," echoed Guðrún darkly. "Why are you here?"

Ísabella made a careful move towards the door.

"I see you," snarled Arnar. "I want you in that corner there, with your mother. Brynjólf, Gunnar, you stay in front of me. Away from the door. When my wife comes back, I would like her to be pleasantly surprised." He paused. "Are you drunk again, Gunnar?"

"Not your business!"

Arnar laughed. "That is why you never amounted to anything. How many times have you now sworn to yourself that you would stop? I'd think that almost dying would finally stop you, but it still wasn't enough. If you had only listened…"

"Then I'd be dead," barked Gunnar. "A great pastor you'd made."

"May I remind you I am not my brother? I am but a simple builder with a simple plan."

"I think you're anything but simple," said Guðrún. "Ísabella, stand behind me."

"That's sweet of you, Guðrún. She's staying where she is. Whoever moves first, gets a knife between their eyes. Understood?" He put down the shotgun, wiped the knife with the bedsheet, then held it up menacingly. "It's not perfectly weighed, but very sharp. Say what you want about Gunnar, but he's great with tools. Well done, Gunnar."

"Go to hell!"

"Are you still emigrating? I thought I'd let you know in advance that there is also prohibition in America."

Before Gunnar had a chance to respond, Arnar lifted a finger to his lips. Everyone stilled, listening to footsteps in the hallway. "Bjarni?" a female voice asked. "Are you there?"

Arnar's gaze turned towards the door. Brynjólf hesitated perhaps half a second too long before attempting to leap towards the bed. The knife struck him in the chest, and he gasped in shock, then dropped to his knees. Ísabella's short, shrill scream died abruptly as a woman stormed in, only to freeze as well, taking in the scene.

Gunnar, who was being bombarded by so many stimuli his mind couldn't process them fast enough, looked at the woman in surprise. He was used to the mental image of a fierce beauty, someone who would look out of place anywhere but the King's residence. In place of the princess he imagined stood a red-faced woman wrapped in a shapeless sheep coat, woollen shawl around her neck, scarf wrapped around her head. It was impossible to determine her age in this light, but she definitely wasn't young anymore.

"Hello," said Arnar politely.

"He's dying!" yelled Ísabella. "We have to get him to a doctor!"

Arnar chuckled. "What a shame you can't go home and telephone him."

"Dear God," said Juana. Her voice was flat, emotionless. Based on Arnar's story, Gunnar expected to see fountains of tears and loud shrieks. But those were provided by Ísabella, at least until Guðrún slapped her in the face and the screaming stopped.

"Come here, wife, sit next to me," said Arnar.

"I never..." started Juana. "Ingvar? No... that's not... How can you be...?"

Arnar shook his head. "Not even you recognise me?"

"You're dead, I don't understand... Why have you killed Bjarni?"

"You could at least do me a favour and pretend you're in shock," barked Arnar. "Sit here next to me, or someone else will die. Not you, not yet. I've got plans for you. Gunnar, give me that knife."

The blacksmith winced. "Not even if you shoot me first."

Arnar pshawed. "Not you. I'll shoot those two," he said, pointing the shotgun towards sobbing Ísabella and steel-faced Guðrún. Despite his best attempts, he couldn't aim correctly. The shotgun was too heavy for his hands that once used to be so strong.

"Go on," said Guðrún. "Waste your bullets so Gunnar can dispose of you."

"Then just the pregnant one... Oh, go to hell. Keep that knife, doctor." Arnar's attention returned to Juana. "Third and last time, sit here next to your rightful husband."

Juana walked around the bed and sat next to Bjarni, her back towards Arnar.

"Turn!"

She turned her head and glared at him.

"Aren't you upset?"

Juana shrugged. "I have nothing left to be upset about."

Gunnar stared at the shotgun, trying to remember what it was that he was forgetting. "It's bent," he said accusingly. "You ruined my father's shotgun. You killed both your brothers, you tried to kill me as well. Now you want to kill Juana. What the hell is wrong with you?"

"Me? It's not me who slept with all three brothers. Including *twins*. I brought a pearl to this country only to lose her to Ingvar. A pastor! He came here, stole my wife, turned everyone against me, made her pregnant..."

"He didn't," said Juana shortly.

"Be quiet. I know what I know. Now I'm rich, they're both dead, and she will either do penance for her sins and return to her rightful husband, or die as well, as she deserves. Who wins? I win."

"You're not rich anymore," said Gunnar.

"Will you shut up?" exploded Arnar. "You survived, well done, now you can kill yourself with your drinking. Don't make me waste a bullet."

"I have sinned, but not the way your sick mind tells you," said Juana. "I have only ever slept with one man. You. The child I carried and you killed was yours. Ingvar wasn't perfect, but he never tried to touch me. Neither did Bjarni."

Arnar shook his head. "No," he muttered. "You're lying, why are you lying? Ingvar said…"

"You just said it yourself," interrupted Guðrún. "He was so scared of you he wrote a goodbye note and put the noose around his neck. He'd have said yes if you asked him if he slept with Niels."

"Juana, why did you marry Bjarni?" asked Gunnar.

"He was nice to me," answered Juana. "Doesn't sound like a lot, does it? But it was enough. I thought I wanted an exciting life full of adventure. I got what I wished for. It turned out that I wanted to be left in peace, to work, have a family. A girl called Helga said that to me many years ago, but I was too stupid to listen. She died recently, but not before all of her dreams came true. None of mine had, except one – I married a man who made me happy." She paused.

Arnar smiled triumphantly.

"I'm talking about Bjarni," she added, and his smile was gone as fast as it appeared. "Do you know what, Arnar? I worked out at the end why you didn't want to marry me, why you tried to keep me away from everyone. As long as I only had you, you owned me. If you decided to get rid of me, you could, and I would have no claim to make, nowhere to go. Is that right?"

"Nobody else wanted you anyway! Not even my brother, if you're telling the truth. And who cares about marriage? Not our Guðrún here, let me tell you…"

"Don't, Arnar," snapped Guðrún. Something about her voice made Ísabella flinch. All of a sudden she didn't want to know her father's name anymore.

"I thought you were special," Arnar continued, not once taking his eyes off Juana. "I came here for you. I never stopped thinking about you. Not for a moment through all those years. And here you are now, ugly, wrinkled, disgusting. Old. Why did I bother?"

"We're all getting old," said Juana. "Bjarni has been dying slowly for the last six months, he's been very sick. You've spared him a lot of suffering, so I guess I'm grateful for that. Ingvar finished his life's work before he died. We never thought about you once after the body was found. I've led a happy life for many years since. Yes, tell me, why did you bother?"

Arnar cleared his throat, then again. "Just tell me the truth," he croaked. "Stop lying and maybe I'll let you live."

"You're a sick, evil man," said Guðrún. "That's what the truth is."

"If you don't shut up, you'll die first." His attention returned to Juana.

"It wasn't mine. I don't believe you for a second."

"Oh yes," she said. "It was. You killed our child, *your* child, in my womb. Out of jealousy over someone who never laid a hand on me. I believed he killed you, and I thanked him in my prayers every night. You think you won some sort of game? Nobody else was playing. We were busy living." Her voice rang with sincerity, and Arnar's lip began to tremble.

"You're lying," he cried, "you must be! Why do you keep lying?"

"Nay," said Gunnar. "She's telling the truth. Here you are, an old man who can't even walk, who murdered his own brothers and his own unborn child, whose wife wants nothing to do with him even if she has to die. You didn't just lose, you lost *everything*–"

With a sharp cry Arnar aimed the shotgun at Gunnar and pulled the trigger.

Click.

"Oh," said Gunnar. "That's what I forgot."

Arnar desperately pulled the second trigger, only to be rewarded with another "click".

"*Afsakið mig*," said Gunnar, then without any effort tore the shotgun from the old man's weak hands. "I never kept it loaded," he continued, kneeling on Arnar's underbelly, then bending to rest his left hand on the old man's throat. Arnar didn't even attempt to defend himself, his face a picture of shock and surprise. "I'm best with hammers," continued Gunnar calmly before raising his fist and slamming it into Arnar's face. The jawbone broke with a juicy crack.

The old man screeched, and his scream turned into a hideous gurgling sound as Gunnar's fists crashed into his face for the second, third, tenth time, pounding rhythmically even when the howling stopped and Arnar's face had turned into red pulp. The blacksmith worked methodically, rhythmically, the way he would have hammered a thick piece of iron. Juana's single, sharp cry pulled him out of his trance, and Gunnar looked down as if surprised. She pushed him away and the blacksmith didn't resist, wiping his forehead with his forearm, covering himself in blood, watching Juana rock back and forth, holding on to Arnar's shirt, crying in loud gulps and yelps.

Ísabella pushed herself past Guðrún and ran towards Brynjólf, crying loudly. "He's dying," she shouted. "Someone help me get him to the hospital! He is dying!"

"I'm not dying," muttered Brynjólf. "But I need to get to the hospital. Look where the knife is."

"In your chest!" shrieked Ísabella.

"On the right side," pointed out the doctor, then coughed, and some blood appeared on his lips.

Guðrún marched towards Brynjólf, pushed her daughter aside, and looked down. "Correct," she said. "By now Arnar forgot where the human heart is. How do we get him to the hospital? Juana, do you have a horse and cart?"

Juana turned slowly and looked at Guðrún as if seeing her for the first time. "We have a car," she said, her voice flat and lifeless again. "I'll drive."

"You know how to drive cars?" asked Gunnar, surprised, leaving alone the beige curtain he was using to wipe blood from his hands.

"It's not that hard," she answered. "Oh, Gunnar, I wish you said the gun wasn't loaded! There's a revolver in a drawer of this side table, I was sitting right there! If only I knew…"

"I forgot," pointed out the blacksmith. "And we were safe anyway. So it was just conversation." He picked up the shotgun and frowned. "He bent it, I told you he bent it. And it's all dirty."

"You better hope Brynjólf doesn't die," said Guðrún sharply. "With a knife in your chest a few extra minutes of *conversation* can make a difference."

"Then let's start moving," said Juana. "Gunnar, help me carry him out. Careful."

The doctor moaned quietly as he was placed in the car. Gunnar's hands were raw, his knuckles scraped nearly to the bone, back sore, but he said nothing. They placed Brynjólf next to Ísabella, who was already holding her husband's hand, whispering to him, kissing his cheek, as tears rolled down her face.

"I'm not feeling so well either," said Guðrún. Her face was pale, and her breathing shallow. "It is my heart, it really is this time. I think I need a doctor too."

"Gunnar," said Juana, "I'm so sorry, there's no space for you. Will you manage? You don't need to do anything here. Just leave it all."

"Aye," said the blacksmith. He looked at his hands again, then watched the car depart. He was already forgotten, and it fit him. But soon there would be people arriving in the house. They would want to see the bodies, examine Gunnar's bloodied hands – he automatically wiped them on his trousers – ask questions. Brynhildur and Anna would be most ruthless. There would be no detail they would leave uncovered. Gunnar would be forced to retell the entire story multiple times, his testimony cross-checked with Juana's and Guðrún's…

The blacksmith briefly went inside the house, emerged a minute later holding his father's shotgun, patting his pocket, and started to walk towards Brynjólf's dwelling where Karl and Ragnar awaited him. As he passed by what used to be Guðrún's inn, he stopped and stared, imagining young Guðrún, Magnús with his silly pipe, panicky Katrín stuck in a corner… He spat into the snow. He'd had enough of all the stories told and untold.

*Sixty-four*, tried the darkness.

"Shut up," said Gunnar aloud, already walking away.

# Epilogue

Brynjólf's wound proved to be deep, but nowhere near mortal. All he needed was rest. Ísabella went into early labour the moment they arrived at the hospital. Guðrún, despite weakly insisting she was completely fine, was put into bed with a large supply of nitroglycerine, which was not the medication she preferred for her heart problems. Brynjólf and Ísabella allowed Juana to stay at their house, fully understanding her refusal to sleep under the roof where both her husbands had died. Had it not been for Brynhildur's burning curiosity, nobody would have remembered to check on Gunnar.

Brynhildur had no qualms about breaking and entering, just in case the blacksmith's life needed saving. She looked at the dried vomit on the floor and shook her head. These were not the proper living conditions for a soon-to-be married man. Then she proceeded to methodically check every nook and cranny of the house, wrinkling her nose at the smell that still hung in the air. To her surprise, the forge was clean and neat. Even the huge anvil shone, and the tools were arranged so neatly she wouldn't have been able to do it better herself. Clearly, Brynhildur reasoned, Halldóra was worth every krona she received. She checked the coals in the fire. Cold.

There was only one thing of interest to be found in the house. In the middle of the table in the kitchen laid a ring. It looked old, scratched, but still beautiful. It was made of gold and some other white metal Brynhildur didn't recognise, both intricately wrapped around each other, a red stone the colour of fresh blood in the middle. Ruby, she thought. Gunnar must have been filthy rich if this was something he left behind – or perhaps he was planning to gift it to his fiancée? Brynhildur tried the ring on, and it fit perfectly. She admired her hand, turning it around to see the reflections of light in the facets of the stone, wondering where Gunnar got it from. From what she knew about his parents it definitely wasn't a family heirloom.

The bed upstairs revolted her, and finding empty bottles hidden in the weirdest spots made her irritated and sad. The dirty blanket in the corner reminded her of the dog, who was nowhere to be found, unlike Karl who had wandered back. Brynhildur decided that Gunnar couldn't have gone too far if he took the dog along but not the horse. Brynhildur briefly looked inside the stable, then left some fodder and water for Karl, not bothering with the manure. She walked around the farm, just in case Gunnar could be found somewhere out there with a broken leg. She briefly examined what probably used to be a shed before it had burned to the ground. Only a rusty corrugated iron roof remained, covering the remains.

Some things would need to be done if Gunnar never returned, she mused as Stjarna carried her home. Someone trustworthy, like herself, would have to take care of selling the whole thing. She found nothing of value in there, except the ring and maybe the forge tools, which meant Gunnar must have taken the money with him. Perhaps that anvil might have been worth something. Technically the place probably belonged to Gunnar's uncle now, but who even knew his name, not to mention his address? Of course, Brynhildur would keep every krona in the bank account, just in case the uncle showed up one day. He probably wouldn't know the exact price the forge went for…

No, she told herself sternly, those were morbid thoughts. Gunnar would be back very soon. It wasn't as though he had a choice. There was no other life for him to lead other than the one Brynhildur had planned out so meticulously. She looked at the ring shining on her finger. It proved he had given up. He might not have been around to present her with the gift, but she was happy to accept it anyway.

There were many other theories about Gunnar's whereabouts.

"Personally," huffed Anna, "I'm very happy he's gone. A good-for-nothing, that's what he was. He was ruining the reputation of the town."

"This town hardly had a reputation as it were," answered Guðrún, who was feeling much better now that she'd left the hospital and could return to her usual medication. "And if it had, then Arnar's return ruined it. Without Gunnar things would have been much worse. To be honest, I don't think anybody but poor Brynhildur noticed he was gone. I have to admit I haven't thought about him much, either."

"I told Brynhildur many times to keep away. He was the worst company for her. Why are you looking at me like this? I'm just telling the truth. He was a disgusting alcoholic, and I am sure he drank himself to death, or jumped off the cliff, like the coward that he was."

"Of course," said Guðrún pleasantly. "What a coward, saving four lives, or five if you include little Bjarni. I have no doubt you are correct." She allowed herself a brief moment of delight at Anna's facial expression. "Nobody found his body though. My bet is that he's alive and well. If I were to guess, I'd say he's living in Reykjavík."

She shared that theory with Brynjólf, Ísabella, and little Bjarni when she visited them at the hospital. Ísabella had no interest in Gunnar at all, completely engulfed in her love for the tiny, wrinkly baby. It was agreed that it was a miracle that the boy had survived such an early birth. It was also clear that fatherhood suited Brynjólf, who sat next to his wife and child, beaming in happiness.

"I think his family lived somewhere near Akureyri," muttered Brynjólf. "Since he looks so much like his father, he would be recognised within minutes. His uncle... the name escapes me..."

"Mother," interrupted Ísabella, immediately forgetting about everything else. "He's grabbing my finger. Look!"

"How sweet," said Guðrún. "He is absolutely delightful." Little Bjarni looked like every other infant she had ever seen, including her own. At the sound of first creaky cry she excused herself as her heart was still in a delicate condition, and she needed rest. Her departure was barely noticed.

Thóra was seen in public crying, said a rumour – or, more precisely, Anna – although hardly anybody could believe such a thing. She withdrew from her duties as a Conservative Woman of Iceland, and Laufey began to breathe easier. When Thóra announced she was leaving to attend to her aunt, who was very ill, everyone nodded in sympathy. Laufey spent two days trembling with excitement, worried Thóra would change her mind, then did something she had dreamt of for ages, yet had never dared.

"Do you have any nice hats?" she asked before the door of the store even shut behind her. Her voice was trembling with excitement.

"Of course we do," said Anna. "What are you looking for?"

"Something unpractical," exclaimed Laufey. "Absolutely no red or black. Pastels."

"What do you think about this one?" asked Anna, presenting something that she had dug out of the "unsold forever" box.

Laufey beamed, seeing the green and pink monstrosity. "It's wonderful!" Then the corners of her mouth dropped slightly. "I don't know why this makes me think of poor Gunnar."

"I don't know either," huffed Anna. "Why don't you try it on?"

"I'll take it! Gunnar was not a happy man," Laufey said confidentially. "Whatever happened to him must be better than the life he had lived here. I'm more sorry for poor Brynhildur, left alone again..."

Brynhildur, who was counting money in the back of the store and frowning over how little there was to count, jerked her head up. *I'll give you poor Brynhildur*, she thought, powerless and furious. This was neither the first, nor the last time those words would be uttered.

"Brynhildur will be just fine," snapped Anna, redirecting the conversation to the other, much bigger scandal. Nobody, including the Reverend, wanted to have anything to do with Arnar's funeral. The body was removed, then after some consideration thrown into the ocean, from the same cliff as another body a long time ago. Guðrún had agreed to inform the Sheriff, who accepted the information, but never did anything with it. What was he supposed to do about a murder of a man who was long dead?

Juana eventually returned home. Her mattress and bedding had been replaced. She shuddered, looking at the empty bed, the only place where she ever felt truly safe, next to snoring Bjarni. If even the dead could come back to life, what other surprises did life hold for her? The only way she would feel safe here again would be sleeping with the revolver under her pillow, she resolved, pulling the drawer open. But the revolver was missing. Juana shut the drawer, then took a bewildered look around. Could she have been wrong? She opened the drawer to check again, just in case she had somehow missed it. Oh, Bjarni... It started with headaches, then his memory started to go, followed by his mind. Most likely Arnar had spared him – and her – many years of suffering. The revolver could have been anywhere, in the stove, thrown into the well, under his clothes... She didn't really know how to use it anyway. A large knife under her pillow would have to suffice.

Brynhildur travelled to the forge and back a few more times until it became clear that Gunnar was not coming back. She did a quick inventory of the house and hung it in the window of the store. One of the items on sale was Karl, who got hungry and lonely enough that she let herself be led into Klettafjörður. Very slowly.

*He owes me*, thought Brynhildur. Her fury was simmering, stewing in itself, constantly expanding. She kept noticing glances cast her way, people exchanging a few quiet words, smiling at her insincerely. *Poor Brynhildur.* She despised being pitied. As time had passed and people moved on to other gossip, she slowly began to relax, reminding herself Gunnar would be found sooner or later.

One day, a new client arrived at the store. It was a young, well-dressed woman. Brynhildur's professional smile faded for a brief moment until the woman took off her gloves, exposing a wedding band.

"Are you new to Klettafjörður?" Brynhildur asked, the first probing question before moving on to the woman's husband, finding out whether there were any unmarried brothers or cousins the right age.

"Yes," said the woman. "We just moved from the country."

"How nice! What brought you here? Family?"

"We bought a house," said the woman. "Down the street, on the corner. We don't know anybody yet."

"I'd be glad to help out," smiled Brynhildur.

"We've heard the stories, of course," continued the woman, lowering her voice. "I'd like those brown plates, four of them, please. Do you have matching cups?"

"The stories? Of course we do. Also four?"

"Yes, please. About the deaths. What a horrible thing to happen. Three men dying in one day! This reminds me, I need soap and a razor for my husband. Still, I mostly feel for the girl."

"Ah, yes, the deaths," said Brynhildur without much interest. "There were only two, though. And I wouldn't call Juana a girl, she's quite old, really… Any particular sort of soap?"

"Anything that will do for shaving, you know what men are like. I meant the other girl, that poor Hildur. She'd been hunting for a husband for so many years, then the moment she got engaged to this doctor, what a hero by the way, she was left to grieve, all on her own again! Between you and me, I've always wondered what was wrong with her… Oh no!" she exclaimed, covering her mouth with her hand. "My manners! I haven't even introduced myself! My name is Helga. Something tells me we'll be good friends."

"My name is *Brynhildur*," said Brynhildur with a voice that could turn drizzle into hail. "Not Hildur. It was a blacksmith, not a doctor. That will be twenty kronur."

"Why, that's a lot…" started the woman, then realisation slowly appeared on her face. Her hands shook as she paid the requested sum without looking up, grabbed her purchases, then escaped, not bothering to say goodbye. Slowly, mechanically Brynhildur followed her, locked the door, returned to the back and sat down on the only chair that fit between the shelves.

*I've always wondered what was wrong with her.* Brynhildur felt sick, her heart beating way too fast somewhere in her throat. *Poor girl, poor Hildur, hunting for a husband for so many years.* How did people know…? She had always been as discreet as possible, yet she'd made an error of judgement, thinking that being the hub of rumours, some of them even true, meant that she was safe from them. Instead, she was clearly interesting enough to be discussed in the *countryside*, behind her own back, no less! Did those people even know what shame meant?

*I've always wondered what was wrong with her.* Anna and Brynhildur would only ever say such words with the best of intentions, to help the poor, non-existent Hildur. They would respect her grief. They would never refer to her as a "husband hunter". They were good women, well-meaning, God-fearing, unlike this… Helga here.

With trembling hands, Brynhildur grabbed a mug that was too cracked to sell, but still good enough to drink from, filled it with cold coffee, then swallowed the disgusting liquid. She was feeling dizzy. *Poor girl, poor Hildur.* Of course Helga was only saying that with the best of intentions, too, she realised with a startle. She, too, probably considered herself to be a good person. But she didn't understand that Brynhildur was doing everything only out of consideration for Gunnar's well-being, for his happiness, selflessly devoting herself to…

Her grip tightened on the mug so hard it broke. Brynhildur looked at her hands in surprise, noticing a few drops of blood. And suddenly she knew the truth, the new truth, the *real* story behind her own motives.

She had never been "hunting for a husband" and there was nothing wrong with her. Brynhildur, a woman pure of heart and soul, dedicated herself to helping people find God in their lives. In fact, she had been learning from Thóra's shining example in order to join the Conservative Women of Iceland. Thanks to her efforts, her beloved Gunnar was on his way to become a real Christian, a proper member of society, liberated from his condition, blessed with a family. Now that the one and only – this was important – love of her life was gone, Brynhildur was grieving, as was only natural in such a situation. She also needed to tend to her mother, whose health was probably going to become frail soon. Sometimes, when people got ill, they needed a doctor to prescribe them medication. Often things went wrong, especially when the doctor's memory was so poor he could barely keep track of people's names, and such reckless attitude to medication could even cause a patient's death. If, God forbid, something like this were to happen to her own mother, Brynhildur would inherit both the store and the adjacent dwelling.

The corners of Brynhildur's mouth went up just a bit. The dizziness stopped.

So many people lived flawed lives without even realising their mistakes. Here, for instance, was a new Helga replacing the old one in the house on the corner. This meant Brynhildur knew her name and address. The new Helga would now do her shopping at the merchant, which meant Ásta would find out everything else. Everyone had dirty laundry, even Brynhildur's own mother was hiding things from her. And if Helga truly was the one pure soul without a single skeleton in her closet, there were always stories to be told in secret, overheard somewhere, most probably untrue, but who knew with strangers who suddenly moved into Klettafjörður out of all places?

The familiar foxy grin appeared on Brynhildur's face for the first time in weeks as she wiped her hands on the turquoise dress she was wearing. This sort of clothing was not suitable for a woman as pious as Brynhildur. Her cleavage would never be exposed to the freezing cold again. From now on, she would only wear black, modest, warm dresses suitable for a woman grieving… *I've always wondered what was wrong with her*, a thought popped into her head, only to be quickly removed. Brynhildur was perfectly fine, except for her heart being broken forever by the death of her fiancée, an unlikely hero whose name and art would never be forgotten.

Absent-mindedly, Brynhildur picked a can of roach poison and fiddled with it. Anna should return within an hour, it would be nice if dinner was already waiting for her.

Now that Thóra was no longer around, it was only natural that Brynhildur would take Laufey under her wing and re-form Conservative Women of Iceland. She would then gain free entrance to every house and the right to judge everyone's piousness, having full support of the pastor and the Church of Iceland. She would devote herself to bringing God's word into people's hearts, make sure the errors of their ways would become clear to them. And if they insisted that they had never done anything wrong, whose words would be believed – those of the sinners, or those of the leader of Conservative Women of Iceland?

Brynhildur exhaled slowly, her foxy smile turning into a polite, warm expression that would accompany her from now on. As she kept playing with the can of roach poison, a reflection of light in the blood-red gem on the ring adorning her finger made her freeze for a moment.

The only obstacle, the only thing that could ruin her new life, was Gunnar. If the blacksmith were to re-appear, the first person he would bump into would triumphantly lead him towards *poor Brynhildur*, who had never stopped grieving him, never took off the ring the blacksmith offered to her as a token of his love right before his unfortunate disappearance. It would be better for Gunnar to be dead by now. Because if he were still alive, she'd find him first, whether he was hiding in America, Denmark, or the smallest village in entire Iceland. He would die a slow and painful death by a thousand cuts, one per each "poor girl" and "poor Brynhildur" she had endured since Sunday, March 28th, 1920.

Thank you for reading *Storytellers* – I hope you enjoyed it.
I would be *most* grateful for a review or a comment on Goodreads,
Amazon, or any other website of your choice. *Takk fyrir!*

The official soundtrack album coming in the spring 2020 to Spotify,
iTunes, Apple Music, and all other streaming and download platforms.

Feel free to contact me at bjorn@bjornlarssen.com

# Credits

Epigraph: an extract from *One Thousand Days in a Balloon* by Salman Rushdie, in *Imaginary Homelands: Essays and Criticism*, 1981-1991, Penguin, 1992, p.432, copyright © Salman Rushdie, 1981-1991.

The anecdote about raisins and powdered sugar is a re-telling of Sigurður Gylfi Magnússon's re-telling of Erlendur Guðmundsson's re-telling of the original Hallgrímur Erlendsson's story. See *Wasteland with Words: A Social History of Iceland* by Sigurður Gylfi Magnússon, Reaktion Books, 2010, copyright © Sigurður Gylfi Magnússon 2010.

I would like to thank Helga Maureen Gylfadóttir, Exhibition Project Manager at Borgarsögusafn Reykjavíkur; Ewa Krawczyk, Assistant Professor, Center for Cell Reprogramming, Georgetown University Medical Center; Kajetan Augustowski; Guðmundur Jónsson, Professor of History at University of Iceland for helping me with research.

All and any mistakes are my own.

# Author's Note

Whilst writing *Storytellers* I have taken certain creative liberties.

Klettafjörður ("Rocky Fjord") is an amalgam of various places and communities I have visited, in and out of Iceland. You will not find it at any particular spot on the map. To use a well worn-out cliché, Klettafjörður is a state of mind.

Where possible, I stuck with the original Icelandic spelling. I made a few small alterations to make the reader's life easier, in particular replacing the name Þóra with Thóra. I left the letter þ intact in the phrase "*þetta reddast*" ("it will all work out fine [in the end]") – read more about the saying at https://www.storytellers.is

I toned down the harshness of Icelandic reality in the 1880s, in particular the health and housing conditions, a lot. In the period described, most transactions were conducted by bartering, as the first bank in Iceland, Landsbanki Íslands was established by law in 1885.

The First World War was referred to as "The Great War" by Icelanders because it brought Iceland its first real wave of financial prosperity. Once the war had ended, the prosperity did as well, almost overnight, between 1919-1920.

For the needs of the book I have somewhat altered the history of blacksmithing in Iceland. One of the first modern forges in Iceland, The Blacksmith's Workshop in Þingeyri was founded in 1913 by Guðmundur J. Sigurðsson. Guðmundur learned the trade in Denmark and returned to Iceland in 1906. The workshop, which was actually a large company offering various metalwork services, still operates as a museum. Gunnar's forge unfortunately isn't available to visitors. Nevertheless, if you ever happen to visit Iceland and would like to see both Bjarni's and Gunnar's dwellings, both can be found at the Árbæjarsafn Open Air Museum near Reykjavík.

I would like to sincerely apologise to everyone who had ever worked at *The Women's Paper (Kvennablaðið)* in the 1920s.

During the prohibition in Iceland, doctors prescribed alcohol as medication for various ailments. The prohibition itself wasn't a success, since one of the main exports from Spain to Iceland was Spanish wine, and once the Icelandic government was threatened they reluctantly agreed to accept the wine again. Nevertheless, beer remained illegal in Iceland until 1989. Read more at http://www.storytellers.is

Despite the fact that I have a black beard and worked as a blacksmith for five years, Gunnar and I are not actually the same person. I feel the need to mention this since my own brother congratulated me on how bravely and openly I wrote about my alcoholism, delirium tremens, and moonshine production. Disappointingly, while I did research methods of moonshine production and Gunnar's medication use, I haven't tested them myself (or on myself). As for delirium tremens, unfortunately I am not able to tell you whether Grendel existed or not, because he threatened me that he'd haunt me non-stop if I revealed this information.

# Acknowledgements

I often wondered how the acknowledgements sections at the end of a book can be so long. Surely nobody even knows that many people? It turns out that the solitary process of writing a book isn't the same as living in a bubble. Therefore...

First, thank you to the unknown person who sent me Ásgeir's "King and Cross" video, which made me check out the album – *In the Silence*, and its Icelandic version *Dýrð í dauðaþögn*. John Grant translated Einar Georg Einarsson's poetry and broke my heart into a million glittery pieces. The three of you created impossible beauty that made me write approximately two million words over the period of two years, travel to Iceland multiple times, and fall in love with all its wonders.

I would like to thank Helga Maureen for going way beyond the call of duty helping me with research, and for being an awesome person in general. Ewa Krawczyk and Kajetan Augustowski contributed medical nightmares... damn you, autocorrect! Medical *information*. Technically I did my blacksmithing research myself, but I wouldn't get far without Casper Prager. Ruth Jeavons helped with certain religious matters, while Mia Moore helped with certain equestrian matters. (Shout-out to my girlfriend Stjarna, a sweet, stubborn mare who proved to me Icelandic horses can be just as self-driving as I described.) Rachel Thorne provided me with copyright help.

Bartosz Sarbiński sent my husband and me to places that even maps have forgotten. (Stukrotne dzięki za Heiðmörk, skórzaku.) Ken Ryan showed us Iceland through his eyes and allowed me to raid his library. Georg Wittlerbäumer and Benjamin Gijzel allowed me to retreat into their Magical Garden, helping me keep the sliver of sanity I still have.

I couldn't be more grateful to all of my beta-readers, critique partners, some of them re-reading the book at its various stages multiple times and giving me fantastic feedback. Special thanks to Anna Aycock, Meghan DeHart, Penni Ellington, Kristen Lamb, Terry Tyler, and Zuzz Wittner. I received help and encouragement from various groups, including Creative Writing Workshop, Writer Unboxed, ALLi, and Bloggess Pals. (KKMF!)

I owe a mountain of gratitude to the editor extraordinaire Megan Dickman of Crystal Clear Resources, who I credit with turning *Storytellers* from a bunch of words into a book. Megan took me so far out of my comfort zone I couldn't even see my comfort zone anymore, had faith in me when I didn't, and every time when I felt I was just done with this book she'd send me an email that would kick me back into gear. Megan, you have no clue how many times I went through your corrections and suggestions, muttered to myself "challenge accepted", then threw myself back into work. Extra thank you for Rachel Starry who put Megan and me in touch.

This book is dedicated to my husband Jos, the best human being I ever met.

Bjørn Larssen was made in Poland. He is mostly located in Amsterdam, the Netherlands, except for his heart which he lost in Iceland. Born in 1977, he self-published his first graphic novel at the age of seven in a limited edition of one. Since then his short stories and essays were published in Rita Baum Art Magazine, Writer Unboxed, Inaczej Magazine), Edurada. pl, Homiki.pl, and Holandia Expat Magazine. He is a member of Alliance of Independent Authors and Writer Unboxed.

Bjørn has a Master of Science degree in mathematics, worked as a graphic designer, a model, and a blacksmith. He used to speak eight languages (currently down to two and a half). His hobbies include sitting by open fires, dressing like an extra from Vikings, installing operating systems, and dreaming about living in a log cabin in the north of Iceland, even though he hates being cold. He has only met an elf once. So far.

This is his first novel.

www.bjornlarssen.com
www.storytellers.is
www.facebook.com/bjornlarssenwriter
www.twitter.com/bjornlarssen